Investigating psychology 2 – From biological to developmental

Edited by Rose Capdevila, John Dixon and Gemma Briggs

This publication forms part of the Open University module DE200 Investigating psychology 2. Details of this and other Open University modules can be obtained from the Student Registration and Enquiry Service, The Open University, PO Box 197, Milton Keynes MK7 6BJ, United Kingdom (tel. +44 (0)845 300 60 90; email general-enquiries@open.ac.uk).

Alternatively, you may visit the Open University website at www.open.ac.uk where you can learn more about the wide range of modules and packs offered at all levels by The Open University. To purchase a selection of Open University materials visit www.ouw.co.uk, or contact Open University Worldwide, Walton Hall, Milton Keynes MK7 6AA, United Kingdom for a brochure (tel. +44 (0)1908 858793; fax +44 (0)1908 858787; email ouw-customer-services@open.ac.uk).

The Open University, Walton Hall, Milton Keynes MK7 6AA

First published 2015

Edited, designed and typeset by The Open University.

Printed in the United Kingdom by Latimer Trend and Company Ltd, Plymouth

ISBN 978 1 7800 7857 1

1.1

Contents

Chapter 1

Do you hear what I hear? Music cognition, preference and identity

Peter J. Rentfrow

Contents

1   Introduction

Consider, for a moment, the last time you listened to music. What was the music? Did you choose it? If so, why? What factors do you think influenced your decision about what music to play? What were you doing when you made your selection? Were you walking, driving, socialising with friends, or maybe hanging out alone? Do you think the activity you were engaged in influenced your choice? How were you feeling when you were considering what music to play? Did your mood affect your musical selection? Have you always liked this kind of music?

Chances are, when you decided which music to play you didn't give a great deal of thought to the factors affecting your decision, but as you will learn in this chapter, there are a number of psychological factors that influence how we experience and engage with music, ranging from developmental processes, through to cognitive aspects and social factors. Indeed, the field of psychology is ideally situated for helping us understand why music plays such an important role in our lives because, as you now know, psychology focuses on a wide range of human experiences – from basic perceptual experience to more complex social processes, such as stereotyping and impression formation. By bringing together theories and concepts from different areas of psychology, this chapter is intended to help you question and understand why music plays such an important role in our lives, and draws together some of the themes already explored in the module.

Learning outcomes

On completing this chapter you should:

- have an understanding of the different perspectives and approaches to investigating music cognition and preference

- have an awareness of the theoretical links between music cognition and identity, personality and decision making

- have an appreciation of the applications of research on music cognition and preference.

---

2   Do you hear something?

Reflecting on your own musical experiences can give you some ideas about your behaviour and the role that music plays in your life. You might, for example, listen to music in the morning while getting ready for the day ahead, maybe listen to it during your morning and evening commute, and perhaps you listen to it when you exercise. Someone else may only listen to music while commuting, while others may only listen to music during their workouts. Reflecting on when and how often you listen to music can tell you something about yourself, but your personal experiences and beliefs are not necessarily shared by others, so if we are to do systematic research on the psychology of music it is imperative that we employ scientific methods that allow us to make reliable comparisons between people. With clearly worded surveys, representative pieces of music, and large representative samples of the population, we can be in a good position to make some valid claims about how people experience and engage with music, in general.

With that in mind, let's start with the question: How often do people listen to music? Results from numerous large-scale survey studies involving several thousand volunteers can provide us with precise information about how often people listen to music. According to these surveys, the typical person in Europe and the United States of America listens to roughly 18 hours of music in an average week. If we assume that a typical person sleeps eight hours a night this means people spend more than 15 per cent of their waking hours with music playing. Given the proliferation of mobile devices, such as smartphones and tablets, which make it even easier to take music wherever we go, people are spending more money on music. In 2010, for example, the global digital music industry was worth approximately US$4.7 billion, an increase of more than 1000 per cent from 2004 (International Federation of the Phonographic Industry, 2011; Motion Picture Association of America, 2007). Some of you, no doubt, will find these figures low based on your experiences, and would have estimated that people spend more time and money on music, while others will think these figures are high relative to your personal habits. These differences in experiences are the very reason why psychologists and social scientists systematically collect data from representative samples of people, because no single person's experiences generalise to the population.

Listening to music is a physical experience; we feel music through sound waves. Some people find particular patterns of sounds, or styles of music, very appealing, while others find them aversive. When I hear John Coltrane's 'A Love Supreme', for instance, I may find it very enjoyable while another person may just hear a harsh mixture of unpleasant sounds. Moreover, the music we listen to can affect us on a variety of levels, from the neurological to the behavioural. Thus, when we listen to music, many different psychological processes are active. But identifying and understanding the ways in which people respond to music first raises a basic, yet fundamental question: What is music?

2.1   Summary

Although personal experiences with music can provide some clues about why music plays an important role in many people's lives, such experiences are subjective. Therefore, effectively understanding the psychological processes that influence how we respond to music requires a systematic methodology.

3   How do we understand music?

When we hear a sequence of sounds, how can we tell it is music that we are hearing and not a car alarm, water pipes clanging, or passers-by chatting? The study of music cognition – or the perception, comprehension, and recollection of music – has grown exponentially in the past few decades and follows a long and distinguished history dating back to the origins of experimental psychology. The Gestalt psychology movement, for example, was founded to address questions about the nature of melody and melodic transformations, and Wundt (1904), Fechner (1966) and Helmholtz (2009) devoted a great deal of their research to understanding the fundamentals of sound. Later, investigators concerned with language acquisition were interested in determining whether music was processed differently to the spoken word. All of these early investigations help provide a solid basis for the study of music cognition, or how it is that we make sense of musical information.

Music can be characterised as a series of tones that change in pitch, duration, amplitude, and timbre over time (Stalinski and Schellenberg, 2012). To understand how we make sense of musical information, it is useful to look at how music cognition develops. Children's attraction to music begins in infancy. While still in the womb, infants show a preference for their mother's singing voice compared to their normal speaking voice (Trehub, 2001). In their first year, infants show preferences for **musical consonance** (or pleasant sounding intervals) over **musical dissonance** (or unpleasant sounding intervals), and for clear rhythmic patterns (Zentner and Eerola, 2011). In studies of this kind infants are seated on their parent's lap while they are played either recordings of rhythmic music or the human voice. Throughout the study, the infants' behaviours are recorded with a video camera. Later, trained judges view the video recordings and code the degree of movement displayed by each infant. In addition to movement to music, in their first year, infants also appear to remember and recognise music for as long as two weeks. Moreover, they can distinguish between different strains of music they have heard compared to music they have not heard. As children develop, their preferences for simple musical structures evolve in favour of more complex music structures.

Musical consonance
Pleasant sounding intervals.

Musical dissonance
Unpleasant sounding intervals.

Activity 1.1:   How can you measure musical preferences in infants?

Can you think of a simple way to test which music infants show a preference for? What might be the difficulties in devising this kind of study?

As you will learn later, there are some rather straightforward methods for assessing how adolescents and adults respond to music. But studying how infants respond to music requires different methods. One of the most common procedures for studying infant reactions to music is 'the head-turn' or 'preferential listening' procedure. In this procedure, infants as young as five months will sit on their parent's lap facing forward, with a speaker and visual display located on their right and another speaker and display on their left. A blinking light will then appear from the display to attract the infant's attention followed by a musical pattern. The music will stop once the child looks away. Another blinking light will appear from the other monitor, followed by a musical pattern that stops when the child looks away. This will happen several times, and each time researchers will measure how long the infant looks in the direction the music is coming from. The underlying assumption is that the longer the infant looks in the direction of the music, the longer the infant is listening to the music. Longer looking or listening suggests that the infant is differentiating the musical pattern from other patterns.

As you can imagine, there is a lot of uncertainty about what is happening while infants are listening to music, like whether or not they enjoy the musical pattern. One way researchers have tried to measure musical enjoyment among infants is through **rhythmic engagement**, or the extent to which infants physically move in response to musical patterns and whether their movements align with temporal aspects of the music. The more rhythmic engagement, the more enjoyment infants appear to derive.

However, early in life, cultural experiences begin to have an effect on music perception and preferences. Using a procedure very similar to the ones used to measure preferential listening in infants, researchers have observed that infants and toddlers begin to better differentiate the

Rhythmic engagement
The extent to which infants physically move in response to musical patterns and whether their movements align with temporal aspects of the music.

musical harmonies and rhythms of their own culture compared to those of other cultures (Hannon and Trainor, 2007; Soley and Hannon, 2010). Studies in North America comparing music perception of infants and adults have shown that infants were much better at detecting incorrect melodies from native and non-native music than were adults (Lynch et al., 1990). Nevertheless, by adolescence, young people experienced more difficulty detecting incorrect melodies in non-native music (Lynch and Eilers, 1991). Research has demonstrated that by the first year of life, infants find it difficult to detect vocal enunciations that are not part of their native language, and the research on music perception suggests that the musical enculturation develops along with language acquisition. Taken together, these findings indicate that as infants begin to differentiate sounds that are specific to their culture, they lose the ability to hear or recognise sounds that are not common to their culture. The research covered so far helps us appreciate the impact of culture, language, and early experiences on music perception, but what are the implications of those early processes on learning or musical preferences?

3.1   Summary

The act of listening to music, something we take for granted every day, involves a highly complex and sophisticated set of cognitive processes. These processes are closely tied to our ability to communicate through language and are shaped, in part, through socialisation during early stages of development. The culture in which an individual is born also has an impact on their perception of both language and musical sounds, with native sounds being more easily recognised than non-native sounds.

4   How does music make me feel?

Given the effect of culture and early experience on music cognition, what other factors come into play when we identify music that we like or dislike? We turn now to the link between the music we listen to and the emotion it elicits.

Pause for thought

Take a moment to reflect on an experience you had in which you were deeply moved by music.

Chances are that you have had at least one strong experience with music. Recall the details of the experience. What music were you listening to? Had you heard the piece before? How did the music make you feel? Were there other people present? Do you have similar reactions every time you hear the music, or was it just on that occasion?

The details of your experience with music can provide clues about why it can have such a profound effect. Sometimes a number of variables are in place that make the impact of the music very powerful (e.g. your mood, the social context, the lighting). This is often true at live music venues, where people have come together for the sole purpose of listening to music. There may be a lightshow that provides a visual display of the music, and the crowd's reaction in turn affects the artists' performance. Other times it may be a very emotional event in which a piece of music is played that somehow captures the essence of the experience and enhances the emotions experienced (e.g. a wedding ceremony, a graduation, a funeral). Either way, what is obvious to everyone is that music can have profound effects on our feelings.

It will therefore come as no surprise that many artists and writers have remarked that the significance of music is that it is able to express emotions that words cannot. This idea implies it is possible to perceive emotions in music; but do people perceive the same emotions from the same music? In other words, if I perceive a song as being particularly happy, do you also perceive it as happy? In addition to perceiving emotion in music, anecdotal evidence suggests that certain kinds of music can affect the way we feel, with some music making us feel elated and enthusiastic, while other music makes us feel depressed and melancholic. Is it that music causes us to feel a certain way, or does the way we feel influence the music we choose to listen to? These are some of the general questions that researchers interested in music and emotion study.

Several empirical investigations have explored questions concerned with the expression, perception, and induction of emotion in music (see Juslin and Sloboda, 2010). The basic paradigm used in these investigations involves presenting participants with various musical pieces and asking them to independently evaluate the extent to which each piece of music expresses various emotions, like joy, sadness, fear, or anger. More specifically, pieces of music are played through headphones. While listening to the music, participants are asked to indicate the extent to which they perceive the music as communicating different emotions. Based on participants' ratings, researchers can evaluate whether the songs were perceived to have similar emotional qualities. The results from such studies show that people generally agree about the emotions that are expressed in music.

4.1   How do we perceive emotion in music?

A different way to explore this issue is to ask if there are particular musical features that make a song sound happy, sad or romantic. A few experiments have attempted to address this question by investigating whether the emotions that listeners perceive in music are the same emotions that composers and performers tried to communicate. In one study, for example, Juslin (2000) instructed professional musicians to perform different musical pieces, and each time to express different emotions, including happiness, sadness, anger or fear. The auditory features of the musical pieces were analysed by music engineers and played to a group of listeners who indicated the emotions they perceived in the music. The findings indicated that certain auditory features (e.g. loudness, tempo, timbre, etc.) were manipulated by the musicians to communicate certain emotions and that these auditory features affected which emotions listeners perceived in the music. These findings indicate not only that we can perceive emotion from music, but that listeners infer the same emotions from the same songs, and that these inferences are based, at least in part, on particular sound characteristics of the music.

The previous studies in this section demonstrate that we can perceive emotion in music and that we are likely to hear the same emotions in the same songs, but perceiving emotion in music is not the same thing as actually having an emotional reaction to music. If you are doing quantitative research on emotion, in which you are trying to assign numerical values to emotional experiences, one of the biggest challenges is figuring out precisely how to measure it. One common way to measure psychological characteristics, like emotion, is with self-reports or surveys that ask people to report on their feelings in general, or at this very moment. This can be a useful method because who knows better what you are feeling than you? But the challenge with this method is that people are not always accurate in their self-reports. This is not because people are inherently deceptive, but because we may not have sufficient insight into how we are feeling, or we may be trying to come across favourably to the researcher. For these reasons, it is common for researchers to use multiple methods to measure emotions, which may include surveys, physiological activity, brain activity, facial muscle activity, or other non-verbal behaviours.

In the case of music and emotion, a number of experiments have examined the question of if and how music moves people by measuring different indicators of emotion. For example, Lundqvist et al. (2009) carried out a systematic investigation of the effects of happy and sad music on listeners' emotions. Participants sat alone in a soundproof room and listened to a number of happy and sad musical clips while their heart rate, skin conductance, body temperature, and facial muscles were monitored. After each musical clip, participants completed a brief survey that assessed their current emotion. Using these various emotion indicators, the researchers found that listening to happy music as compared to sad music generated more self-reported happiness, smiling, skin conductance, and lower body temperature.

Activity 1.2: How do you measure emotional reactions to music?

Consider a particular piece of music that you find very pleasurable. Maybe the piece makes you smile or sends chills down your back.

Now think about another song that you have negative feelings toward. This may be a song that you find irritating or frustrating.

What are the characteristics of the music that you find pleasant? Are there particular sounds or rhythms that you enjoy? What associations do you have with the music? Do you have any memories linked to the song, which may be the reason why you enjoy it so much?

Now what about the song you don't like? What are the musical characteristics of that song? Is there a negative experience linked to the music that contributes to your feelings about it?

In studies on emotional reactions to music, it is often necessary for researchers to use musical stimuli with which the participants have no prior associations. If listeners have associations with the music, any reaction observed in response to it might be the result of a memory or other association and not the result of the music. In such cases, it is impossible to know if the change in mood was from the music itself, or an association the participant had with the music.

In another influential study on music and emotion, Blood and Zatorre (2001) investigated brain activity while individuals listened to highly pleasurable music. As we will discuss later, because there are individual differences in musical preferences, it is very likely that music you find highly pleasurable is not the same music another person will find equally pleasant. So to overcome that obstacle, the researchers instructed participants to come to the laboratory with songs from their personal collection that consistently generated intensely pleasant responses (i.e. chills, or shivers down the spine) and for which they had no strong associations (e.g. memories). Participants then listened to these songs while their brain activity was monitored using positron emission tomography (PET). The results from the investigation revealed which areas of the brain are most active when people are listening to intensely pleasurable music. Interestingly, the pattern of brain activity observed in the study is very similar to the pattern of activity that occurs when individuals consume their favourite foods (e.g. chocolate) or certain narcotics (e.g. cocaine or heroin, as discussed in Book 2, Chapter 5).

Studies investigating the effects of music on emotion are typically carried out in laboratory settings, where multiple variables can be controlled to ensure that changes in emotions are the result of the music and not some other variable. Such controlled experiments are necessary for investigating the causal association between variables. However, laboratory settings can be artificial and unrealistic, so findings obtained from such studies may not generalise to real-world situations. In our daily lives, we choose to listen to music depending on our situation, surroundings, mood, and energy level. For example, we may choose to listen to fast and lively music in an effort to energise us while exercising, to elegant and romantic music to set the scene for a dinner party, and to calming and relaxing music while preparing to go to bed. So, what role does music play in everyday life situations?

In recent years, a number of new methodologies have been developed that are designed to measure the experiences people have in daily life. One common method used for studying people's daily experiences with music is called **experience sampling**. Basically, this method involves asking participants, multiple times a day, a few questions at a time (e.g. What are you doing? How are you feeling? Who are you with? Are you listening to music? If so, what is the title of the song?). Studies using this methodology complement controlled laboratory investigations by revealing whether associations observed in the lab emerge in the real world.

Experience sampling
This method involves asking participants the same few questions at a time, multiple times a day.

A few studies have used the experience sampling method to examine associations between music and emotion. Results from those studies suggest that music elicits emotions in listeners quite frequently and that most of the emotions are positive in nature. For example, Juslin et al. (2008) recruited a group of volunteers to participate in a study on emotions in everyday life. Participants were given a palmtop computer to carry with them for 14 days and told that the computer would prompt them seven times every day to complete a brief questionnaire. The questionnaire was designed to measure participants' recent behaviours (including listening to music) and current mood. By looking at the associations between music listening behaviour and mood, the researchers were able to not only determine how often people listen to music, but also which emotions were associated with music listening episodes. The results revealed that music-induced emotions were experienced in nearly two-thirds (64 per cent) of all the music-listening experiences reported. Additionally, the feelings that were most commonly elicited by music included calmness, happiness and interest. These findings nicely complement laboratory studies by revealing similar results in the real world, and go a step further by revealing which emotions are typically elicited in people's daily musical experiences. Overall, this work suggests that people use music in an effort to generate or to maintain positive affect.

4.2   How does music influence emotion?

According to Juslin and Västfjäll (2008), there are seven psychological mechanisms that are responsible for the emotional effects of music. These mechanisms include:

- cognitive appraisal

- brain stem reflexes

- evaluative conditioning

- emotional contagion

- visual imagery

- episodic memory

- musical expectancy.

Emotional contagion
The spreading of emotion from person to person.

These mechanisms shed light on why it is that music moves us. For example, we may become sad while listening to someone sing a sad song because, as research on **emotional contagion** indicates, we 'catch' the moods and emotions of the people around us. Or, we may become excited while listening to our favourite football team's chant because, as research on conditioning shows, stimuli can become paired, or associated, with specific reactions so that we have positive or negative feelings tied to the stimuli. As you can see from Juslin and Västfjäll's list, the varying mechanisms draw on research from a range of psychology sub-disciplines, including social, cognitive, neurological and developmental areas.

4.3   Summary

Music resonates with people at an emotional level. We can readily perceive emotion in music, and the emotions you perceive are generally the same emotions that others also perceive in the music. This suggests that particular combinations of sounds have come to be associated with certain emotions. Our perceptions are separate from the emotions we experience in response to music. That is, we can perceive a song as depressing, but that does not mean that the music makes us depressed. Several lines of investigation indicate that the emotional experiences we have with music are driven by a set of social, cognitive and biological mechanisms.

5   Why do you like the music you do?

Given the important role that music plays in emotional experience, it may come as no surprise that early music researchers believed that musical preferences served as a portal to the unconscious. For example, the influential British psychologist, Raymond Cattell, suggested that music acts as a catharsis for unexpressed emotions, and that listening to music releases repressed emotional tendencies. Therefore, he argued, musical preferences reflect unconscious motives, needs, conflicts and desires (Cattell and Saunders, 1954), such as a need for achievement or power. It was with this in mind that Cattell and colleagues designed a musical preference test comprising a variety of classical music pieces. The idea was that people's degree of preference for the musical pieces would reflect unconscious aspects of their personalities, like anxiety, paranoia or mania. Although this may be an appealing idea, a crucial aspect of empirical research is the ability to determine whether your theory or test is valid or assesses the very thing that it was designed to measure. At the time in which Cattell's research was being done, and even today, there were no reliable methods for measuring unconscious processes (and because the unconscious is, by definition, outside conscious awareness, self-report surveys are not an option). Consequently, there is no way to determine whether musical preferences actually reveal aspects of the unconscious.

Activity 1.3:   How do you measure what you can't see?

Arguably, one of the most influential psychologists is Sigmund Freud. His theories about the unconscious, the impact of early life experiences on later development, and psychotherapy have inspired much thinking and criticism since they were first introduced. Although the thought that individuals have an unconscious that influences their thoughts, feelings and behaviours may be intuitively appealing, from an empirical standpoint, it is very problematic because there are no valid methods for measuring the unconscious. As a result, we are unable to systematically investigate Freud's claims about the role of the unconscious because unconscious processes cannot be measured.

Of course, there are a number of psychological constructs that cannot be seen, but that researchers have devised ways to measure. One such construct is implicit attitudes, or attitudes that are outside of conscious awareness. A common example is implicit racism, or the idea that we may have implicit attitudes about race, that affect our behaviour but that are not within our conscious awareness. A popular method for assessing implicit attitudes about race is the Implicit Association Test (IAT). Go to the IAT at this website: https://implicit.harvard.edu/implicit/ and take the test on attitudes to race. It will take you about ten minutes to complete.

After taking the test, reflect on the task you were asked to carry out. How might the task capture your implicit associations? Might such a test be used to measure Cattell's ideas about the associations between musical preferences and unconscious processes?

Contemporary theory and research in this area has revised Cattell's ideas by arguing that musical preferences reinforce and reflect aspects of people's personalities, attitudes, values and emotions (Rentfrow and Gosling, 2003; Rentfrow and McDonald, 2010). A crucial distinction between Cattell and current research on music and personality is that current research focuses on conscious psychological processes, and aims to measure these reliably. A considerable amount of research on music and personality focuses on the structure of musical preferences. Studies concerned with the structure of musical preferences address questions such as: Which musical genres do fans of classical music enjoy most? Which musical genres are most strongly related to preferences for rap music? How do the musical genre preferences of classical fans compare to those of rap fans? By addressing these types of questions, research can determine whether there are important dimensions of musical tastes that are defined by preferences for distinct groups of musical genres. Indeed, just as we can describe the objects in our world in terms of three dimensions (i.e. their length, width and height), research on the structure of musical preferences enables us to identify and describe preferences in terms of their key dimensions.

Several studies conducted in Europe, North America, and Asia have examined the structure of musical preferences. The typical method used to measure preferences is to ask participants to indicate the extent to which they like different music genres (e.g. classical, rock, rap, country, etc.) Of course, there are limitations with musical genres in that not everyone has the same idea of what defines a genre and not all songs can be easily categorised into a single genre. So another method for measuring preferences is to play excerpts of actual music to participants and for them to indicate their degree of liking for the music. This latter approach has the advantage of ensuring that everyone's preferences are based on the same stimuli. With music preference data from large samples of volunteers, researchers can employ a statistical technique called **factor analysis** that effectively divides musical preferences into different groups comprising similar styles of music. Across the various studies conducted, the results consistently show that musical preferences can be broken down into approximately five music-preference dimensions (Rentfrow et al., 2011). What are these dimensions and how are we to interpret them?

Factor analysis
A technique that generates a set of factors that summarises the relationships between variables in a correlation matrix.

Activity 1.4:   Finding order in the musical universe

Research on the structure of musical preferences focuses on the ways in which preferences for music group together. Given the vast musical array of songs, artists and genres, how do you think the various styles of music group together? As a thought experiment, consider the list of musical genres below. How might you reduce these 20 genres into a few dimensions of musical preferences? Which genres do you think will group together to form a dimension?

Alternative	Dance	Jazz	Rap
Bluegrass	Folk	New Age	Reggae
Blues	Funk	Opera	Religious
Classical	Metal	Pop	Rock
Country	World	Punk	R&B

Although different researchers prefer different labels, one set of music-preference dimension labels spells MUSIC: Mellow, Unpretentious, Sophisticated, Intense and Contemporary.

- **Mellow:** This preference dimension comprises pieces of music classified mostly as soft rock, R&B, smooth jazz and new age. It is characterised by listeners as romantic, easygoing, quiet and slow. Artists typical of this dimension include Kenny G, Nora Jones, Al Green and Barry White.

- **Unpretentious:** This preference dimension comprises pieces classified mainly as blues, bluegrass, country, religious and folk. It is characterised by listeners as acoustic, simple, calm and heartfelt.

Artists typical of this dimension include Roy Orbison, B.B. King, James Taylor and Joni Mitchell.

- **Sophisticated:** This preference dimension comprises pieces classified primarily as classical, opera, jazz and world, and is characterised by listeners as dynamic, inspirational, smart and complex. Artists typical of this dimension include Miles Davis, Bach, Puccini, Yo Yo Ma and Astor Piazzolla.

- **Intense:** This preference dimension comprises pieces classified as alternative, hard rock, punk and metal and is characterised by listeners as loud, distorted, aggressive and raucous. Artists typical of this dimension include Metallica, Sex Pistols, Ministry and Napalm Death.

- **Contemporary:** This preference dimension comprises pieces classified as rap, dance, funk, reggae and pop, and is characterised by listeners as danceable, lively, energetic and rhythmic. Artists typical of this dimension include Jay Z, Rihanna, Pharrell Williams and Lady Gaga.

The MUSIC preference dimensions provide a useful framework for reducing the vast musical space into a set of basic dimensions. However, it should be kept in mind that, so far, the majority of research concerned with the structure of musical preferences has focused on Western music and collected data from volunteers in North America and Western Europe. Consequently, it is not clear whether the MUSIC framework applies to music from other cultures. Furthermore, most of the musical genres and excerpts used in the research were produced since the mid-1960s, so it is not clear if the MUSIC framework could be used to classify music from older generations. It might be that the model only captures the preference dimensions that are most prominent in the music of today. Nevertheless, we can still use the MUSIC preference dimensions as a framework for developing a testing hypothesis about musical preferences.

5.1   Why do I like the music I choose to listen to?

Does your personality influence your musical preferences? An increasing number of investigations have looked at the correlations between musical preferences and a range of personality and individual difference variables, including the Big Five personality traits (Openness, Conscientiousness, Extraversion, Agreeableness and Neuroticism), political ideology, psychological values, sexual attitudes, self-perceptions, as well as cognitive abilities. Using this information, researchers can examine whether there are correlations between musical preferences and psychological and demographic characteristics. Across the various studies, one personality variable that is consistently found to relate to musical preferences is Openness – or the degree to which a person is creative, curious, imaginative and liberal. Results show that people high in Openness have a tendency to like sophisticated music, especially classical, jazz, and to some extent rock music. Conversely, people who are Extroverted and like spending time with other people generally enjoy listening to dance and rap music. Of course, it should be emphasised that correlation does not equal causation – the correlation between Openness and preference for sophisticated music does not tell us anything about the cause of that association. Moreover, the observed correlations are generalisations based on tens of thousands of people, and it is certainly the case that some people will not fit these results exactly.

So, if personality develops over time, does musical preference also develop and change through the lifespan? A common concern among parents of adolescents occurs if their child begins to listen to 'problem' music. The concern often focuses on whether or not the preference is indicative of psychological or behavioural problems. Perhaps there is good reason for concern because studies have revealed links between problem behaviours, like risk taking, drug use, sexual behaviour, and deviance, and musical preferences (e.g. Arnett, 1991). For example, results from a large-scale investigation of adolescents found that fans of heavy metal and rock music were more likely to engage in forms of self-harm (e.g. cutting), substance abuse and violence, whereas adolescents with preferences for classical and jazz music were more likely to show symptoms of depression. What is unclear from such investigations is whether listening to certain styles of music causes people to behave in particular ways, or whether people who are at risk are more likely to prefer listening to certain styles of music.

Box 1.1   Crossing boundaries: music preference and personality

The vast majority of research on musical preferences and personality focuses on adolescents and young adults. Consequently, we know very little about how musical preferences evolve over the life course. Do preferences stay stable throughout life or do they change over time? Recent research involving a large cross-sectional sample of people aged 12 to 65 examined trends in musical preferences for clues about the stability of preferences and whether developmental changes in personality affect musical preferences (Bonneville-Roussy et al., 2013). The results indicated that musical preferences change over time in ways that appear to reflect key challenges of psychosocial development. For example, preferences for aggressive rock music are highest during adolescence when young people are faced with the challenge of establishing autonomy and independence and when the personality trait Agreeableness is lowest. Preferences for dance and party music peak during young adulthood when individuals are faced with the challenge of finding a long-term intimate partner and Agreeableness begins to increase. Preferences for heartfelt singer-songwriter music and 'elite' music like classical and jazz increase throughout middle adulthood during a period when individuals are concerned with the challenge of having a meaningful and successful life, and the personality trait Openness is high.

Taken together, research on musical preferences and personality suggests that the music people choose to listen to reinforces and reflects information about themselves: their personalities, attitudes, values and psychosocial development. What is not entirely clear from this research is whether preferences shape personality, or vice versa. Many personality theories suggest that our traits remain relatively fixed throughout development, and in light of how much preferences change throughout the lifespan, one hypothesis is that personality influences preferences. However, to the extent that music is a representation of the culture in which one lives, it is conceivable that repeated exposure to particular musical styles, just as repeated exposure to certain values, beliefs and rituals, might shape aspects of personality. Research that measures personality and preferences multiple times, over several years, has the potential to shed more light on this issue.

5.2   Does music help form my identity?

Some researchers suggest that one of the ways in which people use music is to affirm and to discover who they are, i.e. their identity (DeNora, 2000). From this perspective, music can provide a platform for self-exploration, a tool that enables people to engage in self-reflection and think about who they are. When we listen to music, we may not only perceive or experience emotions, we may also have associations with the music that conjure up images or personal characteristics that resonate with us because we either recognise these characteristics in ourselves or wish to embody them. Such images may be linked characteristics like being tough, cool, romantic, creative or sophisticated. So when we listen to music that brings to mind certain personal characteristics, we are engaging in a form of self-exploration, in which we imagine or affirm aspects of our identity. According to research by Tarrant et al. (2002), the identity associations that music brings to mind are among the main factors that determine whether or not we like a piece of music. For example, some classical music is regarded as intellectual or cerebral, and people who want to see themselves as cultured and sophisticated may adopt preferences for such music to come across in a particular way. Similarly, musical styles like hard rock and rap may bring forth feelings of toughness in many listeners, and it may be the feeling of toughness more than the music itself that determines whether or not people like it.

Activity 1.5:   The soundtrack of your life

Take a moment to reflect on the music that has been important to your life and consider what, if anything, that music might reveal about who you are. Perhaps you might find it helpful to divide your life into different chapters that correspond to different periods in your life. For each of the chapters, list some of the songs that were really important to you at the time. As you identify songs for each of the chapters, think about what you were like at that time of your life. What was important to you? Who were the significant people in your life? What were your aspirations? In what ways are these things reflected in the music you listed?

A number of investigations have also studied the associations between musical preferences and self-esteem. Many of these studies are based on social identity theory (SIT, see Book 1, Chapter 3), which is based on the assumption that the demographic and social groups that individuals are members of (e.g. gender, race, student, Londoner, etc.) are a core component of identity (Tajfel and Turner, 1979). SIT is useful for understanding people's attachment to music and its impact on feelings of self-worth because positive information about one's group makes people feel good about themselves whereas negative information about the group can reduce people's feelings of self-worth. With that in mind, researchers have investigated how one's affiliation with music-based social groups, like punks, goths or emos, for example, relates to self-esteem. Findings from these studies show that people adopt values, attitudes, opinions and lifestyles that are in line with those of the music-based social groups with which they identify. The more someone identifies with a group, the more favouritism they show towards that group and more derogation towards out-groups. According to this perspective, this process of putting one's group above all other groups may serve to enhance people's beliefs about themselves and lead to increased self-esteem.

To illustrate this idea, consider the hippies of the 1960s who wore bellbottoms, tie-dyed T-shirts, and sat in circles singing 'Give Peace a Chance', or the punks of the 1970s who wore torn denim jeans, studded leather jackets, colourful Mohawk hairstyles and slam-danced to 'Anarchy in the UK'. These music-based social groups, and others that exist, comprise collections of individuals who share strong preferences for particular styles of music. And because of their strong association with the music, they adopt clothing styles that effectively show their membership within the group. Moreover, they engage in behaviours and express values that are in line with those of other members of the group. The research on music and identity sheds light on the social and psychological reasons people engage in such behaviour.

Another reason why people might align themselves with music-based social groups is to achieve a sense of uniqueness. According to Brewer's 'optimal distinctiveness theory' (1991; 2003), people have opposing needs to belong and to be accepted, on the one hand, and to be unique and special, on the other. Specifically, identifying with a broad social group (e.g. music lover, sports fan, student) does not sufficiently separate oneself from other people, whereas being entirely different from everyone is isolating. According to optimal distinctiveness theory, individuals strive for an optimal balance between fitting in and being unique. Music can help people balance these countervailing needs. For example, Abrams (2009) showed that individuals with preferences for styles of music that were moderately popular invested more commitment to their musical identities compared to individuals with preferences for musical styles with limited or broad popularity. Taken together, all of the research in this area informs our understanding of why music plays such an important role in individuals' lives: music helps people to explore, reflect on, and construct their identities.

5.3 Does music help me form social relationships?

Do your friends like the same music as you? Could you be romantically involved with someone who hated your favourite music? There is a widespread belief that similar musical preferences are essential for social bonding and attraction. This is reflected in online dating websites, Facebook, Twitter, and other social media sites, where people frequently share information about their musical preferences. It is as though information about people's musical likes and dislikes is useful for deciding whether or not you want to form a relationship with them. Indeed, in Nick Hornby's bestselling novel *High Fidelity*, record store clerks, Rob, Dick and Barry, spend their days making lists of all-time-top-ten songs for various occasions and passing judgement on customers' musical tastes. For them, music is essential for determining the compatibility of prospective romantic partners because, as Barry states, 'it's no good pretending that any relationship has a future if your record collections disagree violently' (Hornby, 1995, p. 117). Given all the research on music and emotion, personality and identity, the idea that musical preferences are important for attraction and social bonding may not be entirely fictional.

Beyond simple anecdote, there is empirical evidence that people share information about themselves in order for others to learn more about them and vice versa. For example, Rentfrow and Gosling (2006) examined the online conversations of unacquainted university students who exchanged messages for six weeks in an effort to get to know each other. The researchers found that participants discussed a variety of topics, from school and adjusting to university, to sports and favourite films, but of all the topics covered, music was the most commonly discussed. So it would seem that people believe information about the music they listen to tells others something about who they are. And as you will recall, there are good reasons to think that, because musical preferences are related to emotional experiences, attitudes, personality and identity. As a matter of fact, surveys of people's reasons for listening to music show they believe their musical preferences to reflect information about their opinions, attitudes and lifestyles (Rentfrow and Gosling, 2003).

Given that people use music to learn more about one another, what does information about people's musical preferences communicate about who they are? One line of research has examined this question by studying the stereotypes people have about fans of particular musical styles (see Book 1, Chapter 8 for more on stereotyping). Rentfrow investigated stereotypes about fans of several different musical genres (Rentfrow and Gosling, 2007; Rentfrow et al., 2009) and found that individuals have clearly defined beliefs about fans of certain musical styles and that those beliefs are consensually shared. For example, fans of classical music are thought to be primarily white, upper class, hardworking, quiet, physically unattractive, creative and educated. In contrast, fans of rap music are thought to be sociable, athletic, relaxed and to smoke marijuana. These findings tell us something about the stereotypes of fans of specific musical genres, but as the research on musical preferences indicates, people typically enjoy a variety of musical styles. How might we take that into account when looking at music and social attraction?

Activity 1.6:   Music stereotypes

Take a look at Figure 1.1. Can you tell which kinds of music these people prefer most?

Figure 1.1   Musical preferences are sometimes reflected in other life choices

Another way to examine the information that music communicates about listeners is to look at the impressions individuals form on the basis of real people's musical preferences. For example, Rentfrow and Gosling (2006) recruited university students to take part in a study of music and personality. Participants (who served as targets) completed a personality measure and were asked to generate a list of their top-ten favourite songs. Next, each target's ten favourite songs were played to another group of participants (who served as judges) who rated the targets on various psychological characteristics. The results showed that the judges formed similar impressions of the targets' personalities and that their impressions overlapped significantly with targets' self-reports of their own personalities. These findings suggest that musical preferences can be an effective way to learn something about other people, which may be why music is a popular topic of conversation among people becoming acquainted. More generally, the findings suggest that music can be an effective vehicle for communicating information about oneself.

Knowing about someone's musical preferences can offer us clues as to what they are like, or what they want us to think they are like, which we can then use to decide whether or not we are attracted to them and want to learn more about them. Indeed, studies on musical preferences and attraction show that music can play a decisive role in shaping perceptions of attraction. For example, Zillmann and Bhatia (1989) showed participants clips of videos of potential dating partners along with information about their musical preferences. They found that potential partners who were said to be fans of country and western music were perceived as less attractive compared to fans of other musical styles. The results also revealed that men perceived potential female partners who were said to be fans of classical music as more physically attractive and sophisticated, compared to females with ostensible preferences for heavy metal music. These findings, like the ones described earlier on music stereotypes show that musical preferences can affect how individuals are perceived by others, but it is worth keeping in mind that the specific content of those beliefs most likely vary over time, as the social and cultural connotations of the music changes. Consider, for example, the reaction many parents from the 1930s, 1950s or 1960s had upon first hearing Benny Goodman, Elvis Presley or The Beatles. When those artists entered the scene their music was perceived as wild and their fans unruly. Now, of course, the perception of that music and the people who listen to it is entirely different.

There is some evidence suggesting that individuals are attracted to people who share their musical preferences. For example, in a longitudinal study of friendship formation among adolescents, Selfhout et al. (2009) found that participants who mutually identified one another as best friends had very similar musical preferences. In addition, participants who share similar musical preferences were more likely to become friends compared to participants who had preferences for different styles of music. Similar findings emerged in a study by Boer et al. (2011), in which the researchers examined the musical preferences of college roommates at the beginning of the academic year and again later in the year. Their results revealed that roommates with preferences for similar styles of music were more satisfied in their relationship and were more likely to want to continue being roommates the following year compared to roommates with different musical preferences. Furthermore, the researchers found that the association between preferences and attraction was mediated by value similarity, meaning that the reason why participants were more attracted to roommates with similar preferences was because they also shared similar values and worldviews. These findings point to some of the psychological factors that explain why similarities in musical preferences contribute to social attraction, but it is also likely that people who share similar tastes in music enjoy similar films, books and other activities, which means they will likely spend more time together. Taken together, research on music and attraction indicates that music communicates valid information about people's psychological characteristics and that this information influences people's decisions about who to spend time with and who to avoid.

5.4   The effects of music on thoughts and behaviour

Given the evidence that music has been linked to psychological and interpersonal processes, it is conceivable that music might also have an impact on how people think and behave. This is certainly the concern that many parents have about their children listening to certain kinds of music. Indeed, through the years, parent groups have voiced their concerns about the violent and misogynistic messages in some rap and heavy metal songs, fearing that such messages will have negative effects on their developing children, leading them to behave violently or to adopt negative views towards women. What is the evidence that music has such deleterious effects on listeners?

The bulk of research that has investigated the effects of music has focused on its negative effects. This requires researchers to measure participants before and after listening to music in order to see if a change occurred that could be attributed to the music. For example, to examine the impact of listening to music with violent lyrics on aggression, Anderson et al. (2003) measured participants' self-report level of aggression at the beginning of the study. Then, some participants heard music with violent lyrics, some participants heard music by the same artist that did not have violent lyrics, and other participants heard no music. Finally, feelings of aggression and hostility were measured again. If exposure to music with violent lyrics elicits violent thoughts in listeners, then participants who heard violent music should show an increase in aggression after hearing the music compared to participants in the other two conditions. And that is what the researchers found. Specifically, participants who heard tense-sounding music with violent lyrics displayed higher levels of hostility and reported more aggressive thoughts compared to participants who heard non-violent music or no music at all.

The study by Anderson et al. shows that certain kinds of music can increase aggressive thoughts and feelings, but that does not necessarily mean that music can make people behave aggressively towards others. To determine whether music actually influences behaviour, Fischer and Greitemeyer (2006) designed an elaborate experiment to investigate the impact of listening to misogynistic music on aggression towards women. Upon arriving at the laboratory, participants were told they would be participating in two short studies: one about music and the other about chilli sauces. The first study was ostensibly concerned with attitudes about music, and participants either listened to music with lyrics expressing aggression towards women or listened to neutral music. After listening to the music, participants indicated their liking for the songs and whether they would recommend them to a friend. Immediately after the music part of the study, participants were joined by a male or female confederate (who they believed was another participant) and had to choose either a painfully spicy chilli sauce or a sweet chilli sauce for the confederate to taste. The second part of the experiment was used as a measure of aggression to see if listening to aggressive music influenced which chilli sauce participants selected. Consistent with the researchers' predictions, participants who were exposed to music that expressed aggression towards women were more likely to select the painfully spicy chilli sauce for the female confederate, but not for the male confederate. Taken together, these findings would seem to suggest that parents have good reason to be concerned about what kind of music their children listen to because the evidence seems to suggest that certain kinds of music can have negative effects on the thoughts, feelings and behaviours of listeners.

Although most of the research on the effects of music has focused on the dark side of music, it is reasonable to expect music to have positive effects too. Several studies by Greitemeyer (2009a; 2009b) indicate that when people listen to music with prosocial messages, they are more likely to display empathic behaviour and to help others in need compared to when people listen to neutral music. Additionally, there is evidence that music that portrays a social group in a favourable light has the potential to shape people's beliefs about the group. For example, Rodríguez-Bailón et al. (2009) found that Spanish participants who listened to Flamenco music displayed more favourable behavioural tendencies towards Gypsies compared to participants who listened to classical music. These findings suggest that music has the potential to change how people view others associated with specific types of music.

Research on young children has also demonstrated that *making* music can play a role in increasing cooperation and prosocial behaviour. Kirschner and Tomasello (2010) asked pairs of German four-year-olds to complete tasks either involving making music or not. After learning a song, with associated rhythmic movements, and playing basic percussion instruments, children were asked to complete tasks that required them to cooperate with one another. Compared to pairs of children who had simply played while listening to rhyming words (rather than making music), those who had produced music were significantly more likely to work together to complete the cooperative task and showed more spontaneous helping. Similar effects were also demonstrated by Davies et al. (2013) who found that children who had made music were 30 times more likely to show helping behaviours than those who had listened to a story. The researchers collectively claim this shows how music can allow young children to have shared emotions and experiences that help them to bond with others while demonstrating prosocial behaviours.

Research on music and behaviour has also examined the impact music has in commercial settings. In fact, empirical investigations on the effects of in-store music on consumer behaviour shows that the music played in shops influences how long customers stay in shops, how quickly they move around the shop, and which products they buy (e.g. North et al., 1999; Yalch & Spangenberg, 2000). For example, North et al. (1999) conducted a fascinating study at a wine shop to determine whether music influenced the type of wines customers purchased. Specifically, they worked with a wine connoisseur to create two displays with comparable wines, one that featured a selection of

French wines and another that featured a selection of German wines. Over a period of several days, they alternated the music that was played in the wine shop, with French music played on certain days and German music played on the other days. At the end of the study period, the researchers analysed whether the music played was related to the number of featured wines sold. The results revealed that significantly more German than French wines were sold on days when German music played in the background, whereas more French than German wines were sold on days when French music was playing. Additionally, only 2 per cent of the participants reported that the music factored into their choice of wine (see Book 2, Chapter 3 for further discussion of why this might be the case).

The research on music and consumer behaviour is interesting not only because it reveals how music can be used to manipulate the behaviour of customers, but because it provides one example of how features of the environment can shape our judgements and decisions without our awareness. Indeed, music can influence our behaviour without us even realising it. While shopping, whether for wine or a new pair of trousers, our attention is most likely focused on the product we want to buy, not on the music playing in the background. This is an example of attentional bias, in which our attention is focused on what is salient (wine or trousers), but other features of the environment still find their way into our thoughts and actions, thereby influencing which bottle of wine or pair of trousers we leave the store with.

5.5   Summary

There are many reasons why we like the music that we choose to listen to. So far, research in this area indicates that we choose to listen to music that satisfies and reinforces our psychological needs. It might be music that conjures images of how we see ourselves or how we would like to be seen by others. It may be music that provides cognitive stimulation to occupy our mind, or music that conveys sadness to validate our feelings of disappointment. It might also be music that communicates a message to the outside world that we are strong, independent and unconventional. Whatever the reason is for any given occasion, music is there to comfort us.

6 Concluding thoughts

This chapter began by asking you to think about the music you listen to and the reasons behind your choice. Hopefully, by now, you can see there is a rich and vibrant area of research that brings together theories, concepts and methods from many different areas of psychology with the aim of understanding why we listen to music. Consequently, you will probably not think about your music or the musical preferences of others in quite the same way anymore because now you know that there is empirical research showing that music really does influence the ways in which people think, feel and behave. Moreover, the music that people choose to listen to reflects information about their (developing) identities and personalities, information that we can infer if we know something about their musical preferences. After all, knowing what kind of music someone likes is a good way to determine whether we have shared interests, beliefs or personalities – information that is important when trying to get to know someone.

Given all that we know about the factors that influence the music we choose to listen to and the effects it can have, which song do you want to hear next?

Further reading

- For a thoughtful and engaging overview of the biological basis of musical experiences, Daniel Levitin's book is perfect:

Levitin D. J. (2006) *This is your brain on music: the science of a human obsession*, New York, Dutton.

- Oliver Sacks' book on music offers a highly entertaining and informative overview of music and brain research:

Sacks, O. (2007) *Musicophilia: tales of music and the brain*, New York, Knopf.

- North and Hargreaves' pioneering work is now a classic text for music psychology students:

North, A. and Hargreaves, D.J. (eds) (1997) *The social psychology of music*, Oxford, Oxford University Press.

- This is the most comprehensive review of theory and research on music and emotion:

Juslin, P.N. and Sloboda, J. (eds) (2009) *Handbook of music and emotion*, Oxford, Oxford University Press.

References

Abrams, D. (2009) 'Social identity on a national scale: optimal distinctiveness and young people's self-expression through musical preference', *Group Processes and Intergroup Relations*, vol. 12, no. 3, pp. 303–17.

Anderson, C.A., Carnagey, N.L. and Eubanks, J. (2003) 'Exposure to violent media: the effects of songs with violent lyrics on aggressive thoughts and feelings', *Journal of Personality and Social Psychology*, vol. 84, no. 5. pp. 960–71.

Arnett, J.J. (1991) 'Heavy metal music and reckless behavior among adolescents', *Journal of Youth and Adolescence*, vol. 20, no. 6, pp. 573–92.

Blood, A.J. and Zatorre, R.J. (2001) 'Intensely pleasurable responses to music correlate with activity in brain regions implicated in reward and emotion', *Proceedings of the National Academy of Sciences*, vol. 98, no. 20, pp. 11818–23.

Boer, D., Fischer, R., Strack, M., Bond, M.H., Lo, E. and Lam, J. (2011) 'How shared preferences in music create bonds between people: values as the missing link', *Personality and Social Psychology Bulletin*, vol. 37, no. 9, pp. 1159–71.

Bonneville-Roussy, A., Rentfrow, P.J., Xu, M.K. and Potter, J. (2013) 'Music through the ages: trends in musical attitudes and preferences from adolescence through middle adulthood', *Journal of Personality and Social Psychology*, vol. 105, no. 4, pp. 703–17.

Brewer, M.B. (1991) 'The social self: on being the same and different', *Personality and Social Psychology Bulletin*, vol. 17, no. 5, pp. 475–81.

Brewer, M.B. (2003) 'Optimal distinctiveness, social identity and the self', in Leary, M.R. and Tangney, J.P (eds) *Handbook of Self and Identity*, pp. 480–91, New York, Guilford Press.

Cattell, R.B. and Saunders D.R. (1954) 'Musical preferences and personality diagnosis: a factorization of one hundred and twenty themes', *Journal of Social Psychology*, vol. 39, pp. 3–24.

Davies, R., Ohl, M. and Manyande, A. (2013) 'Making music may improve young children's behaviour', *Science Daily*, British Psychological Society (BPS) [Online]. Available at www.sciencedaily.com/releases/2013/09/130905202851.htm (Accessed 29 March 2015).

DeNora, T. (2000) *Music in Everyday Life*, Cambridge, Cambridge University Press.

Fechner, G. (1966) *Elements of Psychophysics*, Holt, Rinehart and Winston, New York.

Fischer, P. and Greitemeyer, T. (2006) 'Music and aggression. The impact of sexual-aggressive song lyrics on aggression-related thoughts, emotions and behavior toward the same and the opposite sex', *Personality and Social Psychology Bulletin*, vol. 32, no. 9, pp. 1165–76.

Greitemeyer, T. (2009a) 'Effects of songs with prosocial lyrics on prosocial behavior: further evidence and a mediating mechanism', *Personality and Social Psychology Bulletin*, vol. 35, no. 11, pp. 1500–11.

Greitemeyer, T. (2009b) 'Effects of songs with prosocial lyrics on prosocial thoughts, affect, and behavior', *Journal of Experimental Social Psychology*, vol. 45, no. 1, pp. 186–90.

Hannon, E.E. and Trainor, L.J. (2007) 'Music acquisition: effects of enculturation and formal training on development', *Trends in Cognitive Sciences*, vol. 11, pp. 466–72.

Helmholtz, H.L. (2009) *On the Sensations of Tone as a Physiological Basis for the Theory of Music*, Cambridge, Cambridge University Press.

Hornby, N. (1995) *High Fidelity*, London, Penguin.

International Federation of the Phonographic Industry (2011) *IFP Digital Music Report 2011: Music at the Touch of a Button* [Online]. Available at www.ifpi.org/content/library/DMR2011.pdf (Accessed 29 March 2015).

Juslin, P.N. (2000) 'Cue utilization in communication of emotion in music performance: relating performance to perception', *Journal of Experimental Psychology: Human Perception and Performance*, vol. 26, no. 6, pp. 1797–1813.

Juslin, P.N., Liljeström, S., Västfjäll, D., Barradas, G. and Silva, A. (2008) 'An experience sampling study of emotional reactions to music: listener, music, and situation', *Emotion*, vol. 8, pp. 668–83.

Juslin, P.N. and Sloboda, J.A. (eds) (2010) *Handbook of Music and Emotion: Theory, Research, Applications*, Oxford, Oxford University Press.

Juslin, P.N. and Västfjäll, D. (2008) 'Emotional responses to music: the need to consider underlying mechanisms', *Behavioral and Brain Sciences*, vol. 31, no. 5, pp. 559–75.

Kirschner, S. and Tomasello, M. (2010) 'Joint music making promotes prosocial behaviour in 4-year-old children', *Evolution and Human Behavior*, vol. 31, no. 5, pp. 354–64.

Lundqvist, L.-O., Carlsson, F., Hilmersson, P. and Juslin, P.N. (2009) 'Emotional responses to music: experience, expression, and physiology', *Psychology of Music*, vol. 37, no. 1, pp. 67–90.

Lynch, M.P. and Eilers, R.E. (1991) 'Children's perception of native and non-native musical scales', *Music Perception*, vol. 9, no. 1, pp. 121–32.

Lynch, M.P., Eilers, R.E., Oller, D.K. and Urbano, R.C. (1990) 'Innateness, experience, and music perception', *Psychological Science*, vol. 1, no. 1, pp. 272–76.

Motion Picture Association of America, Inc (2007) *Entertainment Industry Market Statistics* [Online]. Available at www.mpaa.org/USEntertainmentIndustryMarketStats.pdf (Accessed 29 March 2015).

North, A.C., Hargreaves, D.J. and McKendrick, J. (1999) 'The effect of music on in-store wine selections', *Journal of Applied Psychology*, vol. 84, no. 2, pp. 271–6.

Rentfrow, P.J. and Gosling, S.D. (2003) 'The do re mi's of everyday life: The structure and personality correlates of music preferences', *Journal of Personality and Social Psychology*, vol. 84, no. 6, pp. 1236–1256.

Rentfrow, P.J. and Gosling, S.D. (2006) 'Message in a ballad: the role of music preferences in interpersonal perception', *Psychological Science*, vol. 17, no. 3, pp. 236–42.

Rentfrow, P.J. and Gosling, S.D. (2007) 'The content and validity of music-genre stereotypes among college students', *Psychology of Music*, vol. 35, no. 2, pp. 306–26.

Rentfrow, P.J. and McDonald, J.A. (2010) 'Music preferences and personality', in Juslin, P.N. and Sloboda, J. (eds) *Handbook of Music and Emotion*, pp. 669–95, Oxford, Oxford University Press.

Rentfrow, P.J., Goldberg, L.R. and Levitin, D.J. (2011) 'The structure of musical preferences: a five-factor model', *Journal of Personality and Social Psychology*, vol. 100, no. 6, pp. 1139–57.

Rentfrow, P.J., McDonald, J.A. and Oldmeadow, J.A. (2009) 'You are what you listen to: young people's stereotypes about music fans', *Group Processes and Intergroup Relations*, vol. 12, no. 3, pp. 329–44.

Rodríguez-Bailón, R., Ruiz, J. and Moya, M. (2009) 'The impact of music on automatically activated attitudes: Flamenco and Gypsy people', *Group Processes and Intergroup Relations*, vol. 12, no. 3, pp. 381–96.

Selfhout, M.H.W., Branje, S.J.T., ter Bogt, T.F.M. and Meeus, W.H.J. (2009) 'The role of music preferences in early adolescents' friendship formation and stability', *Journal of Adolescence*, vol. 32, no. 1, pp. 95–107.

Soley, G. and Hannon, E.E. (2010) 'Infants prefer the musical meter of their own culture: a cross-cultural comparison', *Developmental Psychology*, vol. 46, no. 1, pp. 286–92.

Stalinski, S.M. and Schellenberg, e.g. (2012) 'Music cognition: a developmental perspective', *Topics in Cognitive Science*, vol. 4, no. 4, pp. 485–92.

Tajfel, H. and Turner, A.C. (1979) 'An integrative theory of intergroup conflict', in Austin, W.G. and Worchel, S. (eds) *The Social Psychology of Intergroup Relations*, Monteray, CA, Brooks/Cole, pp. 33–47.

Tarrant, M., North, A.C. and Hargreaves, D.J. (2002) 'Youth identity and music', in MacDonald, R., Hargreaves, D. and Miell, D. (eds) *Musical Identities*, Oxford, Oxford University Press, pp. 134–50.

Trehub, S.E. (2001) 'Musical predispositions in infancy', *Annals of the New York Academy of Sciences*, vol. 930, pp. 1–16.

Wundt, W.M. (1904) *Principles of Physiological Psychology*, London, Sonnenschein.

Yalch, R.F. and Spangenberg, E.R. (2000) 'The effects of music in a retail setting on real and perceived shopping times', *Journal of Business Research*, vol. 49, pp. 139–47.

Zentner, M. and Eerola, T. (2011) 'Rhythmic engagement with music in infancy', *Proceedings of the National Academy of Science*, vol. 107, no. 13, pp. 5768–73.

Zillmann, D. and Bhatia, A. (1989) 'Effects of associating with musical genres on heterosexual attraction', *Communication Research*, vol. 16, no. 2, pp. 263–88.

Chapter 2

What is the point of childhood? Early experiences and social relationships

Andrew Holliman and Sarah Critten

Contents

1 Introduction

Welcome to this chapter on 'What is the point of childhood? Early experiences and social relationships'. We envisage you sitting in a quiet working area, with a coffee in hand and with this book placed delicately on an otherwise clear table in front of you. Is this accurate? Or perhaps you are reading this in a crammed spare room in your house among the laundry, using some virtual learning environment, trying to focus while the cat wants attention, and trying desperately hard not to wake up the children. Is that closer to reality? Regardless of the means and conditions under which you are reading this chapter, you have at least one thing in common with your fellow readers; you have made it to adulthood. This means you have also experienced childhood, which is the focus of this chapter.

So, what do we mean by 'childhood'? Take a look at Activity 2.1 which should stimulate your thoughts in relation to this question.

Activity 2.1: What is childhood?

1   Draw a line down the middle of a sheet of paper (not on this book) and put 'childhood' on one side and 'adulthood' on the other side. Make a list of some distinguishing features you would associate with each. Some of our features under 'childhood' might include playing, a relatively work-free existence, a Sunday bath, and Winnie the Pooh, while under adulthood could be work, stress, commitment, and responsibility (sigh).

2   Now think about how childhood has changed over the course of time. You might think about what it was like for your parents/guardians or grandparents when they were young. Were their childhood experiences different from your own? What about childhood in the present day? How does their experience differ from your own, and that of your parents/guardians and grandparents? Make a list of some distinguishing features that you would associate with childhood for each of these different generations.

3   What about cultural differences in childhood? This time, you might wish to focus on visual images you have of children from different parts of the world such as the UK, China and Kenya, for example. What do they look like? What are they wearing? What are they doing? What kind of daily activities do they engage in? Do they have

any responsibilities? What role do they play in society? You might find it helpful to jot down some of your ideas.

In carrying out the first part of Activity 2.1 you might have identified, initially, some key distinctions between childhood and adulthood. However, in carrying out those that followed (parts 2 and 3) you might well have come to realise that childhood, and your conceptualisation of childhood, is very much dependent upon culture. For example, you might have initially identified that in the UK, and other Western societies, childhood is often seen as a period of dependency with no real work commitments and very limited responsibility. Nevertheless, in many non-Western societies, children work and make a contribution to the family (e.g. by looking after younger siblings) from a very early age (see Figure 2.1). Indeed, the seminal work of Whiting and Whiting (1975) on 'The Six Cultures Study' has long demonstrated vast cultural variability in 'childhood'. Many scholars, such as Lee and Johnson (2007), have subsequently argued that culture should be afforded greater importance in discussions of child development.

Figure 2.1   Children working to support themselves and their family

It may also have become apparent during this activity that culture itself is dependent upon time. For example, in the 1920s, John Watson (1928) argued in relation to child rearing that (Western) children should be treated as young adults and should never be hugged and kissed or allowed to sit on your lap. This is quite different from what is encouraged in Western societies in the present day. You might have considered opportunities for women to work outside the home, the increasing number of children attending childcare centres, or the extensive role many grandparents now play in their grandchildren's lives (see Griggs et al., 2010). There are intra-cultural differences at any given time, too. The point is that we grow up in different physical, social, cultural, economic and historical circumstances, and these integrate to form a 'sociocultural context' that impacts on our experience and conceptualisations of childhood. Childhood is, therefore, a 'social construction'. While most societies view childhood and adulthood as distinct in some way, how they are different and what is expected in childhood is very much dependent on the society in which the children live. It is also noteworthy here that some developmentalists sub-divide childhood into infancy, early childhood, middle childhood and adolescence. For the purposes of this chapter, we consider childhood as the period from birth until late adolescence, although we appreciate that some would perhaps broaden or restrict this focus.

Thus far, the implication is that childhood is socially constructed and that a universally accepted definition or conceptualisation of this seems unlikely. In spite of this, what is clear across cultures is that a great deal of development occurs during childhood. Subsequently, a plethora of research has focused on explaining 'what develops' during childhood and also perhaps the more challenging question of 'why development pursues its observed course' (Goswami, 2008, p. xiii). Research of this kind has strongly influenced our understanding of childhood by illustrating the physical, cognitive and social capabilities (among others) of individuals at this stage of development relative to those in adulthood. These important issues are considered in this chapter.

Pause for thought

Under English Law, at the time of writing, children under the age of ten cannot be arrested or charged with a crime, although they can be banned from public places during particular times (Local Child

Curfew) or placed under the supervision of a youth offending team (Child Safety Order). Children under the age of ten who break the law regularly can sometimes be taken into care, or their parents could be held responsible. Children aged 10–17 years can be arrested and taken to court if they commit a crime; however, they are treated differently from adults (18 years old and over) in that they are dealt with by youth courts, given different sentences, and are sent to special secure centres for young people rather than adult prisons

What are the assumptions underpinning these laws? Why are adults and children treated differently? You might also consider the case of 'Thompson and Venables (James Bulger)' – covered in Book 1, Chapter 5 – which is of relevance to these discussions.

English Law, according to Westcott (2006), draws upon the issues of 'competency' (e.g. an individuals' understanding, rationality and judgement) and 'culpability' (i.e. whether the individual can be considered accountable and blameworthy). The assumption is that children under ten cannot be held accountable because they lack competency (cognitive and social development) and therefore cannot be considered culpable. Parents, however, can bear some responsibility (as noted above). Some of these cognitive and social developments are considered in this chapter.

It is difficult to define and conceptualise childhood. It is socially constructed and influenced by an integration of physical, social, cultural, economic and historical circumstances. Nonetheless, in most societies childhood is seen as somewhat different from adulthood and this is reflected in the laws of those societies. The key question explored in this chapter is: What is the point of childhood? The focus here is on early experiences and social relationships. The chapter considers some of the key cognitive and social developments (among others) that occur during this stage of life and we will argue that, while development certainly does not stop in adulthood, childhood experience is of paramount importance for later development. The point of childhood, we argue, is:

• to survive it (in a literal sense)

• to learn how to control the environment

• to learn how to function well in the wider social context.

These topics form the three major sections of this chapter.

Learning outcomes

On completing this chapter you should:

- have considered how the period of 'childhood' can be defined and conceptualised

- have an understanding of how nature and nurture might interact to shape our development and influence our survival prospects in the earliest stages of life

- be familiar with a range of developmental processes that enable young children to become increasingly aware of, and able to control and manipulate, their environment

- be familiar with more advanced developmental processes that enable older children to function more effectively within a wider social context.

2   How to survive the early years

The introduction made efforts to define and conceptualise childhood, and made the point that experiences in childhood are of paramount importance for later development. This section explores this claim with a focus on the earliest stage of childhood (up to approximately two years of age). We argue that the first point of childhood is merely to survive it. We will consider how **nature** (genes) and **nurture** (environment) might interact to shape our development and influence our survival prospects in the earliest stages of life. We then focus on infant **attachment** given its importance for both survival and development, and consider the precursors of infant attachment and also the extent to which early attachment experience may impact on later social relationships. We note some contemporary views of attachment and provide a summary of an article that 'crosses boundaries' in this area.

2.1   The (not so) incapable human infant

It was inevitable in a chapter of this kind – which explores the development of human characteristics over time – that there would be some consideration of the nature–nurture debate. Nature concerns genetic- or hormone-based explanations (nativism) while nurture concerns anything that is not nature, such as the environment and experience (empiricism). While other chapters on child development might devote a great deal of time and space to discussions about whether human characteristics (e.g. temperament, personality, intelligence) are primarily the result of nature or nurture, we are going to move forward and provide you with our assessment based on present-day understandings. As Sameroff notes:

> Before complexity there was simplicity ... the history of developmental psychology has been characterised by swings between opinions that determinants of an individual's behaviour could be found either in their irreducible fundamental units or their irreducible fundamental experiences.
>
> (Sameroff, 2010, p. 7)

Since then, new perspectives on nature and nurture embracing a multilevel biopsychosocial dynamic systems approach (incorporating

Nature
The inherited biological predispositions of the individual.

Nurture
'Non-nature' influences on development such as personal experience and the social and cultural environment.

Attachment
A positive social and emotional two-way bond between an infant and another person who is usually the primary caregiver.

biology, thought processes, and the social context) have been offered (see Sameroff, 2010) which propose that:

- they (nature and nurture) mutually constitute each other

- development will not occur without both nature and nurture

- nature will influence nurture and vice versa, as captured in current **transactional models** (see Figure 2.2)

- one would not exist without the other.

Transactional models
A view of development where the environment 'transacts' with the individual over time to produce developmental outcomes; thus, both the individual and environment determine the course of development.

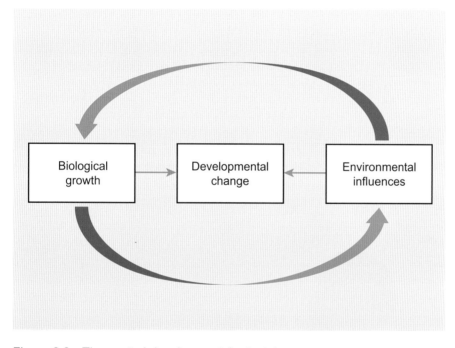

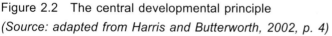

Figure 2.2   The central developmental principle
(Source: adapted from Harris and Butterworth, 2002, p. 4)

An infant's **innate** temperamental **predisposition** (biological), for example, might modify parental thought processes (psychological) and practices (thus, influence the social environment), and these in turn may modify an infant's thought processes (psychological) and behaviour (thus, influenced by the environment), which may then further modify parental thought processes (psychological) and practices (see Kiff et al., 2011). This research on reciprocal relations (Bell, 1968) and transactional models (Sameroff and Chandler, 1975) has led to the most widely held present-day position that all human characteristics result from a complex interaction between nature and nurture and also that while environmental factors influence individuals, individuals also

Innate
Characteristics or abilities present in an individual from birth.

Predisposition
An inclination or tendency beforehand to have particular characteristics or to act or behave in a particular way (often associated with 'nature').

actively influence their environment. Research is now benefiting from advances in molecular genetics and neuroscience, for example, and from interdisciplinary collaboration, which promises to further inform this area of **developmental science**. It is important that you bear all of this in mind throughout this chapter.

Developmental science
The scientific study of age-related changes including, but not limited to, changes in thinking, emotions, behaviour and social relationships.

Pause for thought

Think about human infants (see Figure 2.3). What are they capable of doing (in every sense of the word) and how might these capabilities enhance their chances of survival? You would be forgiven for thinking that all infants do is cry, feed (milk), sleep, and you know what! They seem quite incapable and very vulnerable – after all, most are unable to crawl before six months, and even then, you wouldn't expect an infant of this age to survive without a great deal of care. Contrast this with the infant giraffe that can stand 30 minutes after birth; the pink pigeon that can fly the nest at one month old; the lion cub who is a capable hunter after two years; or the tiger shark who is totally on its own from the second it is born. So, what are human infants able to do to enhance their survival prospects? Hopefully you have some thoughts in relation to this.

Figure 2.3   Social interaction in infancy

You have probably come to the conclusion that the human infant was never going to be an effective hunter. Compared with other species, newborn human infants are quite helpless and highly dependent on others for survival. The traditional explanation for this is that adaptations to bipedalism and an increase in brain size meant that natural selection favoured an earlier birth (reduced to a nine-month gestation period), which also resulted in a comparatively underdeveloped brain at the point of birth. Newborn infants rely heavily on their carers to supply them with nourishment and a warm, safe environment until they are much older; thus, a close relationship (bond) needs to be established between infant and caregiver. To perhaps compensate for a comparatively underdeveloped brain resulting in higher levels of dependency, the evidence suggests that human infants are innately equipped to produce a range of behaviours that influence and control the behaviours of caregivers. Some of the most important behaviours, according to Bowlby (1969), include sucking (for nourishment, but also to reduce distress), cuddling (adjustment of posture to mould to the caregiver's body), looking (eye-to-eye contact as an invitation for the caregiver to respond), smiling (to significant others and through imitation) and, of course, crying (to alert the caregiver that support is needed usually in relation to hunger, temperature or pain). Other behaviours include infants' preference for faces and face-like stimuli (e.g. Fantz, 1961), their highly developed abilities for recognising familiar voices and smells (e.g. DeCasper and Fifer, 1980), and their ability to imitate or copy facial expressions (e.g. Meltzoff and Moore, 1977), among others. These innate infant abilities help influence and control the behaviour of caregivers. This is fundamental to satisfying physiological needs, but also needs for safety and security. Over time, these social interactions become increasingly complex and also reinforce attachment bonds, which will now be given special focus.

2.2 Infant attachment

Attachment is defined as a positive social and emotional two-way bond between an infant and another person who is usually the primary caregiver. As noted previously, infants are born innately prepared to become attached to their primary caregiver, who in most cases is the mother, but it certainly does not need to be – the object of the attachment is usually the individual (referred to as an 'attachment figure') who serves as the infant's primary caregiver (see Section 2.3 on multiple attachments).

Mind map

A type of diagram used to visually organise information where associated ideas are connected to (branch out from) central ideas.

Activity 2.2:   What characterises an attached relationship?

1   Make a list of three people you are 'attached' to and put a circle around each. Create a **mind map** by connecting some descriptors that you believe characterise each relationship.

2   You might also consider how to characterise 'unattached' relationships and look at how these differ from the attached relationships in your mind map.

In carrying out this activity, you might have noted that attached people (who you have listed) seek out each other's company, want to be near each other, gain pleasure from each other's company, feel safe with each other, and can easily pick up their relationship. Unattached relationships are generally the opposite from those characterising attached relationships. While attachment can and does occur in adulthood (as you would hopefully have seen from this activity) it has been argued that in the first three years of a child's life the main task is to form bonds and trusting relationships with other people (Bowlby, 1969).

In Bowlby's (1969) theory of attachment, it was thought not only that infants are predisposed to influence and control the behaviour of caregivers to satisfy needs for safety and security – but that adults, too, are predisposed to respond to these signals at a time when infants are completely dependent on their caregivers for survival. During the development of this attachment relationship, infants become increasingly knowledgeable about the ways in which they are cared for. After around six or seven months of age infants often display 'stranger anxiety' (distress caused by the presence of unfamiliar people) and 'separation anxiety' (distress caused by separation from the caregiver). Bowlby suggested that the infant–caregiver interaction shapes the child's grasp of relationships and that this guides the child's interactions with caregivers and other people in infancy, but also later in life. This was referred to as an 'internal working model of attachment'.

Mary Ainsworth, who worked with John Bowlby in the 1950s, developed the 'strange situation procedure' (Ainsworth et al., 1978), which was designed to assess infants' attachment to their primary caregiver. In seven or eight brief episodes (there are variations of the procedure) infants experience two separations from the caregiver, two reunions with the caregiver, and two interactions with a stranger (one with the caregiver present and one without the caregiver). Throughout the procedure, observers rate the infant on several features, but of most importance is the infant's behaviour with the parent when they are reunited. Three main types of attachment were identified, with a fourth being added later. 'Securely attached' infants (60–70 per cent) would be expected to show discomfort when the caregiver leaves and show happiness when the caregiver returns, recovering quickly from any distress. The remaining 30–40 per cent are classified as 'insecure' in that they have a less positive attachment to their primary caregiver. One form of insecure attachment was classified 'insecure–resistant', or 'ambivalent' – these infants are clingy throughout the procedure and are upset when the mother leaves, but both seek and resist comfort upon reunion. Another form of insecure attachment is 'insecure–avoidant' – these infants are indifferent towards their caregiver throughout the procedure, seem less upset when they leave and may ignore the caregiver on reunion. A final classification was later added 'disorganised–disoriented' – these infants show no pattern of stress coping behaviour during this procedure. The strange situation procedure has enabled researchers to measure the strength of attachment between infant and caregiver. As a result, a great deal of research has focused on both the precursors of secure attachment and the consequences for later development.

2.3 Precursors and consequences of early attachment

An extensive literature has shown that the most crucial predictor of attachment is **maternal sensitivity**; that is, the ability of a primary caregiver (not necessarily the mother) to respond appropriately and promptly to the signals of the infant. Recent research has shown that maternal responsiveness can predict attachment security at both 12 and 18 months (e.g. Raby et al., 2012). In a meta-analysis of 66 studies a moderately strong relationship was found between maternal sensitivity and attachment (De Wolff and van IJzendoorn, 1997) and **randomised interventions** (training) which focused on developing parents'

Maternal sensitivity
The ability of a primary caregiver (not necessarily the mother) to respond appropriately and promptly to the signals of the infant.

Randomised interventions
Where individuals are allocated 'at random' (by chance alone) to receive a particular intervention.

sensitivity towards their infants increased the probability of a secure attachment (Bakermans-Kranenburg et al., 2003) – this experimental research suggests that maternal sensitivity may be causally related to attachment security. It follows that insecure–resistant attachments may result from inconsistent, unresponsive parenting while insecure– avoidant attachments may result from intrusive or rejecting parenting (see De Wolff and van IJzendoorn, 1997). Disorganised attachments may result from abuse or some other kinds of traumatic experiences. In sum, there is strong evidence from this, and from research on twins, for example, who are genetically identical, that attachment security is largely determined by environmental factors such as maternal sensitivity (see Roisman and Fraley, 2008).

However, it is noteworthy that, over recent years in particular, a developing literature examined the possibility that infant attachment behaviours may also be influenced by genetic factors. One example of this is shown in the 'Crossing boundaries' box below. This research illustrates how the study of molecular genetics may help us understand more about the infant–caregiver attachment relationship.

Box 2.1   Crossing boundaries: parenting and attachment security is moderated by genes!

Research has shown that maternal sensitivity influences attachment security (e.g. Ainsworth et al., 1978). Therefore, infant attachment has largely been viewed as a reflection of the quality and security of the infant–caregiver relationship. However, it has also been argued more recently (see Raby et al., 2012, for example) that maternal sensitivity only partly explains infant attachment and that genetic factors may also make an important contribution. Subsequently, more recent studies of infant attachment security have adopted a multiple perspectives approach.

Prospective cohort study

A study where a group of similar individuals (cohorts), who differ with respect to certain factors under study, are followed over time to determine how these factors affect particular outcomes.

Luijk et al. (2011) conducted a study (embedded within a **prospective cohort study** – Generation R) in which the role of both genetic and environmental factors in infant attachment was explored. Infants provided DNA from blood samples at birth, and at 14 months attachment security was assessed (with the strange situation procedure) along with maternal sensitivity. It was found that the minor mineralocorticoid receptor (genes involved in the regulation of stress) moderated the association between maternal sensitivity and attachment security. Infants carrying the minor mineralocorticoid receptor allele were significantly more attached if their mothers showed more maternal sensitivity and were significantly less attached if their mothers showed more extreme 'insensitive' behaviours. It was speculated that infants who are faster and better processors of maternal behaviours in stressful situations might be more susceptible to the effects of both positive care (sensitive responsiveness) and negative parenting (extreme insensitivity). Thus, the infant–caregiver attachment relationship could be moderated by genes!

This study highlights how both genetic and environmental factors may interact to influence infant attachment. While the findings reported here need to be replicated (Roisman et al., 2013) the implications are that progress in the study of infant attachment, or other developmental outcomes, is likely to stem from research that incorporates a broad range of perspectives.

On the 'consequences' of attachment, a great deal of work seems to support Bowlby's concept of 'internal working models of attachment'. This is evident in the wealth of research that has shown continuity in attachment behaviour from infancy to later life. This is especially so if the environment stays relatively stable (Weinfield and Egeland, 2004). For example, it has been shown in a number of studies that 'secure' attachment in infancy is associated with closer, more harmonious relationships with peers (McElwain et al., 2011; Panfile and Laible, 2012), more intimate friendships (Bauminger et al., 2008), and positive romantic relationships and emotional health in adolescence (Englund et al., 2011). Furthermore, in a 20-year **longitudinal study**, Waters et al. (2000) found a 72 per cent correspondence between infant attachment classification and adult attachment (using the **Adult Attachment Interview (AAI)** – Main et al., 1985) providing support for the stability or continuity of attachment classifications; although it should not be overlooked that 28 per cent received a different attachment classification from infancy to adulthood. Indeed, there is evidence that positive or negative environmental changes such as the termination or onset of stress and conflict in the home, for example, can improve or compromise attachment security respectively (Moss et al., 2004). This is why later relationship behaviour is best predicted by attachment measures that are combined from multiple points in time during childhood.

There are, however, some important caveats with respect to the findings reported so far on attachment. The first concerns cultural

Longitudinal study
Studies that monitor and chart the development of psychological variables over long periods of time.

Adult Attachment Interview (AAI)
An interview that taps into adult representation of attachment by assessing general and specific recollections of the relationship they had with their primary caregiver when they were children.

influences. If attachment behaviours are biologically driven then we might presume the patterns of attachment would be consistent across cultures; nevertheless, some variation has been found between different cultures (see Jin et al., 2012, for example). In a large-scale study, van IJzendoorn and Kroonenberg (1988) compared the pattern of secure and insecure attachments across eight different countries (West Germany, Great Britain, Netherlands, Sweden, Israel, Japan, China and the United States of America) using the strange situation procedure. Similarities in attachment type were generally observed across cultures with 'secure attachment' the most common classification. However, it was observed that for Israel and Japan there were far fewer 'avoidant' children and far more 'resistant–ambivalent' children. Although, this could be explained by the fact that in Japan infants are rarely separated from their mothers and therefore separation in the strange situation might come as more of a shock resulting in more ambivalent behaviours and inconsolable crying. Further, higher occurrences of the 'avoidant' classification were observed in West German children, and this was attributed to the emphasis placed on independence by this culture (Grossmann et al., 1985). Thus, attachment classifications, and the interpretation of those classifications, may not be consistent across borders and cultures.

As alluded to earlier, there are many intra-cultural changes in relation to childrearing practices in the Western world, for example increasing numbers of mothers working away from the home, increasing numbers of children in childcare, and an increasing role of grandparents. Contrary to Bowlby's earlier ideas, which appeared to place the blame for delinquent behaviour at the feet of the mother, more recent research has shown that infants can develop 'multiple attachments' to a variety of people (rather than only to a primary caregiver, usually the mother) including fathers, siblings, grandparents, and even employees in childcare settings. There is a developing literature on the equivalent role of fathers (e.g. Belsky and Pasco Fearon, 2008; Feldman, 2003; Lewis and Lamb, 2003) and on the important role played by grandparents (see Figure 2.4) – the latter especially true when there are other stressful life circumstances such as parental conflict (Hicks and Goedereis, 2009). The latter finding may also resonate with the so-called 'Grandmother hypothesis' (see Kim et al., 2014, for example), which essentially holds that grandmothers assist the reproductive success of younger mothers (their daughters) by supporting the upbringing of their grandchildren. Currently, grandparents do not have a legal right to see their grandchildren in some countries such as the UK, but this is the subject of much debate.

Figure 2.4   Grandparents helping out with childcare

Another interesting issue in the present day concerns the influence of childcare on attachment. Childcare is pervasive in the twenty-first century across most Westernised countries. In a thorough investigation carried out in the USA by the National Institute of Child Health and Human Development (NICHD) on more than 1000 children from birth to 16 years it was found that:

- by the age of three, more high-quality childcare experience was positively associated with superior social skills (NICHD, 2002)

- by the age of four, more behaviour problems were observed in those who spent more than 30 hours per week in a day care setting (NICHD, 2003)

- attachment, as measured in the strange situation, was not disrupted if there was high-quality childcare, although poor-quality childcare and less parental sensitivity led to heightened risk (NICHD, 1997).

Other research has shown that infants placed in full-time childcare may be more likely to display insecure attachments than those raised at home (Belsky, 2005); however, this was largely attributable to the conditions of the day care setting rather than the attendance of day care itself. Thus, the impact of childcare on attachment is very much dependent on the quality of day care provision.

2.4   Summary

This section has suggested that the first point of childhood (up to approximately two years) is merely to survive it. It was argued that human characteristics result from a complex interplay (rather than either/or) between nature and nurture. We considered some innate infant abilities that influence and control the behaviour of the caregivers and ultimately enhance their survival prospects. These interactions were also thought to be important for socio-emotional development and the formation of attachment bonds. Attachment between caregiver and infant was considered crucial to the infant's survival. It was also argued that early attachment experiences can impact upon later social relationships and that, while continuity is not guaranteed, secure attachment in infancy creates a positive path that is likely to continue into the later years, if the environment remains consistent.

We also noted the intriguing state of play whereby so many changes are occurring in relation to childrearing, for example mothers working outside the home, children in day care, and the increasing role of grandparents. We also presented a summary of a recent article which 'crosses boundaries' in this research area arguing that the relationship between parenting and attachment security is moderated by genes.

An important theme running through this chapter is that human development is 'two-way' with transactional influences; that is, not only is the child influenced by their environment (e.g. their caregivers), but they are also able to actively influence it.

3   How to control the environment

The previous section showed that although infants come into the world with certain instincts and skills designed to attract caregivers and ensure survival, they are still completely dependent on others. In order to develop (eventually) into independent adults capable of leading our own lives and making our own decisions we need to: gather knowledge about how the world works; start to understand how we think and feel about things; and communicate with those around us to learn from them and influence them to get what we want. Therefore, we argue that the next point of childhood is to gain some control by learning how to understand our environment and how to have an impact on the people around us. We will start by examining how we build up our knowledge and understanding of the world via processes of memory. We will then consider how we start to form our own perspective of the world and understand what we think, feel and believe. Finally we will show how we learn to communicate using both non-verbal and verbal language skills.

3.1   Memory and representations

We all know that infants and young children spend a great deal of their time sleeping. However, beyond giving grateful parents a bit of peace and quiet, sleeping is actually an important part of knowledge gathering and learning to understand the world because many of our memories of what we have done in our waking hours are processed and stored during this time (Graves et al., 2001). It has been argued that during the first few years of life, infants are incredible 'learning machines' laying the foundations for future independence.

Activity 2.3:   What do you remember about your own childhood?

Think carefully about your memories of childhood.

1   What is your earliest memory?

2   In this memory, how old do you think you were?

3   What skills did you develop in the first few years of life that you actually can't remember learning at all?

What researchers of child development never cease to find interesting is why there is a failure to remember anything about the first few years of our lives. This phenomenon is often referred to as childhood amnesia. Activity 2.3 will hopefully have demonstrated that our first autobiographical memories, i.e. the personal stories of our own lives, rarely occur before the age of three years and we generally have no real recollection of major milestones such as learning to interact with and use objects, for example shaking a rattle and building a tower of blocks, learning to walk or learning to talk. A key challenge for researchers is to try and explain this.

A prominent explanation is that there are different types of memory systems (Hayne, 2004). Early memories, or our representations of the world (up to the age of approximately three years), are largely thought to involve the learning of practical skills (e.g. walking); instinctive or automatic reactions to our environment (e.g. avoiding touching the oven because it is hot); and the formation of habits and routines (e.g. washing hands before eating) (Hayne, 2004). These so-called lower forms of memory do not necessarily require conscious awareness or much actual thought and are often referred to as 'non-declarative' (e.g. Squire, 1994) or 'implicit' (e.g. Schachter, 1994) memories. However, while it is true that we might not be able to actually recall how we acquired this type of knowledge, we know that if our brain suffers damage following something like a stroke, or another type of head injury, we have to re-learn skills that we take for granted. We never actually stop developing these types of memories particularly when learning practical skills, but as our memory system and representations of the world become more sophisticated we also start to develop higher order memories that we are consciously aware of and can explain to other people if asked. These are often referred to as 'declarative' (Squire, 1994) or 'explicit' (Schachter, 1994) memories. This might help to explain why it is impossible to tell someone about how you learned to walk but you might be able to give a very entertaining account of the first time you tried to ride a bike and promptly fell off! The former occurred before the age of three and was a non-declarative–implicit memory while the latter occurred at the age of five and was a declarative–explicit memory.

Pause for thought

How is it possible to confirm that infants are actually forming memories and to measure if their memory system is improving?

We know that memories are forming in the first few years of life but how researchers actually produce evidence of this is another key challenge of infant memory research. The trick is focusing upon what young infants can do. One thing that they are very good at is showing boredom in response to something already familiar to them versus a keen interest in something that is new. An early method of investigating this effect was called **visual recognition memory techniques** (e.g. Berlyne, 1958; Fantz, 1958) and involved the ability of infants to look at stimuli. In paired comparison tasks, infants were first shown a stimulus, for example a picture of a dog, and then there was a delay before two further stimuli were simultaneously presented: the picture that the infant had already seen and a new or novel picture. If infants remembered the picture shown earlier they tended to look at it for less time compared to the new picture, which was understandably more interesting (Hayne, 2004). Extending the period of delay between the first and second presentation from minutes to days to weeks, allows researchers to show improvements in memory over time in the first year of life (Olson and Sherman, 1983).

Other methods involve the ability of infants to suck, for example using the high-amplitude sucking technique. Infants will suck harder on a nipple (attached to a pressure transducer) to listen to their mother's voice compared to that of an unfamiliar woman. This indicates a memory for the mother's voice (e.g. DeCasper and Fifer, 1980). Another method involves infants' ability to kick. In the **mobile conjugate reinforcement paradigm** an overhead mobile is attached to an infant's leg via a ribbon (Figure 2.5). When the infant kicks this causes the mobile to move. Infants are first introduced to the procedure and then in follow-up sessions memory for the technique is indicated when infants quickly start kicking as soon as the ribbon is tied on (Rovee-Collier, 1997).

Visual recognition memory techniques
Tests of infant memory involving the visual presentation of novel and familiar stimuli.

Mobile conjugate reinforcement paradigm
A technique used to study infant memory whereby an overhead mobile is attached to an infant by a ribbon tied to their leg. The infant gradually learns that if they kick their leg they can make the mobile move.

Figure 2.5   Infant memory can be measured by the mobile conjugate reinforcement paradigm

These innovative techniques have provided evidence showing how our memory systems improve throughout the first few years of infancy and support the growing knowledge and understanding of how we represent the world.

3.2   Egocentrism and early theory of mind

We have shown that young children have growing abilities of learning and memory in relation to their environment. However, what we have discussed so far has presented infants as little more than sponges soaking up knowledge. What we have not considered is how our own unique perspective upon the world forms, and what we think, feel and believe in relation to it. These are vital processes if we are going to achieve independence.

If you have ever spent much time with a young child aged two to three years, you can be left in no doubt that they have a clear idea of what they want. Failure to comply with their requests can result in tantrums and a refusal to move from the floor of the supermarket (Figure 2.6). Children of this age seem incapable of understanding anything that contradicts their own singular purpose, for example: why do they have to go to bed if they want to continue playing? Why do they have to share their favourite toy with some interloper to their playroom? A key challenge for researchers is therefore to try to explain why this early view of the world is apparently so rigid.

Figure 2.6   Tantrums are a characteristic of the egocentric child

The highly influential theorist and researcher Jean Piaget first tackled this problem in the 1920s by suggesting that a failure to see the world from anything other than your own perspective can be understood as the concept of **egocentrism**. He further refined this idea over the next 40 years while often receiving criticism from other researchers. Nonetheless, essentially, egocentrism suggests that young children do not actively choose to ignore the wishes of others because they are naughty or malicious in any way; instead they do not understand that other people actually have views of their own. They genuinely believe the world revolves around them! It is only when they recognise that every person also has a viewpoint on the world, and crucially that it might be different from theirs, that the effect of egocentrism will

Egocentrism
A lack of awareness that other people have views, thoughts, feelings, beliefs about the world that may differ from your own.

reduce. Once this realisation has occurred, the ability to see the world through another's eyes will develop, for instance: 'Mummy only puts me to bed so that I won't feel tired the next day'.

Subsequently a great deal of research has been conducted to track this development. Piaget suggested it should develop by seven to eight years of age (Piaget and Inhelder, 1967) while subsequent studies suggested this was an overestimation and five years was more appropriate (e.g. Hughes and Donaldson, 1979). In the classic 'three mountains task', children viewed a three-dimensional scene of a mountainous landscape and were first asked to explain what they could see from their own perspective, for instance they might describe being able to see a tree, a house, etc. In the second part of the task children are asked to describe the scene from the perspective of another person sitting opposite them. The view from the other side of the scene will be different from theirs, for example you might still be able to see the tree but not the house. It was suggested that egocentrism had reduced once children were able to understand the fact that just because they could see something it didn't mean another could (Piaget and Inhelder, 1967).

The study of egocentrism has shown that children first have to be aware that they have their own, unique perspective of the world before they can understand another's viewpoint. So what mechanism is underlying this development? This challenging question leads neatly on to a consideration of **theory of mind** development. Coined by Premack and Woodruff (1978) it can be understood as a two-step process:

Theory of mind
The ability to recognise that you have mental states, i.e. thoughts, feelings and beliefs, and to understand and be able to infer the mental states of others.

1   To recognise our own mental states, i.e. that we have thoughts, feelings and beliefs

2   To recognise that other people may have a different mental state to our own and be able to infer what they might be thinking, feeling and believing.

It is suggested that although the second step of the process is not fully formed until the age of four or five years the origins begin much earlier.

A key building block involves the concept of shared attention (see Figure 2.7) where the child and their caregiver will be thinking about and looking at the same thing. An example of this might be an adult pointing to a teddy bear and saying: 'Look, there's your teddy bear'. At that moment both the child and caregiver are thinking about the teddy bear and thus their mental states have coordinated. The recognition that someone else might be thinking about the same thing as you is the first step towards eventually being able to infer what someone might be thinking: the ability of mind reading. Later, children will show an understanding of shared intentions. This requires them to first understand what the intention or want of another person might be before they can collaborate in activities which form the basis of social interactions, for example putting away toys together, rolling a ball to each other (Tomasello et al., 2005). At approximately 24 months children also start to show prosocial or helping behaviours signifying empathy, the ability to understand what somebody else might be feeling (e.g. Cole et al., 1992).

Figure 2.7   A father and child demonstrating shared attention

However, it is the ability to understand what other people believe that has often dominated theory of mind research. By the age of four, children should be able to recognise that other people can have false beliefs and indeed researchers have argued that testing this is the only true way of establishing whether a child can infer the mental state of another (Dennett, 1978). The classic false belief test is the Sally–Anne task (Baron-Cohen et al., 1985) which involves showing children a scenario of two children called Sally and Anne, either via pictures or the use of real-world props (see Figure 2.8).

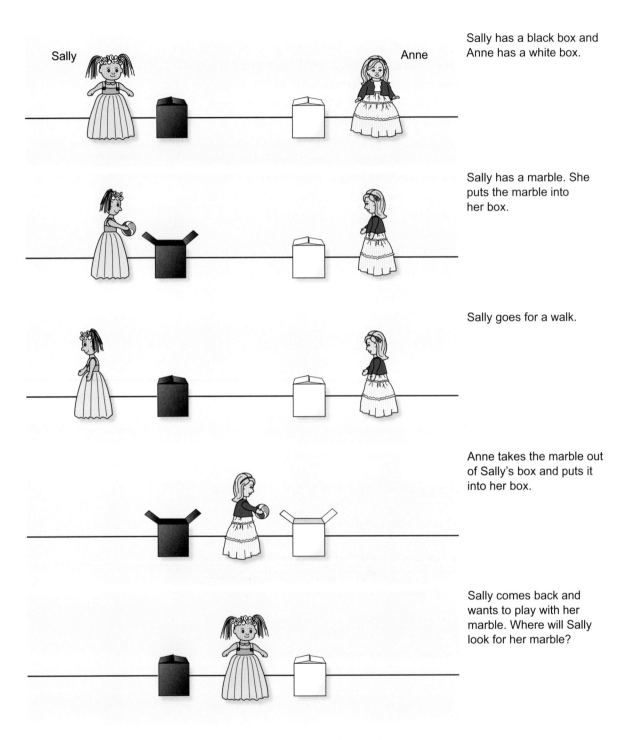

Sally has a black box and Anne has a white box.

Sally has a marble. She puts the marble into her box.

Sally goes for a walk.

Anne takes the marble out of Sally's box and puts it into her box.

Sally comes back and wants to play with her marble. Where will Sally look for her marble?

Figure 2.8   A pictorial version of the Sally–Anne task of false belief

Sally has a marble which she places in her black box before leaving the room. Subsequently 'naughty' Anne moves the marble out of the black box and into her own white box. Sally then returns to the room and children are asked to say where they think Sally will look for her marble. If children understand that Sally falsely believes that the marble is still in her black box (because she doesn't know that Anne moved it) then they will say that she will look for it in the black box. This answer would indicate that the child recognises that people can have false beliefs.

3.3 Language development

We have shown so far that in the first few years of life, children are building up their knowledge of the world through developing memory systems. They are gaining not only a sense of themselves in relation to the wider world, i.e. their own thoughts, feeling and beliefs, but also a growing understanding of other people via social interactions. We will now consider how young children start to achieve some degree of impact and control over the world due to the development of language.

> ### Pause for thought
>
> When first starting to study psychology our concept of language and communication might be somewhat limited to the idea of learning how to talk and hold conversations, i.e. verbal language. However, what quickly becomes apparent when you consider the issue further is that language is so much more than this, and that non-verbal characteristics, such as shared gaze/attention, facial expressions and gesturing, also have to be taken into account.
>
> To illustrate this point you might recollect a conversation you have had recently, or engage in one right now (if there is someone else in the room), and think about the 'non-verbal' communication that is taking place.

We have already seen that infants are born with a preference for looking at faces and listening to voices (Section 2.1). Very rapidly infants also start to imitate or copy adults' facial expressions (e.g. Meltzoff and Moore, 1977) and move their limbs in response to adult speech (Condon and Sander, 1974). As well as helping to form the attachment between infant and caregiver, this also forms the basis for early language development because it is a form of communication. In fact, caregivers and infants can be observed engaging in practice or **proto conversations** (Bateson, 1979) characterised by face-to-face activity; consistent eye contact; and turn taking in smiling, facial expressions, hand movements and pre-speech sounds, for example cooing and babbling. Infants are already influencing their environment by the use of these skills (see Figure 2.9).

Proto conversations
An early interaction between an adult and infant before the infant can speak involving a two-way and turn-taking exchange of gestures, sounds and facial expressions viewed as a 'practice' conversation.

Figure 2.9   A mother and infant engaging in a proto conversation

From the age of 12 months we can start to see a real cross-over between language and theory of mind development. As referred to in Section 3.2, the processes of shared attention and shared intentions are also integral to language development as children learn that objects, people and abstract concepts are represented by words, and that it is through words that knowledge and goals can be shared. Children certainly should not be viewed as passive participants during this process. Prior to speech, children will use gesture, in the form of pointing, to engage adults in conversation and to extract knowledge. Imperative pointing encourages an adult to do something for you, for instance if a child points at a toy it might mean they want you to bring it to them while declarative pointing encourages a child or adult to share attention about something of interest, for example if a child points at a toy it might mean they're trying to engage you in an interaction about the toy and what it is or does (Bates et al., 1975).

From the age of 18 months to four years children learn to say their first words and start to form simple and then more complex sentences, rapidly increasing their ability to gain further knowledge about the world by asking questions and to have an impact on the world by engaging those around them. However, despite the development of verbal language, gesture (see Figure 2.10) continues to play an important role in easing the speaker's burden by improving access to the desired words (Rauscher et al., 1996). This is demonstrated by Activity 2.4, which is based on the work by Pine et al. (2007), and shows how difficult speech can be if we don't have gesture to help us.

Figure 2.10   Gesturing is an important part of the development of language and communication

---

Activity 2.4:   What is the purpose of gesturing?

First, when you have an opportunity, find a willing partner to engage in this activity (if necessary this task could be done via telephone* or Skype if they can't be in the same room as you) and carry out the following:

1   Start by suppressing your gestures, i.e. sit on your hands and then try to explain to your partner what some of the following items are and how you use them (of course not mentioning their names!): umbrella, bow and arrow, fire extinguisher, bag pipe, watering can, binoculars, stethoscope, whisk.

2   From your verbal descriptions ask your partner to identify the items.

3   Did you experience any difficulties? If so, what were they?

4   Were some items harder to describe than others? If so, why do you think that is?

*It would be interesting to further reflect on any additional difficulties for this task if you can't actually see the other person!

The importance of language for increasing the independence of children cannot really be overstated. Indeed the prominent theorist Vygotsky (who you read about in Book 2, Chapter 4) suggested that children's development can be understood as a product of social interaction and it is language that is the main facilitator of this interaction. Linked to this point is the idea that if children are deprived of access to any type of language input prior to puberty they will find it difficult to fully develop grammatical abilities later on. This 'critical period' hypothesis for language (Lenneberg, 1967) did initially find some support via the case studies of so-called wild or feral children. The most famous example of these was Genie who was discovered at the age of 13 years. Abused and neglected by her parents, she had never really been exposed to language and initially could not speak at all. Although intensive speech therapy enabled her to acquire a vocabulary and produce simple phrases she was never able to communicate in grammatically correct, complex sentences (Buddenhagen, 1971). Nonetheless, this hypothesis has been challenged more recently and current thinking suggests that language, like any skill, can be acquired at any time providing circumstances are favourable and a person doesn't have any barriers to learning in a

typical manner, for example a disability of some kind
(Tomasello, 2000).

3.4 Summary

This section has shown that the second point of childhood is to learn
how to control the environment. We argued that first we need to learn
how to understand it and engage in the process of knowledge
gathering. Underlying this are memory systems that become more
sophisticated over time and this is studied using some of the most
innovative methods in psychology. We also considered that as we start
the process of learning we have our own, unique perspective of the
world. As egocentrism decreases and theory of mind develops, we also
gain the ability to understand other people, vital for influencing social
interaction. Finally we have shown that our development of both non-
verbal and verbal language is not only a vehicle for our growing
understanding of the world and other people, it is our most important
skill for controlling and impacting our environment.

4   How to function well in the environment

As children enter the school years they have generally formed close relationships with caregivers and other family members and have started to build up knowledge and understanding of their environment. They have also started to appreciate that they have their own perspective of the world and have gained an initial understanding that other people may see the world differently from them. The next step in the journey towards independence is to function more effectively within a social context. Therefore, we argue that the third point of childhood is to build a wider network of successful relationships beyond immediate family. Inevitably this process is not always easy when faced with the negative behaviours of others and the challenges of interacting in an increasingly digitalised world. We will show how our friendships with peers develop over time and consider the effects of bullying at school. We will then introduce the second order theory of mind and suggest how this allows us to manipulate others. Finally we will explore a very modern concern: the impact of social media on children's friendships and communication.

4.1   Friendships and bullying at school

It is frequently said that your school days are the best days of your life. Now whether you agree with this sentiment or not it is often true that our memories of school are dominated more by our experiences with our peers than our actual academic studies (see Figure 2.11). As children get older and develop into adolescents, feelings and emotions become heightened to the point where friendships and peer influence can be all-consuming while any negative action or comment from a bully can really leave its mark.

Figure 2.11 Friendships develop throughout the school years

Activity 2.5: What does friendship mean to you?

1 First think about your early school days (from four to eleven years old) and write a few notes about your friendships. How many close friends did you have? Was there a best friend? What was the basis of your friendships and what do you think determined your choice of friends? What did you learn from your friendships?

2 Now think about your later school days (from 12 to 18 years old) and repeat the process. Can you see any obvious changes in your friendships as you got older?

Friendships are extremely important in our development and we hope Activity 2.5 has helped you reflect upon your experiences of them and what you learned from them. This is important because lessons about reciprocal relationships, i.e. relationships on a relatively equal power footing (unlike the caregiver–child relationship) can only really be learned with peers. These lessons about how to interact successfully with other people are necessary if we are going to move from the dependence of childhood to the independence of adulthood.

While it is true that we may describe our friendships in a more complex way as we grow older, and the activities we carry out within friendships change considerably over time, the meaning we place on friendship does not necessarily alter. The key characteristic of a friendship is a sense of mutual support and this is actually more powerful than just having the same likes or dislikes. The size of our friendship networks and the time we spend with our friends may also change over time, reaching a peak in adolescence, but it remains the case that good friends help us feel better about ourselves, increase our sense of well-being and provide support through the transitions of life (Hartup and Stevens, 1997). As well as an emotional impact we also gain valuable social skills, such as how to resolve conflict, working with others to achieve goals and self-disclosure, i.e. learning to share our feeling, opinions, etc. which will ultimately prepare us for romantic relationships as well (Hartup and Stevens, 1999).

Unfortunately a lack of close friendships can make it difficult for children socially and this is associated with greater difficulties in transitions, for example moving from primary to secondary school (Berndt and Keefe, 1992). This can lead to a greater need to seek help for emotional and behavioural problems (Rutter and Garmezy, 1983). We should point out that there is a lack of clarity though about what causes what here. Do children feel bad because they don't have any friends, or does the fact that they are naturally less confident make it difficult for them to make friends? Whatever the answer (and with most things it is likely to be a mixture of both) it cannot be denied that negative interactions with our peers during childhood is a challenge that can be difficult to face as we make our way in the world (see Figure 2.12).

Figure 2.12 Bullying can have a negative impact upon social and academic development

There is some disagreement about how to define bullying although Farrington (1993) suggested that it is physical, verbal or psychological attacks or intimidation intended to cause fear, distress or harm to the victim. Other characteristics frequently include an imbalance of power between the perpetrator and the victim, absence of provocation by the victim and repeated incidents over time.

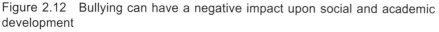

Pause for thought

Do you agree with Farrington's definition of bullying?

How would you define bullying?

Differences in definition between schools may influence how bullying is tackled and sadly being a prolonged victim of bullying can lead to increased levels of depression, anxiety and psychosomatic symptoms (Kaltiala-Heino et al., 2000), feelings of social ineffectiveness and interpersonal difficulties (Craig, 1998) as well as higher absenteeism from school, and lower academic competence (Roland, 2002).

Therefore, effective bullying interventions should focus on empowering victims and helping them to cope to lessen the negative impact rather than just on punishing the perpetrators (Juvonen and Graham, 2001).

4.2   Manipulation and later theory of mind

As we spend more time with our peers our theory of mind skills continue to develop. In Section 3.2 we saw that a major milestone in understanding the perspective of other people was the identification of false beliefs, which occurs around the age of four years. However, theory of mind development does not stop there and over the next few years not only can we understand how other people are thinking and feeling but we can also actively manipulate what they think and how they feel (Gillibrand et al., 2011).

Continuing our earlier discussion, many of the positive manipulations that children learn occur within friendships. We've already seen that friendships are often defined by the quality of mutual support and both children and adults agree that prosocial behaviour is expected (Berndt, 2002). Prosocial behaviours continue to increase throughout the school years alongside a finer understanding of both what might be causing hurt, upset or need as well as how best to remedy it (see Figure 2.13). Children start to routinely help and share with their friends in both day-to-day activities such as school work and in more emotionally charged circumstances, for example sticking up for a friend in a fight or having to cope with the awful realisation that the boy/girl they fancy doesn't reciprocate (Berndt, 2002)! Unfortunately greater understanding of how to manipulate also has a darker side. Indeed one theory of bullying suggests that perpetrators may have superior theory of mind skills compared to their peers because if we truly want to frighten another person or make them feel bad we need to have a true insight into which buttons to press (Sutton et al., 1999).

Figure 2.13 Prosocial behaviour is a positive effect of advanced theory of mind skills

4.3 Social media

When we were younger the only way to see our friends outside of school was to go round to their house or meet somewhere, for instance a park or outside the shops, and the only way to contact them was by a landline telephone or to send a letter through the post. During this century the nature of children's social interaction and communication has undergone seismic shifts and this process doesn't look to be slowing down anytime soon. Children's interactions are being played out in a virtual world due to the growth in social media and its constant availability via various technologies, for example smart phones, tablets, etc. (see Figure 2.14). This has implications for how children and adolescents conduct their friendships, how bullying extends into cyberspace, and how we present ourselves and view others within a digital context.

Figure 2.14   Children are increasingly using new technologies to engage in social interactions

It is difficult to make any clear conclusions about the overall impact. A review from the American Academy of Pediatrics (O'Keefe and Clarke-Pearson, 2011) summarised the research findings gained hitherto. From a positive perspective, the growth of social media has allowed children to be connected in a way that was never previously open to them. This allows the proliferation of friendships outside of school and has encouraged children to learn to communicate in different forms and develop new social skills to maintain those friendships (Valkenburg and Peter, 2007). Furthermore, it provides opportunities to feel more connected to a wider social world where you can exchange ideas, gain information and access creative outputs within communities that wouldn't have been previously open. All of these things will continue to allow children to develop independently beyond their immediate family and socially interact within the wider world (see Figure 2.15).

Figure 2.15 Adolescents taking part in the recent craze for selfies

However, inevitably, there are possible negative impacts on children's development as well. Cyber-bullying extends our traditional definition of bullying (see Section 4.1) into the virtual world. Nevertheless, while the intention of the bullying remains the same, it does differ from face-to-face incidents in a number of ways. It is pervasive at home as well as school (leading to the question of who should tackle it). It can reach a much wider audience, and the perpetrators are not always known due to the anonymous nature of some interactions. However, withdrawal from electronic media can make the impact worse as it can lead to greater social isolation. Moreover, there are particular concerns about sexting, i.e. the sending or receiving of sexually explicit messages, pictures and videos involving children or adolescents, which is actually illegal according to UK law. These incidents can occur without consent or can actually be distributed by the children themselves due to peer pressure or natural urges to experiment without fully realising the possible extent of the exposure. The latter certainly concerns the issue of how children are portraying themselves online and the medium does allow for experiments in identity (Valkenburg and Peter, 2008). Slightly less extreme than sexting are concerns that the use of certain types of media, for example posting personal videos and pictures, can lead to a negative impact on well-being as children feel inadequate compared to peers, heavily scrutinised and pressured to conform to certain ideals of physical appearance (Pea et al., 2012).

This debate is likely to continue to challenge researchers due to the different ways that social media are used by children. Nonetheless, what is becoming more apparent is the role of parents and educators in scaffolding its use and helping children to understand how to protect themselves within this world. In conclusion, a sensible view might be to argue that over time there have been many new developments that (as a society) we are worried may have a damaging effect on our children's social development, for example comics, TV, movies, computer games, but what is important is that children use them appropriately within their social interactions.

4.4   Summary

This section has shown that the third point of childhood is to learn how to function well in the environment, and develop social relationships beyond the immediate family to further our independence. We have shown that peer relationships are the vehicle by which we learn about reciprocal relationships, and friendships promote our sense of well-being and provide support as we develop skills of conflict resolution and team working and cope with the transitions of life. Friendships are particularly important given the inevitability of negative reactions from peers in bullying situations that can leave a lasting effect.

We have argued that underlying this growing understanding of other people are more advanced theory of mind skills that allow us to actively manipulate how others are feeling. This can be manifested within friendships in positive prosocial behaviours or negatively within bullying situations by perpetrators who can skilfully identify vulnerabilities.

Finally, we have provided insight into the changing context by which children are experiencing these interactions, namely the growth of social media and associated technologies. Findings are mixed regarding the possible advantages and harmful effects to children's social development. However, it seems clear that this aspect of childhood has undergone some seismic changes, presenting new challenges for children themselves and for researchers trying to study the phenomenon.

5   Concluding thoughts

So, what can we conclude about this chapter on 'What is the point of childhood? Early experiences and social relationships'. The first conclusion is that 'childhood' is difficult to define and conceptualise because it is socially constructed and rooted in a physical, social, cultural, economic and historical context. Childhood exists as a period of the lifespan where tremendous development occurs. The first challenge we have in the earliest stages of childhood is to survive it and make it through to the later stages. We have seen that evolution has equipped us with many innately specified behaviours designed to influence and control the behaviour of caregivers in our environment when we are particularly vulnerable – this ultimately enhances our survival prospects. These behaviours are also crucial for the attachment relationship, which is not only vital for survival, but also provides a working model for later interactions. Some challenging and contemporary issues were also addressed here such as the theory of multiple attachments, the impact of day care centres, and the possible role of genetics in the infant–caregiver attachment relationship.

A second challenge once we have survived the turmoil of the earliest stage of the lifespan is to learn how to control the environment, and this is underpinned by key cognitive advancements. Significant developments occur in our memory systems allowing us to gather knowledge and learn about our environment. Furthermore, the development of egocentrism allows us to understand that we have a unique view of the world while theory of mind skills help us to understand that others may view the world differently. Alongside this our major tools of communication (non-verbal and verbal language) allow us to have an impact on the environment and start to achieve what we want. However, it was noted that while developments in young children's thinking enables them to act on the environment, it does not necessarily follow that they can act well in the social world.

Lastly, we considered that, as children move progressively away from the family during childhood via the development of peer relationships, we start to form the skills of interpersonal relationships and with second order theory of mind are increasingly able to manipulate others with both good and bad intentions. Finally we highlighted the possible benefits and challenges that children face in navigating these peer relationships within the growing influence of social media.

In sum, the point of childhood, we argue, is first to *survive it*; second, to learn how to *control the environment*; and third, to learn how to *function well in the wider social context*. We will leave you with two quotes about childhood; the first was Andrew's favourite and the second was Sarah's favourite.

In childhood, we press our nose to the pane, looking out. In memories of childhood, we press our nose to the pane, looking in.

Robert Brault

I cannot for the life of me understand why small children take so long to grow up. I think they do it deliberately, just to annoy me.

Roald Dahl, *Matilda*

Further reading

- This article discusses the theory that many attributes of the developmental disorder autism can be potentially understood in the context of a problem with theory of mind development, i.e. 'mindblindness'. This article is useful for both further understanding of the role that theory of mind plays in cognitive and social development and for one theoretical perspective of autism:

Baron-Cohen, S. (1995) *Mindblindness: An essay on Autism and Theory of Mind*, Cambridge, MA, MIT Press.

- This general textbook on developmental psychology is designed for undergraduates and is an excellent overview of key topics in this field. Relevant theory and research is presented in a clear and accessible manner and learning is supported with fun and thought-provoking activities:

Gillibrand, R., Lam, V. and O'Donnell, V.L. (2011) *Developmental Psychology*, Harlow, Prentice Hall.

- This article challenges universal theories of child development and argues that early childhood educators have not been attentive enough to the centrality of culture in a child's development:

Lee, K. and Johnson, A.S. (2007) 'Child development in cultural contexts: implications of cultural psychology for early childhood teacher education', *Early Childhood Education Journal*, vol. 35, no. 3, pp. 233–43.

- This article provides an interesting discussion of the Six Cultures Study of Socialization (SCSS). It argues that more than 50 years on it remains an historical landmark project that inspired future work and exemplifies the possibilities and problems of comparative research on child development:

LeVine, R.A. (2010) 'The six cultures study: prologue to a history of a landmark project', *Journal of Cross-Cultural Psychology*, vol. 41, no. 4, pp. 513–21.

- This article considers how the nature–nurture debate has evolved over time and proposes a unified theory of development that captures the complex interplay between individual and contextual factors:

Sameroff, A. (2010) 'A unified theory of development: a dialectic integration of nature and nurture', *Child Development*, vol. 81, no. 1, pp. 6–22.

References

Ainsworth, M.D.S., Blehar, M., Waters, E. and Wall, S. (1978) *Patterns of Attachment: A Psychological Study of the Strange Situation*, Hillsdale, NJ, Erlbaum.

Bakermans-Kranenburg, M.J., van IJzendoorn, M.H. and Juffer, F. (2003) 'Less is more: Meta-analyses of sensitivity and attachment interventions in early childhood', *Psychological Bulletin*, vol. 129, no. 2, pp. 195–215.

Baron-Cohen, S., Leslie, A.M. and Frith, U. (1985) 'Does the autistic child have a "theory of mind?"', *Cognition*, vol. 21, pp. 37–46.

Bates, E., Camaioni, L. and Volterra, V. (1975) 'The acquisition of performatives prior to speech', *Merrill-Palmer Quarterly of Behavior and Development*, pp. 205–26.

Bateson, G. (1979) *Mind and Nature: A Necessary Unity*, New York, Dutton.

Bauminger, N., Finzi–Dottan, R., Chason, S. and Har-Even, D. (2008) 'Intimacy in adolescent friendship: the roles of attachment, coherence, and self-disclosure', *Journal of Social and Personal Relationships*, vol. 25, no. 3, pp. 409-28.

Bell, R.Q. (1968) 'A reinterpretation of the direction of effects in studies of socialization', *Psychological Review*, vol. 75, no. 2, pp. 81–95.

Belsky, J. (2005) 'Attachment theory and research in ecological perspective', in Grossmann, K.E., Grossmann, K. and Waters, E. (eds) *Attachment from Infancy to Adulthood: The Major Longitudinal Studies*, New York, Guilford Press, pp. 71–97.

Belsky, J. and Pasco Fearon, R.M. (2008) 'Precursors of attachment security', in Cassidy, J. and Shaver, P.R. (eds) *Handbook of Attachment: Theory, Research, and Clinical Applications*, New York, Guilford Press, pp. 295–316.

Berlyne, D.E. (1958) 'The influence of the albedo and complexity of stimuli on visual fixation in the human infant', *British Journal of Psychology*, vol. 49, no. 4, pp. 315–18.

Berndt, T.J. (2002) 'Friendship quality and social development', *Current Directions in Psychological Science*, vol. 11, no. 1, pp. 7–10.

Berndt, T.J. and Keefe, K. (1992) '"Friends" influence on adolescents' perceptions on themselves in school', in Schunk, D.H. and Meece, J.L. (eds) *Students' Perceptions in the Classroom*, Hillsdale, NJ, Erlbaum, pp. 51–73.

Bowlby, J. (1969) *Attachment and Loss: Vol. 1. Attachment*, New York, Basic Books.

Buddenhagen, R.G. (1971) *Establishing Vocal Verbalisations in Mute Mongoloid Children*, Champaign, IL, Research Press.

Cole, P.M., Barrett. K.C. and Zahn-Wexler, C. (1992) 'Emotion displays in two-year-olds during mishaps', *Child Development*, vol. 63, no. 2, pp. 314–24.

Condon, W.S. and Sander, L.W. (1974) 'Neonate movement is synchronized with adult speech: interactional participation and language acquisition', *Science*, vol. 183, no. 4120, pp. 99–101.

Craig, W.M. (1998) 'The relationship among bullying, victimization, depression, anxiety, and aggression in elementary school children', *Personality and Individual Differences*, vol. 24, no. 1, pp. 123–30.

DeCasper, A.J. and Fifer, W.P. (1980) 'Of human bonding: newborns prefer their mothers' voices', *Science*, vol. 208, no. 4448, pp. 1174–76.

Dennett, D. (1978) *Brainstorms: Philosophical Essays on Mind and Psychology*, Cambridge, MA, Bradford Books/MIT Press.

De Wolff, M. and van IJzendoorn, M.H. (1997) 'Sensitivity and attachment: A meta-analysis on parental antecedents of infant attachment', *Child Development*, vol. 68, no. 4, pp. 571–91.

Englund, M.M., Kuo, S.I.-C., Puig, J. and Collins, W.A. (2011) 'Early roots of adult competence: the significance of close relationships from infancy to early adulthood', *International Journal of Behavioral Development*, vol. 35, no. 6, pp. 490–96.

Fantz, R.L. (1958) 'Pattern vision in young infants', *Psychological Record*, vol. 8, pp. 43–7.

Fantz, R.L. (1961) 'The origins of form perception', *Scientific American*, vol. 204, no. 5, pp. 66–72.

Farrington, D.P. (1993) 'Understanding and preventing bullying', in Tonry, M. and Morris, N. (eds) *Crime and Justice: An Annual Review of Research*, vol. 17, Chicago, IL, University of Chicago Press, pp. 381–458.

Feldman, R. (2003) 'Paternal socio-psychological factors and infant attachment: the mediating role of synchrony in father-infant interactions', *Infant Behavior and Development*, vol. 25, no. 2, pp. 221–36.

Gillibrand, R., Lam, V. and O'Donnell, V.L. (2011) *Developmental Psychology*, Harlow, Prentice Hall.

Goswami, U. (2008) *Cognitive Development: The Learning Brain*, Hove, UK, Psychology Press.

Graves, L., Pack, A. and Abel, T. (2001) 'Sleep and memory: a molecular perspective', *Trends in Neurosciences*, vol. 24, no. 4, pp. 237–43.

Griggs, J., Tan, J.P., Buchanan, A., Attar–Shwartz, S. and Flouri, E. (2010) '"They've always been there for me": grandparental involvement and child well-being', *Children and Society*, vol. 24, no. 3, pp. 204–14.

Grossmann, K., Grossmann, K.E., Spangler, G., Suess, G. and Unzner, L. (1985) 'Maternal sensitivity and newborns' orientation responses as related to quality of attachment in northern Germany', *Monographs of the Society of Research in Child Development*, vol. 50, no. 1–2, pp. 233–56.

Harris, M. and Butterworth, G. (2002) *Developmental Psychology: A Student's Handbook*, Hove, UK, Psychology Press.

Hartup, W.W. and Stevens, N. (1997) 'Friendship and adaptation in the life course', *Psychological Bulletin*, vol. 121, no. 3, pp. 355–70.

Hartup, W.W. and Stevens, N. (1999) 'Friendship and adaptation across the lifespan', *Current Directions in Psychological Science*, vol. 8, pp. 76–9.

Hayne, H. (2004) 'Infant memory development: implications for childhood amnesia', *Developmental Review*, vol. 24, no. 1, pp. 33–73.

Hicks, J.H. and Goedereis, E.A. (2009) 'The importance of context and the gain-loss dynamic for understanding grandparent caregivers', in Shifren, K. (ed) *How Caregiving Affects Development: Psychological Implications for Child, Adolescent, and Adult Caregivers*, Washington, American Psychological Association, pp. 169–90.

Hughes, M. and Donaldson, M. (1979) 'The use of hiding games for studying the coordination of viewpoints', *Educational Review*, vol. 31, no. 2, pp. 133–40.

Jin, M.K., Jacobvitz, D., Hazen, N. and Jung, S.H. (2012) 'Maternal sensitivity and infant attachment security in Korea: cross-cultural validation of the Strange Situation', *Attachment and Human Development*, vol. 14, no. 1, pp. 33–44.

Juvonen, J. and Graham, S. (2001) *Peer Harassment in School: The Plight of the Vulnerable and Victimized*, New York, Guilford Press.

Kaltiala-Heino, R., Rimpelä, M., Rantanen, P. and Rimpelä, A. (2000) 'Bullying at school – an indicator of adolescents at risk for mental disorders', *Journal of Adolescence*, vol. 23, no. 6, pp. 661–74.

Kiff, C.J., Lengua, L.J. and Zalewski, M. (2011) 'Nature and nurture: parenting in the context of child temperament', *Clinical Child and Family Psychology Review*, vol. 14, no. 3, pp. 251–301.

Kim, P.S., McQueen, J.S., Coxworth, J.E. and Hawkes, K. (2014) 'Grandmothering drives the evolution of longevity in a probabilistic model', *Journal of Theoretical Biology*, vol. 353, pp. 84–94.

Lee, K. and Johnson, A.S. (2007) 'Child development in cultural contexts: implications of cultural psychology for early childhood teacher education', *Early Childhood Education Journal*, vol. 35, no. 3, pp. 233–43.

Lenneberg, E. (1967) *Biological Foundations of Language*, New York, Wiley.

Lewis, C. and Lamb, M.E. (2003) 'Fathers' influences on children's development: the evidence from two-parent families', *European Journal of Psychology of Education*, vol. 18, no. 2, pp. 211–28.

Luijk, M.P.C.M., Tharner, A., Bakermans–Kranenburg, M.J., van IJzendoorn, M.H., Jaddoe, V.W.V., Hofman, A., Verhulst, F.C. and Tiemeier, H. (2011) 'The association between parenting and attachment security is moderated by a polymorphism in the mineralocorticoid receptor gene: evidence for differential susceptibility', *Biological Psychology*, vol. 88, no. 1, pp. 37–40.

Main, M., Kaplan, N. and Cassidy, J. (1985) 'Security in infancy, childhood, and adulthood: a move to the level of representation', *Monographs of the Society of Research in Child Development*, vol. 50, no. 1/2, pp. 66–104.

McElwain, N.L., Booth–LaForce, C. and Wu, X. (2011) 'Infant–mother attachment and children's friendship quality: maternal mental-state talk as an intervening mechanism', *Developmental Psychology*, vol. 47, no. 5, pp. 1295–311.

Meltzoff, A.N. and Moore, M.K. (1977) 'Imitation of facial and manual gestures by human neonates', *Science*, vol. 198, no. 4312, pp. 75–8.

Moss, E., Cyr, C. and Dubois-Comtois, K. (2004) 'Attachment at early school age and developmental risk: examining family contexts and behavior problems of controlling–caregiving, controlling–punitive, and behaviorally disorganized children', *Developmental Psychology*, vol. 40, no. 4, pp. 519–32.

NICHD (1997) 'The effects of infant child care on infant-mother attachment security: Results of the NICHD study of early child care', *Child Development*, vol. 68, no. 5, pp. 860–79.

NICHD (2002) 'The interaction of child care and family risk in relation to child development at 24 and 36 months', *Applied Developmental Science*, vol. 6, no. 3, pp. 144–56.

NICHD (2003) 'Does amount of time spent in child care predict socioemotional adjustment during the transition to kindergarten?', *Child Development*, vol. 74, no. 4, pp. 967–1005.

O'Keefe, G.S. and Clarke-Pearson, K. (2011) 'Clinical report from American Academy of Pediatrics: the impact of social media on children, adolescents and families', *Pediatrics*, vol. 147, no. 4, pp. 800–4.

Olson, G.M. and Sherman, T. (1983) 'Attention, learning and memory in infants', in Haith, M. and Campos, J. (eds) *Handbook of Child Psychology, vol. 2 Infancy and the Biology of Development*, New York, Wiley, pp. 1001–80.

Panfile, T.M. and Laible, D.J. (2012) 'Attachment security and child's empathy: the mediating role of emotion regulation', *Merrill-Palmer Quarterly*, vol. 58, no. 1, pp. 1–21.

Pea, R., Nass, C., Meheula, L., Rance, M., Kumar, A., Bamford, H., Nass, M., Simha, A., Stillerman, B., Yang, S. and Zhou, M. (2012) 'Media use, face-to-face communication, media multi-tasking and social well-being among 8 to 12-year-old girls', *Developmental Psychology*, vol. 48, no. 2, pp. 327–36.

Piaget, J. and Inhelder, B. (1967) *The Child's Conception of Space*, New York, Norton.

Pine, K.J., Bird, H. and Kirk, E. (2007) 'The effects of prohibiting gestures on children's lexical retrieval ability', *Developmental Science*, vol. 10, no. 6, pp. 747–54.

Premack, D. and Woodruff, G. (1978) 'Does the chimpanzee have "theory of mind"?' *Behavioural and Brain Sciences*, vol. 1, no. 4, pp. 515–26.

Raby, K.L., Cicchetti, D., Carlson, E.A., Cutuli, J.J., Englund, M.M. and Egeland, B. (2012) 'Genetic and caregiving-based contributions to infant attachment: unique associations with distress reactivity and attachment security', *Psychological Science*, vol. 23, no. 9, pp. 1016–23.

Rauscher, F.H., Krauss, R.M. and Chen, Y. (1996) 'Gesture, speech, and lexical access: the role of lexical movements in speech production', *Psychological Science*, vol. 7, no. 4, pp. 226–31.

Roisman, G.I. and Fraley, R.C. (2008) 'A behavior-genetic study of parenting quality, infant attachment security, and their covariation in a nationally representative sample', *Developmental Psychology*, vol. 44, no. 3, pp. 831–39.

Roisman, G.I., Booth–LaForce, C., Belsky, J., Burt, K.B. and Groh, A.M. (2013) 'Molecular-genetic correlates of infant attachment: a cautionary tale', *Attachment & Human Development*, vol. 15, no. 4, pp. 384–406.

Roland, E. (2002) 'Bullying, depressive symptoms and suicidal thoughts', *Educational Research*, vol. 44, no. 1, pp. 55–67.

Rovee-Collier, C. (1997) 'Dissociations in infant memory: rethinking the development of implicit and explicit memory', *Psychological Review*, vol. 104, no. 3, pp. 467–98.

Rutter, M. and Garmezy, N. (1983) 'Developmental psychopathology', in Mussen, P.H. (series ed) and Hetherington, E.M. (vol. ed) *Handbook of Child Psychology, vol. 4, Socialisation, Personality and Social Development*, 4th edn, New York, Wiley, pp. 775–911.

Sameroff, A. (2010) 'A unified theory of development: a dialectic integration of nature and nurture', *Child Development*, vol. 81, no. 1, pp. 6–22.

Sameroff, A.J. and Chandler, M.J. (1975) 'Reproductive risk and the continuum of caretaking casualty', in Horowitz, F.D., Hetherington, E.M., Scarr–Salapatek, S. and Siegel, G.M. (eds) *Review of Child Development Research*, Chicago, University of Chicago Press, pp. 187–244.

Schachter, D.L. (1994) 'Priming and multiple memory systems: perceptual mechanisms of implicit memory', in Schachter, D.L. and Tulving, E. (eds) *Memory Systems*, Cambridge, MA, MIT Press, pp. 233–68.

Squire, L.R. (1994) 'Declarative and non-declarative memory: multiple brain systems supporting learning and memory', in Schachter, D.L. and Tulving, E. (eds.), *Memory Systems*, Cambridge, MA, MIT Press, pp. 203–32.

Sutton, J., Smith, P.K., and Swettenham, J. (1999) 'Social cognition and bullying: social inadequacy or skilled manipulation?', *British Journal of Developmental Psychology*, vol. 17, no. 3, pp. 435–50.

Tomasello, M. (2000) 'Do young children have adult syntactic competence?' *Cognition*, vol. 74, no. 3, pp. 209–53.

Tomasello, M., Carpenter, M., Call, J., Behne, T. and Moll, H. (2005) 'Understanding and sharing intentions: the origins of cultural cognition', *Behavioural and Brain Sciences*, vol. 28, no. 5, pp. 675–91.

Valkenburg, P.M. and Peter, J. (2007) 'Preadolescents' and adolescents' online communication and their closeness to friends', *Developmental Psychology*, vol. 43, no. 2, pp. 267–77.

Valkenburg, P.M. and Peter, J. (2008) 'Adolescents' identity experiments on the internet: consequences for social competence and self-concept unity', *Communication Research*, vol. 35, no. 2, pp. 208–31.

van Ijzendoorn, M.H. and Kroonenberg, P.M. (1988) 'Cross-cultural patterns of attachment: a meta-analysis of the Strange Situation', *Child Development*, vol. 59, pp. 147–56.

Waters, E., Merrick, S., Treboux, D., Crowell, J. and Albersheim, L. (2000) 'Attachment security in infancy and early adulthood: a twenty-year longitudinal study', *Child Development*, vol. 71, no. 3, pp. 684–9.

Watson, J.B. (1928) *Psychological Care of Infant and Child*, New York, W.W. Norton Company, Inc.

Weinfield, N. and Egeland, B. (2004) 'Continuity, discontinuity, and coherence in attachment from infancy to late adolescence: sequelae of organization and disorganization, *Attachment and Human Development*, vol. 6, no. 1, pp. 73–97.

Westcott, H. (2006) 'Children and the legal system', in Wood, C. Littleton, K. and Sheehy, K. (eds) *Developmental Psychology in Action*, Milton Keynes, The Open University, pp. 53–97.

Whiting, J.W.M. and Whiting, B.B. (1975) *Children of Six Cultures: A Psychocultural Analysis*, Cambridge, MA, Harvard University Press.

Chapter 3

How do we know what is right and wrong? Theories of moral development

Paul Ibbotson

Contents

1 Introduction

Pick up any newspaper and you will see stories that have taken on a moral dimension. Matters as diverse as tax evasion, assisted dying and freedom of expression are united in the way they typically provoke a righteous reaction. Unlike a discussion on particle physics for example, the entry bar for joining these moral debates is set quite low. We have an internal moral compass we can consult and being judgemental comes relatively easily to us. The specifics of the debate may change, but many of the underlying moral principles at stake – justice, fairness, rights – are the same ones philosophers have been arguing about for millennia. Moral debates are here to stay.

Some of the moral issues covered in this chapter are considered taboo in many cultures and may elicit some strong reactions. These reactions are as much a part of our human experience as vision, language or memory. The study of morality aims to understand where the principles of right and wrong come from and how they work. Note that this approach is predominantly descriptive rather than normative. That means this research does not take a stance on who or what is morally right (normative approach); rather, it is trying to describe an important part of human social life (descriptive approach). In order to answer these questions we can bring together evidence from psychology, sociology, neuroscience, anthropology and philosophy, as well as comparing ourselves with our nearest living relatives, the chimpanzees. The study of morality has gained insights from all of these domains and is a good example of 'working across boundaries'.

To answer the question: 'How do we know what's right and wrong?' we will look at the development of social and moral judgements throughout childhood, considering whether children go through specific stages of moral development. We will look at whether or not there is a fundamental difference between moral rules and **social conventions**. To do that, we need to look at research into behaviour and beliefs within and across different cultures. We will then look at the role of emotions in moral reasoning and whether evolution via natural selection has shaped our species' unique moral sense. Finally, we consider the relationship between what people say they will do (moral judgement) and what they actually do (moral behaviour). To get started, read the following story in Figure 3.1. Decide whether you think what Julie and Mark did was wrong.

Social conventions
Behaviours that serve to coordinate social interactions in social systems such as rules about clothing and food. They are argued to be arbitrary and changeable.

Pause for thought

Figure 3.1   A moral dilemma

Julie and Mark are brother and sister. They are travelling together in France on summer vacation from college. One night they are staying alone in a cabin near the beach. They decide it would be interesting and fun if they tried making love. At the very least it would be a new experience for each of them. Julie was already taking birth control pills, but Mark uses a condom too, just to be safe. They both enjoy making love, but they decide not to do it again. They keep the night as a special secret, which makes them feel closer to each other.

Haidt et al. (1993) presented this story to many people. Like the majority of their participants, you probably had a gut reaction that what Julie and Mark did was wrong. After the initial reaction of 'eugh!' you may have struggled to explain *why* it was wrong. Note that the story has been cleverly crafted so as to counter the most common objections about why what they did was wrong. For example, the siblings used two forms of contraception so that inbreeding is not a consideration; the story makes it clear that they were not emotionally hurt; it takes place in private so the act could not offend the community; and Julie and Mark agree never to do it again so it would not interfere with future relationships. Eventually, participants are left with no rational justification that they can articulate and talk instead of their gut reaction: 'I don't know, I can't explain it. I just know it's wrong'. Haidt calls this kind of reaction '**moral dumbfounding**'– we know it is wrong but struggle to explain why. When reading these two further examples below you might think that they are unpleasant, but try to identify who the victim is in these stories. If you think there is no victim where does the unpleasant feeling arise from?

> A family's dog was killed by a car in front of their house. They had heard that dog meat was delicious so they cut up the dog's body, cooked it and ate it for dinner. Nobody saw them do it.
>
> A man goes to the supermarket once a week and buys a dead chicken. But before cooking the chicken, he has sexual intercourse with it. Then he cooks it and eats it.

People have gut feelings about these scenarios and thousands of others like them. They elicit strong moral convictions in people about what is right and wrong – some actions are just considered to be wrong even if they don't hurt anyone – and they often struggle to rationalise the convictions after the fact. Where do these sentiments come from? How do they develop over our lifetime? How do children come to know right from wrong?

Moral dumbfounding
A gut reaction that an act or thought is morally wrong, but an inability to articulate why it is wrong.

Learning outcomes

On completing this chapter you should:

- have knowledge of the key features of moral judgements and moral behaviour

- have an understanding of the differences between moral rules and social conventions

- be able to identify the role that culture and norms play in our moral sense

- be able to give examples of the way in which emotions regulate the moral sense

- have considered how the prosocial nature of humans compares with that of our closest living evolutionary relatives.

2   The development of social and moral judgements

This section looks at some of the classic developmental studies on social and moral judgements. You will see how Piaget, Kohlberg and Turiel built on one another's work to develop a theory of moral development. To start, there is a discussion of a theme that was relevant to all their work – the interaction of genes and environment.

2.1   Nativism and empiricism

Nativism

Nativist positions focus on knowledge that is organised in advance of experience. It argues moral knowledge and emotions are an instinct; a product of our evolutionary history with a strong genetic basis.

For a long period of time, the debate about the source of our moral nature was polarised between **nativism** and **empiricism**. Nativism argues that moral knowledge and emotions are instincts; products of our evolutionary history with a strong genetic basis (Darwin, 1871; Hauser, 2006). Another way to think about nativism is to consider it as those elements of our nature that are organised in advance of experience. For example, fish are born expecting water. They have gills, scales on their skin, fins and so on. Some people have argued that just as fish are born expecting water, so humans are born expecting culture (e.g. Tomasello et al., 2005). We are born with the capacity to acquire culture through social learning, imitation and intention reading in a way that sets us apart from other animals.

Empiricism

Empiricist positions focus on knowledge that is gained from observation or experience. Empiricism argues whatever morals we have as adults must have been learned during childhood. Under this view moral development can be thought of as a process of acquiring behaviours and internalising the standards and values of a society.

Empiricism, by contrast, emphasises the role of learning in development ('empirical' means from observation or experience), so whatever morals we have as adults must have been learned during childhood (Locke, 1690). According to this view, moral development can be thought of as a process of acquiring behaviours (Skinner, 1971) and internalising the standards and values of a society (Aronfreed, 1968). Like many of the big ideas, the ancient Greeks got there first and debated the role of nature and nurture over 2000 years ago. Meno asked Socrates, 'Can you tell me, Socrates, whether virtue is acquired by teaching or by practice; [or] whether it comes to man by nature, or in what other way?' (Plato, *Meno*).

The nativist–empiricist debate is often presented as if it were a choice we have to make. This is misleading for a number of reasons. First, as you will see, what is considered right and wrong varies between cultures and in some cases is correlated with other aspects of cultural life. Equally true, however, is the fact that our closest evolutionary relatives do not acquire the same moral sentiments as us, even when raised in human cultures. This means there is something in human nature that allows the development of human morals. As Cohen (1999, p. 68) put it: 'Nature limits and channels nurture.' So it is possible to think that we have the capacity to acquire a human repertoire of moral sentiments *and* that these are shaped by the particular social and cultural contexts within which a person lives.

Second, the boundary between genes and environment is being blurred by the study of **epigenetics** (from the Greek 'around' the gene). This is the study of how the environment can regulate how particular genes work within an individual's lifetime. For example, monozygotic twins, who share all of their genes, can in rare cases have different eye colours. Small differences in the environment that each twin experiences in the womb are thought to change the expression of the eye colour gene. More complex examples exist where the environment causes certain genes to become active, which leads the organism to search out different environments which results in other genes being switched off and so on. For example, the ants shown in Figure 3.2 have the same genome but very different bodies and behaviour – soldiers, common labourers, and queens. Epigenetics allows us to study the effect of the environment in regulating how particular genes work within an individual's lifetime.

Epigenetics
From the Greek 'around' the gene, epigenetics studies how the environment regulates how particular genes work within an individual's lifetime.

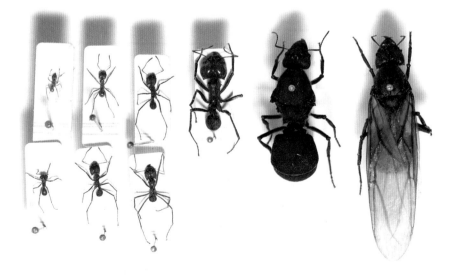

Figure 3.2   Same genes, different bodies (and different behaviour)

Third, identical twins raised together are not perfectly correlated on either physiological or psychological measures (Plomin, 1994; Plomin and Daniels, 1987). Experiments with inbred animals show that when twins are raised in environments that are strictly controlled for similarity (implanted into the same womb, raised in the same cage with the same lighting, food and water), they show about as much variation in physiological and behavioural measures as those outbred or wild (Gartner, 1990). These differences are thought to arise from molecular chance processes or small variations in the environments. For example, even identical twins in the womb cannot occupy the same space at the same time. As such, they will be exposed to slightly different conditions. These initial tiny variations might initiate a complex cascade of consequences that affect the course of development. In summary, the evidence suggests that a simple 'genes plus environment' model fails to explain all the variation we see in an individual, and we need to start thinking about the role that chance events, or randomness, plays in development as well as the interaction between genes and environment.

2.2   Constructing a moral sense

In the previous section you began to see the limitations of thinking in terms of either nature or nurture. In the early part of the past century Jean Piaget tried to move beyond the restrictions of thinking in this dichotomy. He developed a third option to nativism and empiricism; one that was to become very influential in moral theory and developmental psychology in general. 'Rationalism' argued that children work out morality for themselves or 'construct' it as Piaget said in *The Moral Judgment of The Child* (1997). This argument is in keeping with a long philosophical tradition from Aristotle and Kant to more modern versions such as Rawls (1971) who argued children's moral development involves the construction of judgements about welfare, justice and rights through social interactions.

Piaget was initially interested in the development of molluscs and insects such as caterpillars. Before long, he applied the same framework of stage-like development to children. He began by looking at the kind of errors children made about everyday physical objects. For example, if I pour water from a tall thin glass to a short fat one, I think the volume of water has stayed the same, whereas children younger than six think the volume has changed. Moreover, he argued there is little use explaining this 'principle of conservation' to children of this age. Until their cognitive development is at an appropriate stage, and they are given the right kind of experience, they will simply not grasp the concept. Their understanding of volume is neither innate nor learned from adults – this is why rationalism is a third option to nativism and empiricism. Up until this point in history people had thought of children as essentially being little adults. Arguably Piaget's greatest contribution to developmental science was to show that children's thinking is qualitatively different from that of adults, and he developed some of the experimental procedures used to study that difference, many of which are still in use today.

When Piaget turned his attention to studying moral development he started by playing simple marble games with children (Piaget, 1997). He sometimes deliberately broke the rules and pretended not to know what he had done. When the children corrected the mistakes they revealed something about their ability to respect rules, take turns, and resolve disputes. Piaget noticed that the development of moral understanding could be described by the same framework of stage-like progression he had described for the physical world. Just as a three-year-old is not at the right stage to understand the conservation task, so they are also not ready to grasp the concept of fairness – no matter how often you tell them about it. It was noted at the start of this chapter that a lot of moral dilemmas are variations on themes of justice, fairness, and rights. With his simple marble games, Piaget was hoping to tap into these basic building blocks of our moral sense and say something about how these develop. Thus, he claimed that through experience of collaboration and competition with one another, children begin to construct a sense of fairness. Piaget acknowledged development is not always sequential in the way in which the concept 'stage' implies, noting that features of children's thinking appear in adults, while sometimes features of adult thinking appear in children. He claimed that when children are cooperating with equals, '… there is an adult in every child and a child in every adult' (Piaget, 1932, p. 85). Thus, Piaget's main contribution to the understanding of moral development was to suggest that moral knowledge is self-constructed through interaction with others.

2.3   Stages of moral development

Piaget's early work was extended by Lawrence Kohlberg in the 1960s (Kohlberg, 1969, 1976). Kohlberg used short stories, simple enough for children to understand yet subtle enough that they would reveal something about the way children thought about right and wrong. For example, when a child was presented with a question such as: 'Should a girl reveal that her younger sister has lied to her mother?' it wasn't whether the child said 'yes' or 'no' that interested Kohlberg but the reasons they gave when they explained their answer. When Kohlberg coded, analysed and quantified the children's responses to hundreds of these dilemmas he proposed a six-stage progression that characterised their development (Table 3.1). When children are young they typically start out using simple rules of thumb to judge what is right and wrong – heuristics that have worked well enough in the past to be of some use to them. For example, when trying to navigate the complex world of adult moral reasoning, a rule such as 'if a person is punished then what they did must have been wrong' seems a useful place to start from the perspective of the child. Echoing Piaget, Kohlberg called the first two stages of moral judgement 'pre-conventional' because they are reminiscent of the Piagetian stage at which children also judge the physical world by superficial features – 'if the glass is taller it has more water in it'. From five years old onwards, children move on to the two 'conventional' stages, where they begin to reason about rules and social conventions. According to Kohlberg, children at this age care about conformity and respect for authority as they learn to negotiate the constraints adults place on them.

Table 3.1 Kohlberg's stages of moral development

Stage 1	The morality of obedience: Do what you're told
Stage 2	The morality of instrumental concordance and simple exchange: Let's make a deal
Stage 3	The morality of interpersonal concordance: Be considerate, nice and kind: you'll make friends
Stage 4	The morality of law and duty to the social order: Everyone in society is obligated to and protected by the law
Stage 5	The morality of consensus-building procedures: You are obligated by the arrangements that are agreed to by due procedures
Stage 6	The morality of non-arbitrary social cooperation: morality is defined by how rational and impartial people would ideally organise cooperation

Pause for thought

Consider the following dilemma.

Heinz's wife was dying from a particular type of cancer. Doctors said a new drug might save her. The drug had been discovered by a local chemist and Heinz tried desperately to buy some, but the chemist was charging ten times the amount it cost to make the drug and this was much more than Heinz could afford. He could only raise half the money, even after help from family and friends. He explained to the chemist that his wife was dying and asked if he could have the drug cheaper, or pay the rest of the money later. The chemist refused saying that he had created the drug and was going to make money from it. Heinz was desperate to save his wife, so later that night he broke into the chemist's and stole the drug.

Ask yourself:

1 Should Heinz have stolen the drug?

2 Would it change anything if Heinz did not love his wife?

3 What if the person dying was a stranger, would it make any difference?

4 Should the police arrest the chemist for murder if the woman died?

By asking these questions Kohlberg hoped to discover the ways in which moral reasoning changed as people grew older (Kohlberg, 1969).

Piaget suggested that after puberty children become capable of abstract thought, for example reasoning about categories and making analogies. Kohlberg similarly found that at this stage children start thinking for themselves about the nature of authority, the meaning of justice, and the reason behind rules and laws. In this stage children have begun to base their explanations on the *spirit* of the law rather than the *letter* of the law. Piaget thought this shift was achieved by a decline in egocentrism and a corresponding increase in the ability to take roles and assume another's perspective. In the two 'post-conventional stages' (Stages 5 and 6 in Table 3.1) adolescents typically value honesty, and respect laws and rules. Importantly, however, they can also justify when these rules should be disregarded if they are at odds with higher values such as justice and fairness. So, a large part of being human is to feel pulled in different directions – to have conflicting attitudes and beliefs. In this period children are learning to weigh competing moral motivations, for example, 'be kind' versus 'tell the truth'. This is when individuals show increased expertise in moral reasoning and, in Kohlberg's view, become 'moral philosophers' who are trying to work out a coherent ethical system for themselves (Kohlberg, 1969).

2.4   Moral rules and social conventions

Despite Piaget and Kohlberg's crucial contributions to the study of child development, it could be argued that the research methods they employed were bound to find a developmental trend, simply because older children are better at articulating their reasoning than younger children. This issue of task demands on children is still relevant in modern developmental psychology research. Researchers must question whether they are actually measuring something about development rather than measuring the child's increasing ability to complete the task. For this reason, eye-tracking has become a popular technique in developmental psychology in recent years because it places low demands on the child compared to asking them complex questions: if one is interested in the first appearance of a moral concept then it might be better to find a technique that doesn't depend on complex language. Elliot Turiel, a student of Kohlberg, attempted just this. He simplified the stories Kohlberg had used by requiring only a yes/no answer, in this way 'controlling' for language development. These stories were typically about children who break the rules in some way, for example: a boy goes to school wearing his everyday clothes even though the school requires a uniform. 'Is it OK, what the boy did?' 'What if the teacher said it was OK for the boy to wear his normal clothes – then would it be OK?' 'What if this happened in another school, where they don't have any rules about uniforms, then would it be OK?' When the task demands are reduced (i.e. less complex language is used), children as young as five usually say that the boy in this example was wrong to break the rule but it would be OK if the teacher gave him permission, or if it happened at another school. This is an important point. Turiel argued that children recognise that rules about clothing, food and many other aspects of life are social conventions, which by their nature are arbitrary and changeable (Turiel, 1983). If you ask children about actions that hurt others – a girl who pushes a boy off a swing because she wants to use it – nearly all of the children say the girl was wrong. Furthermore, children say she would be wrong if the teacher said it was OK and even if it happened at another school where there were no rules against this kind of behaviour. Thus when faced with a moral transgression, children work out the direct consequences of the act and may arrive at the conclusion it was wrong. However, when observing a social convention violation, children must infer the wrongness of the behaviour from features outside the event. For example, children learn to take a critical perspective on authority especially when it conflicts with moral intuitions. Damon (1977) found that young children reject parental commands to engage in acts that violate moral rules, such as instructions to steal or cause harm to another person. Children of six years or older judged laws that discriminate against individuals on the basis of age, income or appearance to be wrong and that breaking them was acceptable (Helwig and Jasiobedzka, 2001).

Turiel (1983, p. 3) defines moral rules as relating to 'justice, rights, and welfare pertaining to how people ought to relate to each other'. He argues that the realisation that moral rules are special, unalterable and universal (i.e. not culturally specific) is the foundation of all moral development. In all the cultures Turiel examined, children made a distinction between moral rules and conventional rules, even though the content of those rules varied (Hollos et al., 1986; Nucci et al., 1983). This became known as the 'domain approach'. The **moral domain** pertains to issues of harm, fairness and rights, and the social

Moral domain
A moral sense that is thought to relate to issues of harm, fairness and rights.

convention domain is composed of behavioural uniformities that serve to coordinate social interactions in social systems.

As an example of this kind of reasoning in action, the following transcript is of a five-year-old boy in one of Turiel's experiments (Turiel, 1983, p. 62). The boy gives his response to a hypothetical story. The first conversation refers to whether it is right for a school to allow hitting. Because hitting is about harm this is supposed to be a moral issue.

Boy:	No, it is not OK.
Interviewer:	Why not?
Boy:	Because this is like making other people unhappy. You can hurt them that way. It hurts other people, hurting is not good.
Interviewer:	Mark [the boy in the story] goes to Park school. Today in school he wants to swing but he finds that all the swings are being used by the other children. So he decides to hit one of the children and take the swing. Is it OK for Mark to do that?
Boy:	No. Because he is hurting someone else.

In the next example the conversation is about whether it is right to allow children to remove their clothes (a social convention issue). The social rule being discussed here is 'do not remove your clothes at school'.

Boy:	Yes, because that is the rule.
Interviewer:	Why can they have that rule?
Boy:	If that's what the boss wants to do, he can do that.
Interviewer:	How come?
Boy:	Because he's the boss, he is in charge of the school.
Interviewer:	Bob goes to Grove School. This is a warm day at Grove School. He has been running in the play area outside and he is hot. So he decides to take off his clothes. Is it OK for Bob to do that?
Boy:	Yes, if he wants to he can because it's the rule.

Although in both cases the head teacher is 'the boss in charge of school', in the 'moral rule' scenario this authority does not matter but in the 'social convention' scenario it does. Turiel concluded:

With regard to clothing, he accepts the rules of the school as
stipulated, but with regard to hitting he does not. Permitting
children to remove their clothes is judged by him as acceptable
because of the rule and because the boss (i.e. the head of the
school) has the authority to impose the rule or practice. When it
comes to permitting children to hit each other, however, this boy
is unwilling to grant the boss the authority to institute or
implement the rule.

(Turiel, 2003, p. 118)

Thus, it appears that children understand that not all rules are created
equal. For example, four- to six-year-olds are happy to accept
commands to stop fighting (a moral issue) as equally legitimate whether
those commands come from adults or children (Laupa et al., 1995).
However, when it comes to turn-taking or interpretation of game rules
(a conventional issue) children give priority to adults.

Now let's consider how moral rules and social conventions are relevant
to the kind of human stories we encounter every day in the news (see
Figure 3.3)

Pause for thought

Figure 3.3   Moral rules and social conventions

Identify a recent news story, for example by looking on the BBC news website, and try to analyse it from the perspective of a moral rule or social convention. For example, a news story about whether you should recline seats on a plane might be more towards the social convention end of the spectrum whereas a news article about abortion might be considered towards the moral rule end of the spectrum.

What makes one news story fit into the moral category but another not?

Can you see any difficulties with dividing the world into moral rules and social conventions?

Are these categories stable across time?

Are they consistent across cultures?

> Do these categories capture the diversity and changing nature of the human moral sense?

2.5   Personal preference and morality

A sense of autonomy and personal responsibility is also related to the developing moral sense. Research has shown that young children identify personal preference as distinct from the moral and social conventional domains. For example, Nucci (1981) found that US primary schoolchildren judged issues such as choices about friends, appearance (clothing, hairstyle) and preferences for leisure activities as up to the child to decide. Seven-year-old children stated that there should not be a rule governing these matters because it is a matter of personal choice. In contrast, moral issues are thought to be universal and unchangeable.

For example, while it sounds fine to say, 'I like jazz but I don't care if you listen to it or not', it sounds odd to say 'I don't like to murder people but I don't mind if you do!' However, when thinking about this division between personal preference and morality, we find they are not as stable over time or as clear-cut as this example suggests. The same behaviour can be treated as personal preference or moral behaviour depending on the time and place and the person making the judgement. For example, Rozin (1997) noticed that there are two main kinds of vegetarian: those who avoid meat for health reasons (e.g. to reduce dietary fat) and those who avoid meat for moral reasons (e.g. respecting the rights of the animals). When compared with the 'health vegetarians', the 'moral vegetarians' offered more reasons for their meat avoidance; had a greater emotional reaction to meat; were more likely to treat meat as a contaminant, and were more likely to think other people should be vegetarians. Note the normative language of *should*.

As well as shifts in attitudes by individuals, over a longer period societal shifts in attitude can mean that issues that were once considered amoral take on a moralised nature: advertising to children, fracking, plastic bags, violence on television, IQ tests, wearing fur, and food additives. At the same time, many behaviours have moved in the opposite direction, switching from moral wrongdoing to a lifestyle choice: divorce, illegitimacy, marijuana use, masturbation, sodomy, oral

sex and atheism. This shows that to get a fuller picture it is necessary
to study this topic across boundaries.

2.6   Summary

Evidence suggests we should be thinking of a dynamic interaction
between the environment and genes and not the 'either–or' options of
the nativist–empiricist debate. Early researchers in the field suggested
that development consists of a series of stages: Piaget claimed that
moral knowledge is self-constructed as children interact with others
whereas Kohlberg proposed a six-stage progression in children's
reasoning about the social world. Turiel built on these findings yet
removed unnecessary task demands placed on children by designing
tasks that didn't require sophisticated language abilities. More recent
research has demonstrated that the moral domain pertains to issues of
harm, fairness and rights that are said to be universal and
unchangeable. Conversely, the social convention domain is composed
of behavioural uniformities that serve to coordinate social interactions
in social systems, such as rules about clothing and food, which are
argued to be arbitrary and changeable. When an historical and
sociological perspective on the nature of moral development is
included the boundaries between social convention and moral rules
become fuzzier.

3   Beyond harm and fairness

In the 1980s, one of Kohlberg's students, Carol Gilligan, identified some issues with Kohlberg's original research. She pointed out that his research was based on highly homogenous samples – white American school boys. Gilligan replicated his research with participants who were girls and from different cultural backgrounds, and found that while Kohlberg has identified a moral hierarchy based on 'justice', moral hierarchies could be based on other values, such as that of 'care'. This helped to move the debate beyond morality as a single concept, such as 'harm', 'human welfare', 'happiness' or 'justice'. This section explores a more pluralistic view of moral reasoning that acknowledges a stronger role for cultural variation.

3.1   Cultural variation

As hinted at above, the distinction between moral rules on the one side and social conventions on the other might be less distinct than originally proposed. For example, there are many practices, particularly from non-Western cultures, which do not seem related to harm and fairness. To understand the role of cultural variation we need to take a step back from moral reasoning for a moment and look at the ways societies are organised. Social anthropologists have identified two broad classes of society structure. Most societies are characterised by a **sociocentric approach**, placing the needs of groups and institutions first and subordinating the needs of individuals. A sense of civic duty, social harmony, obedience to authority and respect for hierarchy are highly valued. In contrast, the **individualistic approach** makes society the servant of the individual. Personal choice, autonomy and rights are valued here (Shweder and Bourne, 1984). So as cultures differ in how they see individuals and groups, so does the concept of 'self'. What it means to be an individual is dependent on the way the society is organised. It turns out that this has an effect on the kinds of things that people think are moral issues.

Most research on moral development has been conducted in so-called WEIRD cultures: Western, Educated, Industrialised, Rich and Democratic. Research conducted in other cultural contexts, however, has qualified and complicated the findings of such research. Richard Shweder, a psychological anthropologist, found large differences in how Oriyans (residents of Orissa, a state on the east coast of India)

Sociocentric approach
A broad classification of culture that places the needs of groups and institutions first and subordinates the needs of individuals. This framework emphasises duties, social harmony, obedience to authority, and hierarchy.

Individualistic approach
A broad classification of culture that makes society answer to the needs of the individual. This framework emphasises individual choice, personal autonomy, and rights.

and Americans thought about personality and individuality (Shweder et al., 1987). Shweder argued that this led to differences in how they thought about morality. Furthermore, he criticised the framework of Kohlberg and Turiel for being written by and for an individualist framework and doubted its relevance for sociocentric societies, such as the society of people from Orissa. Shweder thought that in reality the boundary between preventing harm (moral rule) and social conventions (regulating behaviours) would be much more culturally variable than had been suggested. To test these ideas he interviewed a matched sample of over 600 people from Orissa and Chicago, including 360 children ranging from five to thirteen years of age. He presented them with thirty-nine short stories in which someone does something that might violate some kind of rule (Figure 3.4).

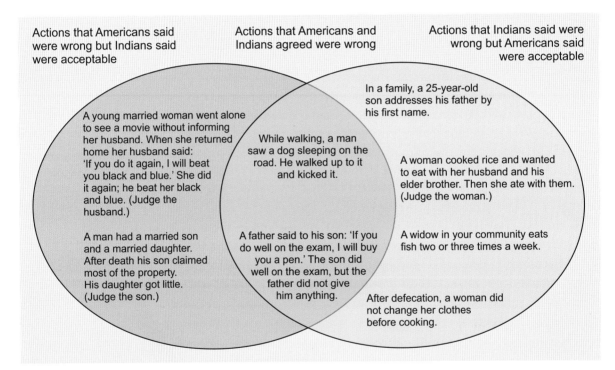

Actions that Americans said were wrong but Indians said were acceptable

Actions that Americans and Indians agreed were wrong

Actions that Indians said were wrong but Americans said were acceptable

A young married woman went alone to see a movie without informing her husband. When she returned home her husband said: 'If you do it again, I will beat you black and blue.' She did it again; he beat her black and blue. (Judge the husband.)

A man had a married son and a married daughter. After death his son claimed most of the property. His daughter got little. (Judge the son.)

While walking, a man saw a dog sleeping on the road. He walked up to it and kicked it.

A father said to his son: 'If you do well on the exam, I will buy you a pen.' The son did well on the exam, but the father did not give him anything.

In a family, a 25-year-old son addresses his father by his first name.

A woman cooked rice and wanted to eat with her husband and his elder brother. Then she ate with them. (Judge the woman.)

A widow in your community eats fish two or three times a week.

After defecation, a woman did not change her clothes before cooking.

Figure 3.4   Cultural differences and similarities based on some of the thirty-nine stories used in Shweder et al. (1987)

Findings revealed that in India, where the society is sociocentric, practices relating to food, sex, clothing and gender relations were almost always judged to be moral issues rather than social conventions. The scope of what people thought were moral issues clearly went well beyond a framework of harm, fairness and rights. For the people of Chicago, where the society is more individualistic, the moral order is constructed around the protection of individuals and their personal freedom. Even for the five-year-old Orissan children, the practices of food, clothing and gender relations had become moralised in a way that they had clearly not been for the Chicago children. Shweder's work shone a light on the role of cultural variation in what counts as moral. Moreover he showed it is possible to predict some of this variation if one takes a look at how the society is organised.

3.2 The morality of evolution and politics

Following Shweder, further research has concluded that the moral domain varies by culture. Of course that does not mean morals vary arbitrarily, and certainly does not rule out a universal capacity for human-like morality. For example, Haidt and Joseph (2004) suggest some dimensions of morality that are candidates for being universal but are also modified by culture, what they call **moral foundations theory (MFT)**. They believe that morality developed in humans because it helped us solve adaptive challenges – essentially an evolutionary psychology approach to the study of morals. Each culture then constructs virtues, narratives and institutions on top of these foundations, creating the variation we see in what is considered moral. The five foundations are:

1 **Care/harm**: This foundation is related to our long evolution as mammals with attachment systems and an ability to feel (and dislike) the pain of others. It underlies virtues of kindness, gentleness and nurturance.

2 **Fairness/cheating**: This foundation is related to the evolutionary process of reciprocal altruism – you scratch my back, I'll scratch yours. It generates ideas of justice, rights and autonomy.

3 **Loyalty/betrayal**: This foundation is related to our long history as tribal creatures able to form shifting coalitions. It underlies virtues of patriotism and self-sacrifice for the group. It is active any time people feel that it's 'one for all, and all for one.'

4 **Authority/subversion**: This foundation was shaped by our long primate history of hierarchical social interactions. It underlies virtues of leadership and followership, including deference to legitimate authority and respect for traditions.

5 **Sanctity/degradation**: This foundation was shaped by the psychology of disgust and contamination. It underlies religious

Moral foundations theory (MFT)
A theory that proposes several innate and universally available psychological systems are the foundations of 'intuitive ethics'. These moral foundations, it is argued, developed in humans because it helped us solve adaptive challenges in our evolutionary past.

notions of striving to live in an elevated, less carnal, nobler way. It underlies the widespread idea that the body is a temple that can be desecrated by immoral activities and contaminants (an idea not unique to religious traditions).

The main message here is that there seems to be some inbuilt repertoire of moral and emotional sentiments that are shaped by the particular social and cultural context a person finds themselves in. Haidt uses an analogy with taste receptors to illustrate this point. Humans are all born with the same five taste receptors: sweet, sour, salt, bitter and umami (the savoury taste of foods like meat and mushrooms). Geography and history have meant cultures have evolved massively different cuisines, yet they are all variations on the same theme of these five building blocks. Moral foundations theory is an attempt to identify the building blocks of morality. There is now good evidence (e.g. review by Graham et al., 2009) not only that these moral foundations generalise to other cultures but that they also have an important bearing on peoples' political ideology and their stance on debates such as gay marriage, abortion, art and welfare spending. In Activity 3.1 you will use moral foundations theory to see which way your moral compass points.

Activity 3.1:   Where does your moral compass point?

This activity is based on the moral foundations questionnaire (MFQ) (Graham et al., 2008). Work your way through the two parts of this questionnaire using the grid in Figure 3.5 to record your scores.

Question	Your response	Question	Your response	Question	Your response	Question	Your response	Question	Your response	Question	Your response
1		2		3		4		5		6	
7		8		9		10		11			
12		13		14		15		16			
17		18		19		20		21		22	
23		24		25		26		27			
28		29		30		31		32			
	Harm/ Care		Fairness/ Reciprocity		In-group Loyalty		Authority/ Respect		Purity/ Sanctity		

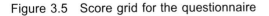

Figure 3.5   Score grid for the questionnaire

Part 1. When you decide whether something is right or wrong, to what extent are the following considerations relevant to your thinking? Please rate each statement using this scale:

[0] = not at all relevant (This consideration has nothing to do with my judgements of right and wrong)

[1] = not very relevant

[2] = slightly relevant

[3] = somewhat relevant

[4] = very relevant

[5] = extremely relevant (This is one of the most important factors when I judge right and wrong)

1   Whether or not someone suffered emotionally.

2   Whether or not some people were treated differently than others.

3   Whether or not someone's action showed love for his or her country.

4   Whether or not someone showed a lack of respect for authority.

5   Whether or not someone violated standards of purity and decency.

6   Whether or not someone was good at maths.

7   Whether or not someone cared for someone weak or vulnerable.

8   Whether or not someone acted unfairly.

9   Whether or not someone did something to betray his or her group.

10 Whether or not someone conformed to the traditions of society.

11 Whether or not someone did something disgusting.

12 Whether or not someone was cruel.

13 Whether or not someone was denied his or her rights.

14 Whether or not someone showed a lack of loyalty.

15 Whether or not an action caused chaos or disorder.

16 Whether or not someone acted in a way that God would approve of.

Part 2. Please read the following sentences and indicate your agreement or disagreement using this scale:

[0] = Strongly disagree

[1] = Moderately disagree

[2] = Slightly disagree

[3] = Slightly agree

[4] = Moderately agree

[5] = Strongly agree

17 Compassion for those who are suffering is the most crucial virtue.

18 When the government makes laws, the number one principle should be ensuring that everyone is treated fairly.

19 I am proud of my country's history.

20 Respect for authority is something all children need to learn.

21 People should not do things that are disgusting, even if no one is harmed.

22 It is better to do good than to do bad.

23 One of the worst things a person could do is hurt a defenceless animal.

24 Justice is the most important requirement for a society.

25 People should be loyal to their family members, even when they have done something wrong.

26 Men and women each have different roles to play in society.

27 I would call some acts wrong on the grounds that they are unnatural.

28 It can never be right to kill a human being.

29 I think it is morally wrong that rich children inherit a lot of money while poor children inherit nothing.

30 It is more important to be a team player than to express oneself.

31 If I were a soldier and disagreed with my commanding officer's orders, I would obey anyway because that is my duty.

32 Chastity is an important and valuable virtue.

Working out your score

When you have completed the questionnaire, add up the six numbers in each of the five columns and write each total in the box at the bottom of the column. The box then shows your score on each of five psychological 'foundations' of morality. Scores run from 0–30 for each foundation. (Questions 6 and 22 are just used to catch people who are not paying attention. They don't count towards your scores).

The average politically moderate American's scores are: 20.2, 20.5, 16.0, 16.5 and 12.6.

Liberals generally score a bit higher than that on harm/care and fairness/reciprocity, and much lower than that on the other three foundations. Conservatives generally show the opposite pattern.

For more information about moral foundations theory, scoring this form, or interpreting your scores, see: www.MoralFoundations.org. To take this

The questionnaire that you just completed has been completed by 132,000 people in an online experiment. The results are displayed in Figure 3.6.

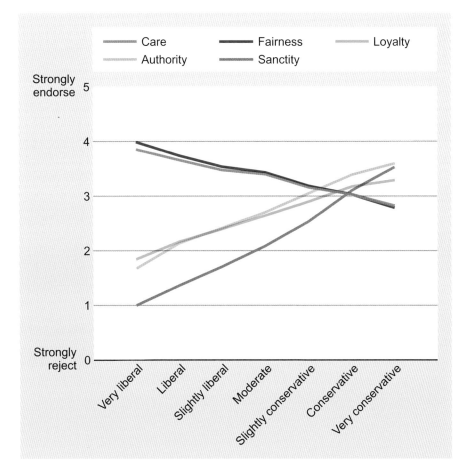

Figure 3.6   Scores on the MFQ from 132,000 participants in 2011 *(Source: www.YourMorals.org)*

The general pattern of results has been replicated many times and shows that the moral compass of liberals points primarily to the care/ harm foundation, with additional support from the fairness/cheating foundation. Conservatives, especially religious conservatives, use all six foundations, including loyalty/betrayal, authority/subversion and sanctity/degradation. What did the moral foundations questionnaire reveal about your moral compass?

3.3   Summary

Shweder raised the possibility that the distinction between the moral and mere convention is not fundamental to moral development but is a cultural artefact – a by-product of the way a society is organised. Moral foundations theory proposes that several innate and universally available psychological systems are the foundations of 'intuitive ethics'. Haidt believes that morality developed in humans because it helped us solve adaptive challenges of our evolutionary past. There is some evidence to suggest that these moral foundations have an important bearing on peoples' political ideology and their stance on debates such as gay marriage, abortion, art and welfare spending.

4   Moral behaviour

In the next activity we look at the subject of altruism, which can be defined as unselfish concern for the welfare of others (see Figure 3.7). It is also usually implied that such concern may be to the disadvantage of the altruist but to the benefit of others (see Book 1, Chapter 5).

Figure 3.7   Donating blood can be considered an act of altruism

---

Activity 3.2:   What would a truly altruistic act look like?

For each scenario below try to think of motivations for these seemingly altruistic acts.

1   A mother leaps in front of a car saving her son but dies in the process.

2   One co-worker buys another a cup of coffee.

3   A guy gives money to a tramp in front of his girlfriend.

4   A man anonymously gives to a charity and tells no one about it.

Discussion

1 Because the child shares half of the mother's genes, this could be an example of inclusive fitness, leading Hamilton (1964a, 1964b), who developed the concept of inclusive fitness, to famously joke that he would willingly die for two brothers (who he is half related to) or eight cousins (who he is one eighth related to).

2 Because the people in this scenario work with each other and probably see each other regularly there could be a reasonable expectation that the favour will be returned. This could be an example of reciprocal altruism or 'you scratch my back, I'll scratch yours'. You may have seen this kind of relationship break down when someone knows they are going to leave a job. 'The shadow of the future' casts over them, they know they will not be accountable for their actions and prosocial behaviour reduces.

3 This generous act could potentially be explained by a kind of second-order theory of mind reasoning on behalf of the man. 'I think that she believes men who give to charity are nice. In that case I'll give some money to this guy in order to win her favour.' So the altruistic act in this case is motivated more for his own reputational concerns than a genuine desire for the well-being of the tramp. Note that this begs the question of why the girlfriend might value altruism in the first place.

4 Here there are no obvious genetic or reputation motivations, nor can the man reasonably expect that the favour will be returned. What we are left with is a so-called 'warm glow' – the satisfaction and pleasure someone might feel when doing this act. Note this begs the question of why people feel good about giving in this way and whether a warm glow can be considered a benefit.

Much of the research discussed so far has focused on morality. However, it seems fair to question how well these judgements and sentiments relate to what people *actually* do – acts of moral behaviour – like those you have just considered in the activity.

Are we naturally selfish or cooperative? This is an age-old philosophical debate known as the 'perfectibility of man'. Either human nature is essentially selfish and individualistic, unless tamed by culture, or humans are born virtuous and are corrupted by society. As with the genetics–environment debate, this kind of either–or thinking doesn't do justice to the complexity of the situation. The reality is that young children are both competitive and cooperative. In this section we will see that although young children can be selfish they are more cooperative than we might expect if we take a comparative psychology approach. The next section looks at the behavioural evidence from children that attempts to answer the question of how we become moral beings. Evidence suggests that even young children have concerns for the well-being of others in the group, at the same time as looking out for their own individual interests (Tomasello and Vaish, 2013).

4.1   Collaboration and commitment

Joint activities involve people working together to achieve a shared goal (See Book 2,Chapter 4). But at what point do humans demonstrate a desire to collaborate with others? Evidence suggests that from a young age children want to participate in joint activities and show commitment to them. For example, if the cooperation breaks down they will try to re-engage their partner out of a motivation to continue the activity together rather than by themselves (Warneken et al., 2006; Warneken and Tomasello, 2007). Importantly, this is true even when the activity does not require two people to achieve the goal, suggesting children do not see people in these contexts as a means to an end but as collaborative partners (Warneken et al., 2012).

Opting out of collaborative activities when you have previously displayed some commitment to the cause runs the risk that you will upset or disappoint others. Toddlers seem to understand the implications of backing out of these cooperative pacts – they feel responsible for them, try to honour them or apologise if they break them. For instance, when working jointly with a partner on a task that should result in both children receiving a reward, three-and-a-half-year-olds continue to work until the partner has also received a reward, even if they received their own reward earlier in the process (Hamann et al., 2012).

4.2   Sympathy and helping

In addition to commitment to shared goals and collaboration with others, young children and even infants demonstrate remarkable prosocial tendencies (Figure 3.8), for example picking up accidentally dropped objects or opening doors for an adult whose hands are full. Children seem to know something about the adults' intentions in these situations as they don't offer help when the adult has deliberately thrown objects down or shows no intention of opening a door for themselves (Warneken and Tomasello, 2006, 2007).

Out-of-reach

A person accidentally drops an object on the floor and unsuccessfully reaches for it.

Physical obstacle

A person wants to put a pile of books into a cabinet, but she cannot open the closed doors because her hands are full.

Wrong result

A book slips from a stack as a person attempts to place it on top of the stack.

Wrong means

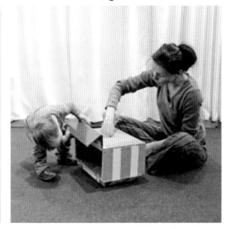

An object drops through a hole into a box and the person unsuccessfully tries to grasp it through the small hole, ignorant of a flap on the side of the box.

Figure 3.8   Examples of helping tasks for young children developed by Warneken and Tomasello (2006)

Pause for thought

The 'remarkable' prosocial capacities noted here must be put in context. Parents might object at this point that *their* child is not always a shining beacon of cooperation. Remember that the bigger question we are trying to answer is the *human* capacity for prosocial behaviour and culture *compared* with other species. Human children's cooperative nature is remarkable when *compared* with other great apes whose cooperation is largely organised around a framework of dominance. Put a random group of chimpanzees in a room and a fight will probably break out. Put a random group of humans together in a room and the same thing is unlikely to happen. What makes the difference? A child raised in human culture will acquire the moral norms of that society whereas a chimpanzee will not. What makes the difference? To understand morals we are thinking about human development in two different senses:

1   How an individual develops through their lifetime.
2   How our species developed over history.

The prosocial nature of toddlers' actions is even more clearly demonstrated when they help at some cost to themselves (Svetlova et al., 2010), or when they have nothing to directly gain from helping. For example, when a 12-month-old infant sees an adult searching for an object that they know the location of, they point to direct the adult's attention to it (Liszkowski et al., 2006, 2008). The behaviourist interpretation of this behaviour would be that prosociality has been encouraged through a system of rewards and punishment. However, in a recent study, the helpfulness of 20-month-old children *decreased* when they were materially rewarded for their helpful behaviour. In contrast children who were not rewarded at all, or who received only verbal praise, maintained a high level of helpfulness throughout (Warneken and Tomasello, 2008).

Warneken + Tomasello. – 2008

Further research has demonstrated that young children also begin to provide comfort and assistance to those in emotional distress, such as another child who is in pain after bumping their knee, or who is upset about their broken teddy bear (e.g. Bischof-Köhler, 1991; Eisenberg and Fabes, 1998; Zahn-Waxler et al., 1992). Experimental work has also shown that infants have an early preference for prosocial characters. Hamlin et al. (2007) put on a puppet show for six- to ten-month-old infants in which a puppet climber struggled to climb up a hill and sometimes a second climber came along and helped the first puppet from below. On other occasions a different puppet appeared at the top of the hill and bashed the climber down the hill. A few minutes later the infants saw a second puppet show where the climber looked back and forth between the helper puppet and the hinderer puppet and then snuggled up to the hinderer. The infants stared at the scene longer – indicating surprise – when the climber snuggled up to the hinderer compared to the helper. This suggests the infants had a stronger expectation that the climber would choose the helpful puppet. This methodology takes advantage of one thing infants are very good at – getting bored. The basic idea is that they will look at something longer when they are surprised by it and therefore interested in it. When the experiment was over the infants were much more likely to reach for the helper puppet than the hinderer puppet when both were placed in front of them. This is important as it is fairly uncontroversial to claim that nobody likes to be hit. If infants were hit directly by the puppet (leaving aside the ethics of such an experiment!) it is pretty clear that they would not want to play with that character. What this experiment shows is a kind of third party judgement about character: infants saw how these characters were behaving towards each other and that guided their own personal preferences. These prosocial judgements translate into prosocial action. For example, by two years of age, toddlers help those who were helpful to them in previous interactions more than those who were not helpful (Dunfield and Kuhlmeier, 2010). Just a year later, children reduce their prosocial behaviour towards an individual who caused or intended to cause harm to another individual (Kenward and Dahl, 2011; Vaish et al., 2010).

4.3   Equality and sharing

If infants and young children can demonstrate an awareness of prosocial behaviours, does this mean they have an appreciation of equality and the need to share? Research shows that three-year-old children who have obtained rewards by working collaboratively with each other divide up their rewards (e.g. stickers, marbles and sweets) equally rather than monopolising them, even when the resources could easily be monopolised (Warneken et al., 2011). When compared with chimpanzees the difference is marked. In similar collaborative situations, chimpanzees have a strong tendency to compete over the resources. The sharing of spoils for chimpanzees usually follows the dominance hierarchy within the group and this places limits on the scope of potential collaborative activities they can take part in (Melis et al., 2006) (See Box 3.1). Three-year-old children can divide up their rewards equally after a collaborative activity – but *only* if they have worked together to achieve the goal (Hamann et al., 2011). Similar prosocial sharing behaviours have been witnessed in **naturalistic observations** too, with infants as young as eight months of age readily sharing toys with other infants, adults and even strangers (e.g. Hay, 1979; Rheingold et al., 1976; Young and Lewis, 1979).

Children become increasingly sensitive to the character of the people they are sharing with or potentially sharing with. By about four years of age, children share (even at a cost to themselves) with their friends more than with non-friends or strangers (Birch and Billman, 1986; Moore, 2009), and by eight years of age, children share more with their in-group than their out-group members (Fehr et al., 2008; see Chapter 3 of Book 1).

When deciding how to divide resources children start out by using the rule of thumb 'fair is equal' – everyone gets the same amount. By five or six years of age children have a more sophisticated understanding of what constitutes a fair share. By this age the concept of fairness takes account of the recipient's need, merit and amount of work they have put in to obtaining the resource. Children have also learned to disregard irrelevant characteristics such as the persons' height or age (e.g. Damon, 1975, 1977; Hook and Cook, 1979; Sigelman and Waitzman, 1991; see also Enright et al., 1984). It is interesting to note that in Western societies the 'pull' of equity-based reasoning often outweighs the pull of other justice principles and this point is arguably explained by the earlier discussion of the distinction between individualistic and more sociocentric societies. Equity, par excellence, is an expression of individualistic conceptions of fairness.

Naturalistic observations A study where researchers take advantage of naturally occurring events, rather than themselves manipulating variables.

> Box 3.1 Crossing boundaries: what do chimpanzees know about sharing?
>
> In this chapter we have studied the idea of morals from multiple perspectives: the anthropological and ethnographic studies of Shweder; the evolutionary perspectives of Haidt; the developmental studies of Piaget, Kohlberg and Turiel; and the philosophical insights of Rawls. Also, in the next section you will read about the

neuroscience discoveries of Damasio. We have already seen how the study of morals can benefit from these multiple perspectives because researchers use converging lines of evidence to understand how morals work. In this box we consider a different way in which the topic of morals sprawls across boundaries – that between human and non-humans. By comparing ourselves to our nearest evolutionary relatives we can understand how we have changed since we separated from a common ancestor as recently as 4 million years ago. The idea here is that we need to know what we share in common in order to understand what makes us unique. So, if we were to study the lives of chimpanzees and humans as completely separate disciplines it would be an arbitrary biological division (we all share a common ancestor if we go back far enough) and it would be a missed opportunity to see what insights we can gain from crossing these boundaries.

Recent comparative research has addressed the question of the evolutionary origins of human morality. In a recent paper in *Nature* Hamann et al. (2011, p. 328) compared the sharing behaviour of toddlers and chimpanzees. Two- and three-year-old children played a game in pairs that involved pulling on two ropes. The ropes brought a board towards them with two marbles at each end. The twist was that the apparatus was set up such that one of the marbles would roll towards one of the children. So one of the children ended up with three marbles and one child had one – even though they had both put in the same amount of work (pulling the rope) to get the marbles. Two- and three-year-olds seemed to have a sense that keeping the three marbles to themselves in this situation was not an appropriate response. Around 50 per cent of the two-year-olds and 70 per cent of the three-year-olds offered the 'extra' marble to the other child. Importantly this was only true when they had worked together to obtain the marbles. If the marbles were already in reach the children did not feel obliged to share.

The setup for the chimpanzee experiment was slightly more complicated but it essentially tested the same capacity for collaboration and sharing. Instead of using marbles the researchers used something much more incentivising to a chimp – grapes. In the chimp version of the experiment, collaboration or no collaboration made no difference – they kept the same amount of grapes in both conditions, regardless of whether it was 'fairly' obtained or not. The title of the paper was called 'Collaboration encourages equal sharing in children but not in chimpanzees' and could reflect an important difference in the moral foundations of us and our nearest evolutionary relatives. The researchers argue this kind of activity – putting our heads together to achieve a shared goal – is a 'fairer test' of our cooperative tendencies as it better reflects the cooperative situations our ancestors faced.

Think about some of the difficulties and challenges of conducting this type of research. For example, researchers had to use different rewards in each experiment, so is a grape as rewarding for a chimp as a sweet is for a child? Does it matter?

4.4 Moral emotions and the brain

The research outlined in this chapter has supported the contention that humans are unique in our moral understanding, awareness and behaviour. But how is this behaviour represented in the brain? In this final section we briefly consider the role that emotions play in our moral sense and how they are instantiated in the brain.

Neuroscientist Antonio Damasio (1994) investigated the emotional basis of morality by studying patients who had suffered brain damage to the ventromedial prefrontal cortex (just behind and above the bridge of the nose). Following this damage the patients were unable to experience emotions – looking at the most cheerful or horrific photographs elicited nothing. They showed no deficits in IQ but when it came to making decisions about their life – work and friends – they either made extremely poor decisions or no decisions at all. One of the functions associated with the ventromedial prefrontal cortex is to integrate conscious deliberations and emotions. In the case of these patients, it seemed that this ability was seriously impaired. Damasio's interpretation of these findings was that gut reactions are necessary to think rationally. For these patients the only way to make a decision was to examine the potential costs and benefits of each option but with none of the emotional content that guides this process in healthy adults. Consequently the lives of these patients soon fell apart.

The claim here was that reasoning *requires* passion. Remember the story of the siblings, Julie and Mark? People make a moral judgment about this story that is quick and emotional but find it hard to justify (moral dumbfounding). When the violation is based on a taboo scenario (incest, sex with a dead chicken, eating a pet), moral reasoning was mostly an after-the-fact search for justifying the decision they have already made. Damasio's research helps to provide the neurological grounding for the psychology of morality.

4.5   Summary

Studies looking at sympathy, helping, cooperation and sharing show young children have concerns for the well-being of others in the group at the same time as looking out for their own individual interests. Recent comparative research has addressed the question of the evolutionary origins of human morality. They suggest humans' tendency to distribute resources equitably may have its evolutionary roots in sharing resources after collaboration. Damage to areas of the brain that integrate conscious deliberations and emotions can impair people's moral judgement.

5   Concluding thoughts

We have taken a long and winding road to answer the question: 'How do we know what's right and wrong?' We have looked at the development of moral judgements throughout childhood, considering whether children go through specific stages of moral development. We have looked at whether there is a fundamental difference between moral rules and social conventions. To do that, we needed to look at research that considered behaviour and beliefs within and between different cultures. We then looked at whether evolution via natural selection has shaped our species' unique moral sense by selecting certain 'moral foundations'. We saw how these foundations can predict personal political ideologies that manifest themselves later in life. We considered the relationship between what people say they will do (moral judgement) and what they actually do (moral behaviour). Finally, we considered how our moral behaviour compares with our nearest ancestors and the role emotion has in regulating the moral sense.

A lot has been learned from over a century of research on morality but, of course, this has opened up many new frontiers and exposed gaps in our knowledge. Instead of pointing out the empirical holes in what is known, I would like to conclude with a thought about a distinction raised at the start of this chapter. We started by saying that research on morality in general does not take a stance on who or what is morally right (normative approach); rather, it is trying to describe an important part of human social life (descriptive approach). One interesting direction for the future of this field can be posed as a question: Does scientific enquiry have any business in recommending what we ought to do? Scottish philosopher David Hume said you cannot derive an 'ought' from an 'is'. By this he meant you cannot derive what ought to be the case (a normative judgement) on the basis of statements about what is (a descriptive approach). Is that true? Can we subject matters of morals to the scientific methodology?

A book by neuroscientist Sam Harris, *The Moral Landscape*, has begun to question Hume's claim (Harris, 2010). Imagine one society routinely practises female genital mutilation on its infants and one does not. Is it a scientific question to ask which one of these societies brings about the greatest well-being to its citizens? One could argue there is a testable hypothesis (mutilation has no effect on well-being) with a variable (mutilation versus no mutilation) and a measure (well-being).

The issue is controversial and begs the question of whether we could define 'well-being' without assuming a moral stance, therefore creating a somewhat circular debate. For the time being, reflect on what you have learned from the descriptive approach to human morality and debate with friends and family whether science will ever be able to tell us what we ought to do.

Further reading

- Why do 'justice' and 'fairness' mean different things to different people? Why is it easier to see the flaws in others' arguments rather than our own? Using moral psychology, ancient philosophy and political analysis Haidt discusses the biological and cultural origins of our moral sense:

Haidt, J. (2012) *The Righteous Mind: Why Good People are Divided by Politics and Religion*, London, Penguin Books Ltd.

- The subtitle of this book is 'how science can determine human values'. This provocative book argues that science can go beyond telling us how we are; it can tell us how we ought to be:

Harris, S. (2010) *The Moral Landscape*, London, Random House Group Ltd.

- How do we measure morality in young children? How do children understand the concept of fairness and equality? What is the evolutionary basis for morality and the role of culture? To answer these questions this book critically discusses topics such as neuroscience; theory of mind; gender, sexuality, prejudice and discrimination:

Killen, M. and Smetana, J. (2013) *Handbook of Moral Development*, 2nd edn, Hove, Psychology Press.

References

Aronfreed, J. (1968) *Conduct and Conscience: The Socialization of Internalised Control Over Behavior*, New York, Academic Press.

Birch L.L. and Billman J. (1986) 'Preschool children's food sharing with friends and acquaintances', *Child Development*, vol. 57, no. 2, pp. 387–95.

Bischof-Köhler, D. (1991) 'The development of empathy in infants', in Lamb, M.E. and Keller, H. (eds) *Infant Development: Perspectives from German Speaking Countries*, pp. 245–73, Hillsdale, NJ: Lawrence Erlbaum Associates.

Cohen, D.B. (1999) *Stranger in the Nest: Do Parents Really Shape their Child's Personality, Intelligence, or Character?*, New York, John Wiley.

Damon, W. (1975) 'Early conceptions of positive justice as related to the development of logical operations', *Child Development*, vol. 46, no. 2, pp. 301–12.

Damon, W. (1977) *The Social World of the Child*, San Francisco, Jossey-Bass.

Darwin, C. (1871) *The Descent of Man and Selection in Relation to Sex*, Amherst, NY, Prometheus Books (this edition 1998).

Damasio, A.R. (1994). *Descartes' Error: Emotion, Eeason, and the Human Brain*, New York, G.P. Putnam.

Dunfield, K.A. and Kuhlmeier, V.A. (2010) 'Intention-mediated selective helping in infancy', *Psychological Science*, vol. 21, no. 4, pp. 523–7.

Eisenberg, N. and Fabes, R. (1998) 'Prosocial development', in Damon, W. (ed. in chief) and Eisenberg, N. (vol. ed.) *Handbook of Child Psychology, vol. 3, Social, Emotional, and Personality Development,* 5th edn, New York, Wiley, pp. 701–78.

Enright, R.D., Bjerstedt, O. Enright, W.F., Levy, V.M. Jr, Lapsley, D.K., Bus, R.R., Harwell, M. and Zindler, M. (1984) 'Distributive justice development: cross-cultural, contextual, and longitudinal evaluations', *Child Development*, vol. 55, no. 5, pp. 1737–51.

Fehr, E., Bernhard, H. and Rockenbach, B. (2008) 'Egalitarianism in young children', *Nature*, vol. 454, no. 28, pp. 1079–84.

Gartner, K. (1990) 'A third component causing random variability beside environment and genotype. A reason for the limited success of a 30 year long effort to standardise laboratory animals?', *Laboratory Animals*, vol. 24, no. 1, pp. 71–7.

Graham, J., Haidt, J. and Nosek, B.A. (2008) The Moral Foundations Questionnaire, available online at: www.YourMorals.org (Accessed 11 June 2015).

Graham, J., Haidt, J. and Nosek, B.A. (2009) 'Liberals and conservatives rely on different sets of moral foundations', *Personality Processes and Individual Differences*, vol. 96, no. 5, pp. 1029–46.

Haidt, J. and Joseph, C. (2004) 'Intuitive ethics: how innately prepared intuitions generate culturally variable virtues', *Daedalus*, vol. 133, no. 4, pp. 55–66.

Haidt, J., Koller, S.H. and Dias, M.G. (1993) 'Affect, culture, and morality, or is it wrong to eat your dog'?' *Journal of Personality and Social Psychology*, vol. 65, no. 4, pp. 613–28.

Hamann, K., Warneken, J. Greenberg, J.R. and Tomasello, M. (2011) 'Collaboration encourages equal sharing in children but not in chimpanzees', *Nature*, vol. 476, pp. 328–31.

Hamann, K., Warneken, F. and Tomasello, M. (2012) 'Children's developing commitments to joint goals', *Child Development*, vol. 83, no. 1, pp. 137–45.

Hamilton, W. D. (1964a) 'The genetical evolution of social behavior: I', *Journal of Theoretical Biology*, vol. 7, no. 1, pp. 1-16.

Hamilton, W. D. (1964b) 'The genetical evolution of social behavior: II', *Journal of Theoretical Biology*, vol. 7, no. 1, pp. 17-52.

Hamlin, J.K., Wynn, K. and Bloom, P. (2007) 'Social evaluation by preverbal infants', *Nature*, vol. 450, pp. 557–60.

Harris, S. (2010) *The Moral Landscape*, London, Random House Group Ltd.

Hauser, M. (2006) *Moral Minds: How Nature Designed our Universal Sense of Right and Wrong*, New York, Harper Collins.

Hay, D.F. (1979) 'Cooperative interactions and sharing between very young children and their parents', *Developmental Psychology*, vol. 15, no. 6, pp. 647–53.

Helwig, C.C. and Jasiobedzka, U. (2001) 'The relation between law and morality: children's reasoning about socially beneficial and unjust laws', *Child Development*, vol. 72, no. 5, pp. 1382–93.

Hollos, M., Leis, P. and Turiel, E. (1986) 'Social reasoning in IJO children and adolescents in Nigerian communities', *Journal of Cross-Cultural Psychology*, vol. 17, no. 3, pp. 352–76.

Hook, J.G. and Cook, T.D. (1979) 'Equity theory and the cognitive ability of children', *Psychology Bulletin*, vol. 86, no. 3, pp. 429–45.

Kenward, B. and Dahl, M. (2011) 'Preschoolers distribute resources according to recipients' moral status', *Developmental Psychology*, vol. 47, no. 4, pp. 1054–64.

Kohlberg, L. (1969) 'Stage and sequence: the cognitive–developmental approach to socialization', in Goslin, D.A. (ed.) *Handbook of Socialization Theory and Research*, New York, McGraw Hill.

Kohlberg, L. (1976) 'Moral stage and moralization: the cognitive–developmental approach', in Lickona, T. (ed.) *Moral Development and Behavior: Theory, Research, and Social Issues*, New York, Holt, Rinehart, & Winston, pp. 84–107.

Laupa, M., Turiel, E. and Cowan, P.A. (1995) 'Obedience to authority in children and adults', in Killen, M. and Hart, D. (eds) *Morality in Everyday Life*, New York, Cambridge University Press, pp. 131–65.

Liszkowski, U., Carpenter, M., Striano, T. and Tomasello, M. (2006) '12- and 18-month-olds point to provide information for others', *Journal of Cognition and Development*, vol. 7, no. 2, pp. 173–87.

Liszkowski, U., Carpenter, M. and Tomasello, M. (2008) 'Twelve-month-olds communicate helpfully and appropriately for knowledgeable and ignorant partners', *Cognition*, vol. 108, no. 3, pp. 732–9.

Locke, J. (1690) *An Essay Concerning Human Understanding*, Nidditch, P.H. (ed.), Oxford, Clarendon Press (this edition 1979).

Melis, A.P., Hare, B. and Tomasello, M. (2006) 'Engineering cooperation in chimpanzees: tolerance constraints on cooperation', *Animal Behaviour*, vol. 72, no. 2, pp. 275–86.

Moore, C. (2009) 'Fairness in children's resource allocation depends on the recipient', *Psychology Science*, vol. 20, no. 8, pp. 944–8.

Nucci, L. (1981) 'The development of personal concepts: a domain distinct from moral and social concepts', *Child Development*, vol. 52, no. 1, pp. 114–21.

Nucci, L., Turiel, E. and Encarnacion-Gawrych, G. (1983) 'Children's social interactions and social concepts in the Virgin Islands', *Journal of Cross-Cultural Psychology*, vol. 14, no. 4, pp. 469–87.

Piaget, J. (1997 [1932]) *The Moral Judgment of the Child*, New York, The Free Press.

Plato, *Meno, Plato in Twelve Volumes, vol. 3*, trans. W.R.M. Lamb (1967), Cambridge, MA/London, Harvard University Press/William Heinemann Ltd.

Plomin, R. (1994) *Genetics and Experience: The Interplay between Nature and Nurture*, Thousand Oaks, CA, Sage.

Plomin, R. and Daniels, D. (1987) 'Why are children raised in the same family so different from one another?', *Behavior and Brain Sciences*, vol. 10, pp. 1–60.

Rawls, J. (1971) *A Theory of Justice as Fairness*, Cambridge, MA, Harvard University Press.

Rheingold, H.L., Hay, D.F. and West, M.J. (1976) 'Sharing in the second year of life', *Child Development*, vol. 47, no. 4, pp. 1148–58.

Rozin, P. (1997) 'Moralization', in Brandt, A.M. and Rozin, P. (eds) *Morality and Health*, New York, Routledge, pp. 379–401.

Schmidt, M.F.H. and Sommerville, J.A. (2011) 'Fairness expectations and altruistic sharing in 15-month-old human infants', PLoS ONE, 6 (10), e23223.

Shweder, R. and Bourne, E. (1984) 'Does the concept of the person vary cross–culturally?', in *Culture Theory*, Shweder, R.A. and LeVine, R. (eds.), Cambridge, Cambridge University Press, pp. 158–99.

Shweder, R.A., Mahapatra, M. and Miller, J. (1987) 'Culture and moral development', in Kagan, J. and Lamb, S. (eds) *The Emergence of Morality in Young Children*, Chicago, IL, University of Chicago Press, pp. 1–83.

Sigelman, C.K. and Waitzman, K.A. (1991) 'The development of distributive justice orientations: contextual influences on children's resource allocation', *Child Development*, vol. 62, no. 6, pp. 1367–78.

Skinner, B.F. (1971) *Beyond Freedom and Dignity*, New York, Knopf.

Svetlova, M., Nichols, S. and Brownell, C. (2010) 'Toddlers' prosocial behavior: from instrumental to empathetic to altruistic helping', *Child Development*, vol. 81, no. 6, pp. 1814–27.

Tomasello, M. and Vaish, A. (2013) 'Origins of human cooperation and morality', *Annual Reviews of Psychology*, vol. 64, pp. 231–55.

Tomasello, M., Carpenter, M., Call, J., Behne, T. and Moll, H. (2005) 'Understanding and sharing intentions: the origins of cultural cognition', *Behavioral and Brain Sciences*, vol. 28, no. 5, pp. 675–91.

Turiel, E. (1983) *The Development of Social Knowledge: Morality and Convention*, Cambridge, Cambridge University Press.

Turiel, E. (2003) 'Resistance and subversion in everyday life', *Journal of Moral Education*, vol. 32, Reprinted in L. Nucci (ed.) (2005) *Conflict, Contradiction, and Contrarian Elements*, Mahwah, NJ, Lawrence Erlbaum, pp. 115–30.

Vaish, A., Carpenter, M. and Tomasello, M. (2010) 'Young children selectively avoid helping people with harmful intentions', *Child Development*, vol. 81, no. 6, pp. 1661–9.

Warneken, F. and Tomasello, M. (2006) 'Altruistic helping in human infants and young chimpanzees', *Science*, vol. 3, no. 11, pp. 1301–3.

Warneken, F. and Tomasello, M. (2007) 'Helping and cooperation at 14 months of age', *Infancy*, vol. 11, no. 3, pp. 271–94.

Warneken, F. and Tomasello, M. (2008) 'Extrinsic rewards undermine altruistic tendencies in 20-month-olds', *Developmental Psychology*, vol. 44, no. 6, pp. 1785–8.

Warneken, F., Chen, F. and Tomasello, M. (2006) 'Cooperative activities in young children and chimpanzees', *Child Development*, vol. 77, no. 3, pp. 640–63.

Warneken, F., Grafenhain, M. and Tomasello, M. (2012) 'Collaborative partner or social tool? New evidence for young children's understanding of joint intentions in collaborative activities', *Developmental Science*, vol. 15, no. 1, pp. 54–61.

Warneken, F., Lohse, K., Melis, A.P. and Tomasello, M. (2011) 'Young children share the spoils after collaboration', *Psychological Science*, vol. 22, no. 2, pp. 267–73.

Young, G. and Lewis, M. (1979) 'Effects of familiarity and maternal attention on infant peer relations', *Merrill-Palmer Quarterly of Behaviour and Development*, vol. 25, no. 2, pp. 105–19.

Zahn-Waxler, C., Radke-Yarrow, M., Wagner, E. and Chapman, M. (1992) 'Development of concern for others', *Developmental Psychology*, vol. 28, no. 1, pp. 126–36.

Chapter 4

Are boys and girls born or made? Understanding the development of gender

Jane Callaghan

Contents

1 Introduction

When a baby is born, what is one of the first questions we tend to ask proud new parents? 'What is it?' 'Is it a boy or a girl?' What do we mean when we ask this kind of question? What are we *doing* when we ask this kind of question? What assumptions do we have about what is important in human experience and interaction? After all, the answer to the question 'What is it?' is rarely 'It is a human being'. Our first questions around new babies tell us something about what is important about identity in our culture. Is the baby healthy? Is the baby a boy or a girl? Gender functions as a core identifier in our social interactions. We tend to assume it is one of the most important things about an individual, something that has a strong influence on behaviour, on the way we interact with others, and the life choices we make (Figure 4.1).

Gender
The socially constructed roles, actions, thoughts, feelings and behaviours that a particular culture associates with being men or women or being masculine or feminine.

Figure 4.1   Is it important that one of the first questions we ask when a baby is born is 'What is it?'

But what do we mean by **gender**? Is it the same thing as **sex**? And what about sexuality or sexual orientation?

The American Psychological Association (APA) defines sex as 'a person's biological status ... typically categorised as male, female or

Sex
Biological characteristic of being male or female.

Intersex
Having ambiguous sex characteristics. For example, having features of both male and female genitalia.

Gender identity
A person's sense of self as gendered. Typically this is understood as your feeling of being masculine or feminine.

Non-binary gender
Gender identities that are not neatly categorised as either masculine or feminine; sometimes referred to as genderqueer. Binary gender classifies gender into two: masculine and feminine.

intersex' (APA, 2012, p. 11). Biological sex is indicated by factors like external genitalia, internal reproductive organs and sex chromosomes. In contrast, the APA suggests that gender 'refers to the attitudes, feelings and behaviours that a given culture associates with a person's biological sex', and **gender identity** is 'one's sense of oneself as male, female or transgender' (APA, 2012, p. 11). Thus biological sex refers to the biological qualities of 'maleness' or 'femaleness', while gender refers to the more cultural and socially constituted attitudes, feelings and behaviours associated with being 'masculine', 'feminine', or **non-binary gender**.

From a very young age, infants and children appear to be aware of differences in gender, and seem to adapt their reactions to their social world to some perception of gender. For instance, Serbin et al. (2002) found that 18-month-old infants presented with pictures of men and women performing gender conforming and non-conforming tasks tended to look longer at non-conforming images (Figure 4.2), suggesting an understanding that they were unfamiliar and thus unusual (as noted in Chapter 2).

Figure 4.2   Serbin et al. (2002) found that young toddlers looked for much longer at gender non-conforming behaviours, like the man putting on lipstick, or the woman using the hammer

There are observable differences in children's play behaviour from about the age of three onwards, with boys more likely to be involved in rough and tumble play, while girls are more likely to engage in play that mimics nurturing roles (Hines, 2011) and in creative and pretend play (Gmitrova et al., 2009). But how do we make sense of these differences in play behaviour?

As we move through this chapter, we will explore how psychologists make sense of the phenomenon of gender, and the development of gender identity and gender 'differences' in children and young people. A core theme in this chapter is whether we can make sense of gender as determined by biology, by social processes, or by an interaction of the two. We will contrast **essentialist** accounts of gender identity (explanations that focus on innate or biologically driven gender differences) with explanations of gender as something that is learned, acquired or socially constructed.

Essentialism
The idea that objects have an essence that makes them what they truly are. Gender essentialism is the notion that human identities are essentially gendered, i.e. that being masculine or feminine is a core part of being human and that our gendered essence is determined by biology.

Activity 4.1:   What is gender?

Without thinking too hard about it, quickly jot down a list of words that you think characterise a 'typical' man or woman, boy or girl. Write ten words for 'masculine' and ten for 'feminine'. Look at the two lists and see if you can identify any patterns.

In a sentence or two write down what you think gender is. Look at your two lists, and consider whether you think that sex differences are natural and inevitable. How do you think boys become boys and girls become girls?

Learning outcomes

On completing this chapter, you should:

- be able to engage with the question 'how do we become gendered?'

- be able to explore psychological understandings of 'gender', gender differences and gender identity

- be able to explain four theoretical approaches to understanding gender and gender difference (biological, cognitive, social cognitive and interactionist theories)

- be able to think critically about our taken-for-granted assumptions about gender.

2   Do humans come in two kinds? Biological theories of gender development

This section considers the idea that we are 'born gendered', or that gender identity and gender difference develop as a consequence of biological maturation.

When my daughter was little, I often took her to baby groups and play groups where infants and toddlers were brought along to play together while their parents looked on, exchanged stories and drank tea. I was often struck by the comments parents made about their children. Pointing to a six-month-old who had accidentally whacked his hand into the face of a baby, an adult might exclaim 'Oh, look at Harry! He's such a typical little boy. So rough and tough', or observing a two-year-old daughter, dressed head to toe in sparkles and pink, 'oh, she does love to dress like a fairy'. More generally, many parents will note that they offered their babies and young children gender neutral toys to play with, but that boys 'just preferred' trucks and guns and construction toys, and girls 'naturally' gravitated towards dolls and dressing up. These exclamations often express a common-sense understanding that boys will be boys, girls will be girls, and that there is something innate and indisputable about gender differences in behaviour.

Sexual dimorphism
Categorisation of organisms into two sex types: male and female; the physical or behavioural differences associated with biological sex.

Many of our common sense and popular accounts of gender and gender differences arise from biological accounts. These accounts tend to assume that differences between boys and girls, and between men and women are best understood as *sex differences*, and that these sex differences are rooted in fundamental biological differences between male and female bodies.

Gender dimorphism
The assumption that gender comes in two kinds, masculine and feminine, that maps only sexual dimorphism.

Let us consider some of these biological explanations of the development of gender roles and identities in children. Biological explanations largely draw on a presumption that **sexual dimorphism** predicts **gender dimorphism**. In other words, the biological explanation suggests that human beings come in two types – male and female – and that this biological difference predicts the difference we see in gender roles (masculine and feminine).

2.1   Animals at heart? Evolutionary accounts of gender

Evolutionary psychological explanations of gender are often used in popular culture to make sense of apparent differences between men and women, boys and girls. Evolutionary theory assumes that gender differences are biologically based, and can be explained by **sexual selection** theory. Evolutionary theory suggests that all animals are intrinsically motivated to ensure the passing on of their genetic material. Sexual selection refers to the strategies species have evolved to improve their chances of reproductive success. This approach proposes that observed gendered differences in social interaction, thought processes, and emotional expression are there to maximise individual and species' chances of ensuring that their genes transfer to the next generation (Buss, 2011; Buss and Schmitt, 2011).

A key assumption in evolutionary explanations of gender difference is that it is rooted in differential parental investment in offspring by males and females, and an associated division of labour. This difference in parental investment begins from conception, with human females having a larger and more prolonged investment in offspring from the outset. Human eggs are larger and fewer in number than sperm. This means that a single male can fertilise many females. This creates conditions in which men must compete for a scarce resource – women they can impregnate. This offers some explanation for differences in levels of aggression in men and women. Further, the reproductive success of males depends on how many females they mate with, but the reproductive success of females does not. This should predict that women will be more discriminatory in partner choice (Buss, 1989). Sex differences in social, intellectual and emotional functioning emerge in relation to these differences in relative parental investment according to evolutionary theorists such as Geary (2010) and Pinker (2003), and are best explained with reference to the principles of sexual selection.

One of the biggest threats to genetic survival for humans is our long gestation period (approximately 40 weeks), and our children's long period of dependency on adult carers. While most species are able to bear multiple offspring (for instance, litters of kittens), the females of some species – including humans – can only bear a fairly small number of children at once (without significant assistance). Because gestation in humans is prolonged, and most typically involves just one offspring

Sexual selection
In evolutionary theory, sexual selection is a mechanism of natural selection. Natural selection refers to the way that organisms that are better adapted to their environment are more likely to survive and reproduce. Sexual selection refers to the selection of characteristics that makes individuals in a species more attractive to the opposite sex, and therefore more likely to enjoy reproductive success.

per pregnancy, human females necessarily invest considerable resource in each baby they carry. Humans have also evolved to have relatively large heads, and so birth must take place relatively early in the lifecycle if the infant is to pass through the birth canal safely. A cost of human beings' relative intelligence is that they are born developmentally earlier and are consequently more dependent than most other species. As a result, post-natal parental investment is also prolonged because human infants are more 'helpless' than other species. To ensure our offspring survive long enough to reproduce themselves, parents need to provide a sustained period of nurturance. This is particularly the case for human mothers who are biologically adapted to bear and nurture offspring.

In contrast, as previously noted, human males are able to produce more offspring, more frequently, and so their biological investment in individual offspring is lower. In terms of the notion of survival of the fittest, human males can 'afford' to invest less in each individual offspring. Evolutionary theorists suggest that this greater investment by human females in their offspring predicts their development of more nurturing and emotionally responsive qualities that enable them to provide a more sustained level of care.

However, this prolonged period of dependency also predicts that human reproductive success is more likely if females are able to attract a mate who also invests time in caring for offspring. While infants are dependent on their mothers for nurture and care, in a hostile environment both mother and infant are vulnerable to hunger, predation and other dangers. Evolutionary approaches indicate that because of this, to maximise chances of reproductive success, both males and females must invest in offspring, but that their labour is divided to support this. In short, females provide nurture and care, while males provide protection, food and other necessities. For this reason, evolutionary theorists argue, males have adapted characteristics that enable them to function effectively as protectors and providers – they are more aggressive, more oriented to search for resources outside the domestic sphere, and so on. In contrast, evolutionary theorists would suggest that human females must invest more in both child rearing and in maintaining a pair bond with their mate, and so have developed characteristics focused on nurturing and emotional labour.

What are the implications of this framework for an understanding of gender, gender roles and gender differences? Within an evolutionary framework, gendered differences in abilities and behaviours are understood as necessary adaptations to specific challenges to reproductive success (Figure 4.3).

Figure 4.3   Did gendered division of labour evolve to increase our reproductive fitness, by providing human offspring with a better chance of survival in a predatory world?

Evolutionary psychology suggests that gender differences in abilities and behaviours are hardwired. It should be noted that evolutionary theory does not predict that men and women will be entirely different: rather, men and women will only exhibit gender differences in circumstances where challenges to reproductive fitness might have operated differently for males and females (Buss and Schmitt, 2011). Indeed, some gendered differences in children's behaviour have been noted that might support an evolutionary explanation. As we have already noted, boys engage in more rough play than girls – perhaps reflecting a tendency for greater aggression that can enable males to compete more effectively for a range of resources necessary for survival and reproductive success, including access to mating opportunities (Geary, 2005, 2010). Girls also tend to engage in more parent-play, and spend more time developing close friendships (Hines, 2011). Nonetheless, it is important to remember that this approach is, necessarily, a speculative one, with many of its claims being untestable (Eagly and Wood, 2011; Wood and Eagly, 2002).

2.2   Did my brain make me do it? The role of hormones, brain structure and function in the development of gender

As we have seen, evolutionary psychology suggests there are evolutionarily driven differences between males and females. Biological accounts of gender outline the underpinning structural and hormonal differences in brain and biology that might produce these gendered behaviours. A 'brain organisation theory' of gender (Jordan-Young, 2012; Liao et al., 2012) suggests that our brains develop in a gendered manner as a consequence of the organising influence of prenatal and perinatal sex hormones, which produce sex differentiation of the brain. That is, sex hormones act on the human embryo in the womb and shape foetal development in sex differentiated ways. The genes that determine the developing foetus's sex are found in the 23rd pair of chromosomes, the X and Y chromosomes – male zygotes have XY chromosomes while females have XX. The presence of the Y chromosome produces the differentiation of the gonad into testes, and begins the hormonal process that results in sex differentiation. However, the process of masculinisation or feminisation of embryos is not solely dependent on chromosomal information – indeed XX and XY embryos tend to feminise without the presence of masculinising influences (Grumbach and Conte, 1998). Becoming biologically male is dependent on the masculinising influence of hormones, specifically

Androgens
Male sex hormones.

Testosterone
The hormone that stimulates the development of male secondary sex characteristics.

androgens. It is these sex hormones that determine the development of male or female genitalia. It is also these same sex hormones that brain organisation theory presumes produce sex differences in male and female brains (Jordan-Young, 2010). From around the sixth week of foetal development, the primordial foetal gonads develop into testes, and begin to produce **androgens**, including **testosterone**. If enough testosterone is produced, then male external genitalia form at about nine weeks' gestation and full masculinisation of the developing foetus is achieved between 12 and 16 weeks. Without these factors, feminisation continues (Lenroot and Giedd, 2010).

Androgens play a role in all neural development (male and female), but their increased presence in male foetal development has a stronger effect on the development of asymmetry in the cerebral cortex, with male brains showing greater volume, but more lateralisation, while female brains are characterised by proportionally more dense corpus callosa (Baron-Cohen et al., 2005). In other words, male brain structures are larger overall, but the connective tissue between the hemispheres of the brain is more developed in females. This kind of brain structure difference is seen as evidence for greater integration of brain function (and for instance, the notion that women are 'better at multi-tasking' – a claim that it should be pointed out has very limited evidence to support it! See Stoet et al. (2013), as well as Book 2, Chapter 2. There is some evidence that newborn babies exhibit differences in brain structure that are similar to sex differences observed in adult brains – for instance newborn male brains have larger volumes of grey and white cortical matter than female brains (Gilmore et al., 2007).

Brain organisation theorists suggest that this early foetal exposure to sex hormones does not just produce male and female genitalia, but also organises the brain in a gendered way, producing 'sex typical' patterns of behaviour, interests, cognitive styles, and sexual desires. This organisation of the brain is illustrated through 'neural network' images that map out the way that gendered brains are purported to function (Figure 4.4). This brain differentiation, established as part of foetal development, develops further when children reach puberty and their bodies are flooded with sex hormones. At this time, we observe rapid physical changes in boys' and girls' bodies as they reach physical and sexual maturity. Most children will move into puberty between the ages of 10 and 17 – for girls, sometime between 10 and 15 years of age, and for boys, between 11 and 17. (Younger entry into puberty is associated with industrialisation and improved nutrition, see for example Atay et al., 2011; Jaruratanasirikul et al., 2014). For girls the most significant physical event will be the onset of menstruation (the menarche), while for boys, it is the first experience of ejaculation (spermarche). Over a period of several years, both sexes acquire body hair, girls' bodies become more curved, boys' acquire more muscle density, facial hair and their voices become deeper. At a neurological level, puberty is associated with increasing myelination of the cells in the prefrontal cortex, speeding up electrical impulses and the transmission of information in this part of the brain (Yakolev and Lecours, 1967; Nagy et al., 2004). This, combined with a process called synaptic pruning (reducing 'surplus' synaptic connections in the grey matter of the brain), enables faster transmission of messages within the brain, and enables young people to think in abstract ways, plan and use logical reasoning (Blakemore and Choudhury, 2006). Synaptic pruning is more inhibited in boys than in girls (Blanton et al., 2004) and this, together with their greater hemispheric dominance, is a possible explanation for gender differences in speech development between boys and girls (Lenroot and Giedd, 2010). Girls develop various aspects of language earlier than boys. For instance, girls on average begin to speak and develop a more sophisticated grammar earlier than boys. This is seen as a result of the specialisation of the left hemisphere of the brain for language as children develop – inhibited synaptic pruning, combined with the greater integration of hemispheric activity of the brain, may result in the slower development of this specialisation. Some studies have noted that, even where boys and girls have similar cognitive abilities, there are differences in boys' and girls' rates of neural activation when performing similar tasks. These studies suggest great neural efficiency for girls (Christova et al., 2008).

Brain organisation theory therefore naturalises the notion that men and women are 'born different', and that boys and girls develop different abilities, thought processes and behaviours based on this biologically determined differentiation. Observers of the rapid physical and neurological changes that occur in adolescence have also noted the significant psychological and social changes that typically occur as young people move through puberty. For example, a difference that is often described in developmental psychology is an observed difference between boys' and girls' visuospatial and verbal abilities, a difference that seems to emerge in puberty (Burman et al., 2008; Chung and Auger, 2013). Also, sex differences in rates of psychological difficulty begin to emerge in puberty, with girls experiencing an elevated risk of mood related or internalising 'disorders', like depression, anxiety, eating disorders (Nolen-Hoeksema, 2001; Carter et al., 2012; Rutter, 2007), while boys are more at risk of 'externalising' behaviours or 'acting out' behaviours like conduct 'disorders' and attention deficit hyperactivity disorder (ADHD) (Zahn-Waxler et al., 2008). It has also been noted that boys are more at risk of autistic spectrum conditions, something Baron-Cohen et al. (2005) hypothesise is linked to hormone exposure in the foetal environment.

MALE BRAIN

FEMALE BRAIN

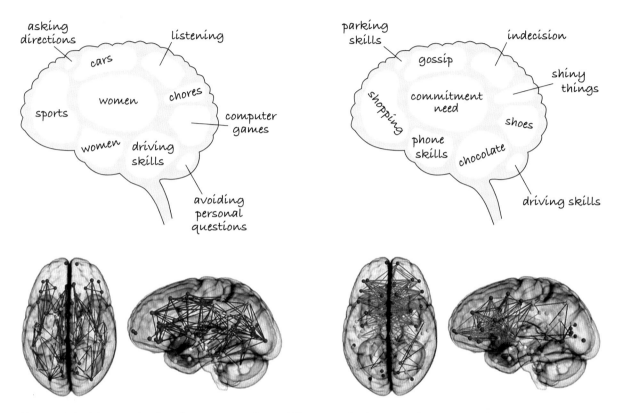

Figure 4.4   Neuroscientists have mapped out differences in the neural networks of the male and female brain. But are these kinds of differences sufficient to explain differences in behaviour and ability? What role might culture play in predicting gendered behaviour?

However, a critical examination of sex difference research in psychology demonstrates that it is largely characterised by small effect sizes, and difficulties in isolating the relative contribution of hormones to behaviour and behaviour to hormones. In other words, the observed differences are actually very small, and don't seem sufficient to account for the range of gender differences that we see in human behaviour and abilities, and the particular effect of specific hormones is not well explained. For example, aggressive behaviour seems to elevate levels of testosterone; however, increasing testosterone also appears to produce aggression (Berenbaum et al., 2011). That is, it is not clear which comes first – the hormone or the behaviour – as they are mutually productive. It is clear that the interaction of gender and biology is more complex than a simple or **determinist** reading of brain

Determinist
The philosophical idea that external causes, rather than human agency, causes behaviour, identity and social interactions.

organisation theory might suggest. For instance, while incidence of conduct disorder (a psychological diagnosis associated with antisocial and disruptive behaviour) may be more common in boys than in girls, research indicates suggests that when looking at boys and girls with conduct issues, the strongest predictor of aggressive behaviour is not male or femaleness, but negative parenting and impoverished socio-economic environments (Berkout et al., 2011). Looking at differences in things like maths performance, it is clear that boys and girls have negligible differences in cognitive ability in maths, and yet boys significantly outnumber girls as high maths performers (Miller and Halpern, 2014). While biological factors like hormones, brain structure and brain function may well influence gender roles, gendered differences in behaviour, emotion and cognition, and gender identity, it seems unlikely that a biological approach alone offers a sufficient explanation for these differences (Hines, 2011; Jordan-Young, 2010). The complexity of determining the relationship between biology and social influence in the construction of gender identity is illustrated by the case of David Reimer, reported in Box 4.1.

Box 4.1   John–Joan–John

The tragic case of David Reimer (Money and Erhardt, 1972) – reported in the media as the 'John–Joan–John' case – illustrates the complexity of the way that culture and biology intersect in the production of gender. It is a case that is 'claimed' by both biological and social determinists as evidence of their particular take on gender identity.

Behaviourists believed that gender – like all human behaviours – was entirely learned, and that babies were born ungendered and became gendered as they learned their gender roles from the culture in which they grew up.

In 1966, 'John' was born biologically male, but as a baby his penis was irretrievably damaged during a minor surgery to correct phimosis (a minor condition where the foreskin does not retract properly). The decision was made to reassign John's gender, and to remove his testicles while he was still an infant to facilitate his feminisation. 'Joan' was dressed and raised as a girl, and was given feminising hormones in puberty to help her to grow up female. Joan was also offered counselling to help her become female.

Joan was treated by a leading gender specialist, John Money, who confidently asserted that her treatment had been a success and that she had been successfully reassigned a feminine gender identity.

In contrast, Milton Diamond (1997), who also worked with Money on this case, suggested that this transition had never been successful, and that before reaching adulthood, Joan had reverted to a masculine identity, married and had children. David Reimer committed suicide in 2004.

This case was initially presented as evidence for the plasticity of gender identity – that gender was *acquired* through socialisation processes. As it became clear that John had reverted to a masculine identity, proponents of the biological approach suggested that it 'proved' that gender programming was biologically driven, established in utero, and was not reversible.

What do you think this case illustrates? Might there be factors beyond the individual's biological programming that explain this individual's identification, first as feminine, then as masculine? Is it possible to isolate either biology or society as causing gender identity in this case?

2.3   Summary

This section has explored biological and evolutionary explanations of gender. These biological explanations of gender and the development of gender typed behaviour explain gender as a hardwired and natural phenomenon. Biological explanations suggest this hardwiring is linked to the action of hormones in the uterine environment, and later in adolescence, which makes the emergence of sex differences inevitable. These hormones facilitate the development of brain structure and brain function in gendered ways. We have explored evolutionary explanations that indicate gender differences emerged naturally as a biological adaptation to ensure survival and reproductive fitness. Critics of this approach suggest that apparent differences in brain structure and brain function are not sufficient to explain the complexity of gendered behaviour.

3   Cognitive models of development – ages and stages?

Cognitive models of gender development suggest that gender perception and gender identity develop as a consequence of physical maturation and accompanying cognitive development. As was discussed in Chapter 3 of this book, Kohlberg (1966) extended Piaget's understanding of cognitive development to consider how, like other cognitive skills, perception and understanding of gender might develop in sequential stages. Kohlberg used a series of reasoning tests to describe children's perception and understanding of gender, and the development of gender identity. He outlined three stages of gender identity development:

1   Gender identity – the child develops an awareness of the existence of boys and girls, men and women, and begins to label him/herself as a boy or a girl.

2   Gender stability – the child develops an understanding that gender identity is stable and remains the same over time.

3   Gender constancy – the child becomes aware that gender does not change based on change of appearance or dress.

Gender labelling has been found to play a role in the development of gender typed behaviour. For instance, Zosuls et al. (2009) conducted a longitudinal study in which they explored the association between the production of gender labels for self and others, and the emergence of sex typed play. They found that gender labelling was present from an average of 19 months of age for boys, and 17 months for girls, and that the presence of gender labels predicted an increase in sex typed play. Girls and boys who described themselves and others in gendered ways tended to play in more gender-typical ways, with boys involved in more instrumental and rough play, and girls in more social and nurturing play. Of course while there may be an association between gender labelling and the emergence of gendered behaviour, it is impossible to evidence that gender labelling underpins this behaviour, and it seems likely that a more complex range of factors is in play here.

Kohlberg developed this set of stages based on experiments with children of different ages, in which he posed questions to explore their gendered reasoning. These included questions such as: 'Are you a boy or a girl?', 'Could you be a boy or a girl if you wanted to?', and 'Will you be a mummy or a daddy when you grow up?' Slaby and Frey (1975) developed a structured assessment tool, the gender constancy interview, to validate Kohlberg's model. This is summarised in Table 4.1.

Table 4.1

Stage	Age (years)	Experimental questions asked	Characteristics of the stage
Identity	1½–2	'Is this doll a boy or a girl/a man or a woman?' 'Are you a boy or a girl?'	The child can correctly label self and others as male or female
Stability	3–4	'When you were a baby were you a boy or a girl?' 'Have you ever been a (opposite sex label)?' 'Will you be a mummy or a daddy when you grow up?'	The child understands people retain the same gender throughout life
Constancy	6–7	'If a boy puts on a dress, will he be a girl?' 'If you played (boys'/girls') games, would you be a boy or a girl?' 'Could you be a (boy/girl) if you wanted to be?'	The child understands that gender is not dependent on changes in appearance (e.g. hair, clothes)

This theory assumes that gender identity and gender perception develop sequentially in stages, and that the capacity to understand gender and gender roles rests on the ability to identify correctly, and in a stable way, with the 'correct' sex. Children who answer the gender questions 'wrongly' are seen as making gender mistakes, and are assumed to be developmentally delayed. This approach was taken up by Zucker et al. (1999) in their work on **gender identity 'disorders'**, with children who do not identify with their assigned biological sex (i.e. children who are born biologically male, but identify as girls/ women, or vice versa). They found that children with gender identity 'disorder' tended to experience a developmental lag in their perception of gender constancy – they did not see gender as constant, but as something they could change if they wanted to, by changing their

Gender identity disorder
A diagnostic category describing people whose gender identity is different from their assigned biological sex.

appearance or their behaviour. This was understood by Zucker, and by Kohlberg and Slaby and Frey before him, to reflect a developmental difficulty, an error in cognitive processing, that needed to be corrected.

Activity 4.2:   Gender rights and wrongs? Applying Kohlberg's model

Have a look at the set of questions and characteristics outlined in Table 4.1. What assumptions are being made about gender? What assumptions are being made about how gender works? Think about the following story:

> From as long ago as I remember, I was a girl. I had a penis and a boy's name, and my parents called me their son. But none of those things fitted with my sense of who I was. As I grew older, and my body started to change with puberty, I found it more and more upsetting to be called 'Peter', and to wear boy's clothes. I started to try on my sister's dresses, in secret, and I preferred to be around her friends rather than my own – to be one of the girls.

What does the Kohlberg model suggest about this kind of experience? How would this model understand this child's discomfort with being a boy, and particularly their sense that being a boy or a son did not 'fit'? What do you think about this example?

In this kind of understanding of gender identity development, gender is presumed to be stable, fixed and permanent. Gender cannot shift or change; it simply is. Appropriate gender identity is understood to map on to biological sex. This theoretical approach naturalises gender identity, and frames gender non-conformity in childhood as a 'gender mistake'.

This kind of approach also illustrates the way that taken-for-granted social assumptions can become naturalised in research practice. It is not possible to be gender non-conformist in this model. If, as a biological female, you answer the question 'Are you a boy or a girl?' as 'I am a boy', you are simply seen as getting that question *wrong*. Moreover, not only are the gender-conforming labels naturalised in this model, but so too are assumptions about gender roles themselves. To be a 'proper girl', the child must necessarily want to 'be a mummy' – she must fit with dominant ideas about heteronormative reproductive sexuality. In other words, she must fall in with taken-for-granted assumptions that good women will grow up, have a male partner and have babies. This theoretical approach shows us how taken-for-granted social assumptions about gender can be embedded in research, and how an unreflected description based on social norms can become reframed in psychological theory as a prescription for those norms.

Pause for thought

Think about the assumptions that Kohlberg's study makes about the nature of gender. Is all gender non-conformity in children a 'gender mistake'?

3.1 Summary

Cognitive approaches to the development of gender suggest that gender identity develops through sequential stages. The cognitive model presumes these stages are driven by biological maturation – we 'grow' increasingly gendered as we mature physically. Children who do not develop gender identity, consistency and stability are seen as making 'gender mistakes', and variations from binary gender identity are understood as a 'cognitive error'.

4   Social cognitive approaches to gender identity development

While cognitive approaches see gender as emerging, naturally, as part of a process of maturation, social cognitive approaches explore gender as something that we perceive and learn about through an interaction of cognitive processes and social processes.

4.1   Just like my dad? Gender and socialisation

Socialisation
The process whereby we learn and adapt to social norms.

Bussey and Bandura (2004) suggest that gender develops as a result of three reciprocal and interacting factors – personal and environmental factors and behavioural patterns. Gender is understood as acquired (rather than developed through maturation, as Kohlberg suggested) through **socialisation**, and through three learning processes: **tuition**, **enactive experience** and **observational learning**. Children are directly taught about gender (tuition) when parents and other socialisers explicitly teach them about being a boy or a girl. This can be achieved through direct teaching about what is, and is not, appropriate behaviour for a particular gender or direct teaching of gender role behaviour (Figure 4.5). For example, in some families, girls might be taught how to cook or change nappies, while boys learn to kick footballs or fix cars. In this way, children learn explicitly and directly the gendered behaviours expected for their particular sex.

Tuition
In social learning theory, being taught expected behaviours and attitudes explicitly and directly.

Gender can also be taught through gender essentialist statements. These are specific messages children are given about appropriate behaviour for men and women that suggest differences in behaviour, attitudes and experiences are natural and innate (e.g. statements like 'boys will be boys', when observing boys playing rough).

Enactive experience
In social learning theory, enactive experience refers to circumstances where individuals learn through direct personal action and experience.

Finally, children can learn gender through enactive experiences. This refers to the way that we learn gender typed behaviour based on reactions to our own actions. So for example, when a little boy gets upset and is told 'big boys don't cry', he learns that crying is not acceptable behaviour for a boy. Similarly, a girl who is praised as 'a good girl' for washing dishes or for playing cooperatively with her friends has learned from these reactions that this is a desirable behaviour for a girl. This can be achieved more subtly too through the censoring of gender inappropriate behaviours. For instance, an adult might comment 'Oh look how funny, she likes playing with trains!' or

Observational learning
Learning that takes place by watching the action of others, and the consequences of those actions.

Figure 4.5   Vintage sexism: what did children learn about gender from these kinds of images?

'He's not really carrying a handbag, he just needs something to carry his cars and trucks in'. These kinds of statements communicate the apparent inappropriateness of atypical gendered behaviours. Observational learning involves observing the consequences of other people's behaviour and making decisions about whether or not to imitate that behaviour. For example, if children see others behaving in gender non-conformist ways, and then see them teased or bullied as 'sissies' or 'tomboys', they are less likely to imitate that behaviour themselves.

Pause for thought

Think about your own experiences growing up. What messages were you given about 'good behaviour' for boys and girls? How were those messages communicated to you? Try to think of examples that fit each of the three forms of learning that Bussey and Bandura identified: tuition, enactive experiences and observation.

While it is self-evident that the kinds of social messages Bussey and Bandura describe are influential in producing gender typing and gender identities, it is important to consider some of the assumptions that gender socialisation as a concept makes about children and the way they learn. Children are seen in this model as *absorbing* social messages about gender in a relatively passive way. They are taught, they observe, they imitate. This suggests that children take on gender roles with little reflection – that they see gender role models, that they are told information about good ways to behave, and that they repeat the things they are taught. But does this really fit with our lived experience of gender? Did you just observe what your mother or father did and then decide to repeat those patterns? Or were you perhaps a little more reflexive and more conscious in the way that you took on, or rejected, ideas about what it meant to be a boy or a girl, a man or a woman? Think critically also about how gender would be transmitted from one generation to a next. If children only acquired gender through passive observation and repetition, would our understandings of gender change over time, or would they remain static? Have a look at Figure 4.6. If you compare social consensus in contemporary UK culture on what it means to be a woman to social consensus in 1954, it is clear that our assumptions about femininity have changed dramatically. Our gender roles have also changed a great deal. But how can we explain that through a simple socialisation model?

Figure 4.6   Has family life remained the same over the past 50 years? Are gender roles the same? How do you think changes in gender roles might have taken place?

In recent years, concerns have been expressed about shifting social representations of gender and their implications for the development of gender identity. In 2010, the APA released an updated version of the its 2007 report on the sexualisation of girlhood and its implications for girls and young women (APA, 2010). This report points to the pervasiveness of increasingly sexualised images of girlhood, querying its implications for socialisation, and for the construction of gender schema for girls. The APA report suggests that sexualisation operates on a continuum, from a sexualising gaze that positions girls and young women as objects of desire, through to active sexual exploitation of young women. The APA task force indicates that the interface of these socialising influences and their implications for the construction of problematic gender schemas for girls will have a negative impact on girls' self-esteem and their identities as young women. They note that girls 'grow up in a milieu saturated with sexualising messages' (APA, 2010) and that the pervasiveness of increasingly sexualised images of girlhood functions to normalise an objectified representation of girlhood. Instances of the sexualisation of ordinary everyday girlhood can be found throughout popular culture. Consider the gendering of girls toys, for example the highly sexualised Bratz dolls shown in Figure 4.7 (Opplinger, 2009), the availability of sexy underwear for pre-teens (Brooks, 2008), and the sexualisation of girlhood in child beauty pageants (Heltsley and Calhoun, 2003).

Figure 4.7   Do toys like Bratz dolls offer an overly sexualised image of girlhood?

Representations of girls and women in song lyrics are highly sexualised, and this representation is not restricted to particular kinds of music. Pardun et al. (2005) highlight several examples:

- 'So blow me bitch I don't rock for cancer/I rock for the cash and the topless dancers' (Kid Rock, 'f*ckoff', 1998)

- 'Don'tcha wish your girlfriend was hot like me?' (Pussycat Dolls, 2005)

- 'That's the way you like to f*** . . . rough sex make it hurt, in the garden all in the dirt' (Ludacris, 2000)

- 'I tell the hos all the time, Bitch get in my car' (50 Cent, 2005)

- 'Ho shake your ass' (Ying Yang Twins, 2003)

The APA task force suggests that sexualisation includes a cultural component, an interpersonal component, and an element of self-sexualisation. Girls constitute their self-identity through modelling and related socialisation processes. They learn how to behave socially, and how to see themselves as gendered people, through the social processes and interactions they observe. This shapes their expectations of themselves, as well as other people's expectations of them and behaviour in relation to them.

However, critics of this approach have noted that, in common with other accounts of socialisation, there is little space for young people's **agency** in these explanations (Egan and Hawkes, 2008). Children are represented as passively positioned in relation to overwhelming social pressures, and these pressures are described in the APA task force document as if girls were uniquely and specifically victimised by these images of girlhood. There seems to be little concern with how young men's identities might be constituted in relation to dominant and problematic representations of masculinity.

Agency
The capacity of an individual to act or take action.

Pause for thought

Do you think boys are subject to socialisation pressures through media imagery about 'being a boy' and 'being a man'? Are there similar pressures on boys to those described by the *APA Task Force on the Sexualisation of Girls* (APA, 2010)? What might some of those pressures be?

4.2 Social cognition – schemas and stereotypes

Alternative **social cognitive models** explore how gender is developed as children actively attend to, select and use social information. Children do not passively observe or learn about gender, they are not passive recipients of gender information. Rather they are active knowers, interacting with a complex social world. A social cognitive approach to gender assumes that it is a 'social category system built around the distinction between male and female' (e.g. Leinbach et al., 1997, p. 107). Social cognition suggests that gender is not biologically determined, but rather that it is a cognitive phenomenon – a conceptual category – built from social information that is mapped on to a biological distinction between the sexes. Gender is not so much in our bodies, as it is in our thoughts about our bodies, concepts that are

Social cognitive models
The cognitive processing of social information, including perceiving, considering and explaining people, events, relationships and social issues.

built through social consensus. Martin and Ruble highlight how different this approach is from a focus on socialisation:

> Cognitive perspectives on gender development assume that children are actively searching for ways to find meaning in and make sense of the social world that surrounds them, and they do so by using the gender cues provided by society to help them interpret what they see and hear. Children are wonderfully skilled in using these cues to form expectations about other people and to develop personal standards for behavior, and they learn to do this very quickly and often with little direct training.
>
> (Martin and Ruble, 2004, p. 67)

Gender schema theory

A social cognitive theory that suggests that children learn about what it means to be masculine or feminine from their culture.

Gender schema theory, proposed by Martin and Halverson (1981), notes that social information about gender is not simply 'absorbed', but that children are actively engaged in thinking about their social context to produce their understanding of gender. As you read earlier in Book 1, Chapter 8, schema is a cognitive construct, referring to a hypothetical 'file' within the 'filing system' of our cognitive processes. These function as cognitive heuristics (rules of thumb) that organise and summarise our experiences of the social world. A gender schema contains all our knowledge, understanding and social expectations of gender. In this sense, gender schemas can be seen as socialised cognitive networks of sex and gender roles. You will remember that schemas are adaptive cognitive structures that help us to manage complex social information – ready-made concepts that we have built up through social experience, and that help us to make sense of and react to our social world. Schemas are established but relatively flexible cognitive structures. While we might have a working understanding of what it means to be a man or a woman, this understanding is not rigid or fixed. It is open to new information, and can be re-evaluated and adjusted depending on that new incoming information. The categories that form the basis for schemas can be re-defined, reshaped, split or joined, based on new social information.

Children with very strong gender schemas are more prone to stereotyped perceptions and behaviours. You read about stereotypes in Book 1, Chapter 4 of this module. What influence do you think stereotypes have on the development of gender? Significant research evidence indicates that children use stereotypes from an early age.

Stereotypes are more rigid schematic representations that function more like blanket rules than flexible cognitive guidelines.

Martin (1989, 1993) suggests that stereotypes are made up of two kinds of associations:

- Vertical associations connect gender attributes to biological sex. For example a vertical association connects together biological category (female) and preference (toys), to form the idea that 'girls like dolls'. This component of stereotyping is in evidence in very young children.

- Horizontal associations draw together clusters of gendered associations in older children and adults, for instance connecting the idea that girls like dolls with the idea that girls also like playing house, and that playing house and playing with dolls are feminine behaviours. This kind of association develops for own-sex when children are four–six years old, and for own and other sex by about the age of eight.

As we have already discussed (Serbin et al., 2002), infants as young as 24 months seemed to recognise and be puzzled by gender non-conformist behaviour. Serbin and her colleagues also conducted experiments to explore the preferences of children aged 12, 18 and 24 months for gender-typed toys, and whether they could match pictures of gender-typed toys to male or female children (Serbin et al., 2002). They found that all children showed preferences for gender stereotypical toys by 18 months, and that girls (but not boys) associated stereotypical toys with the 'matched' gender. By 31 months, boys showed a preference for using male dolls to imitate masculine stereotypical behaviours (Poulin-Dubois et al., 2002). Gender stereotyping therefore emerges quite early for young children, with toddlers exhibiting preferences for gender-typed toys and actions, and evidencing early abilities to label gender typical items and behaviours. In early childhood, gender stereotypes emerge as blanket rules about gender, rather than as flexible guidelines. Martin (1989) presented young children with vignettes, like:

> 'Tommy is a boy, Tommy's best friend is a girl and Tommy likes to play house.'

He found that despite clear information about Tommy's gender non-conformist preferences, children under the age of six tended to claim that Tommy prefers playing with boys and cars, suggesting that children rely on gender stereotypical material in making sense of their social world, even when presented with contrary information. This implies that younger children have not yet developed the kind of cognitive flexibility necessary to enable the use of gender schemas flexible guidelines, but that in early to middle childhood, gender stereotypes are rigid and not easily open to adaptation or re-definition. Stereotyped responses increase with age for children through middle childhood, but their schematic flexibility also increases as children become more tolerant and accepting of variability and exceptions to dominant gender stereotypes. For instance, looking at leisure activities Cherney and London (2006) found that, while there were clear gender differences in leisure preferences for boys and girls, as girls grew older, their preferences for toys, games and sports became less feminine – suggesting that gender typing grows more flexible for girls as they approach their teenage years. Children acquire extensive knowledge of gender stereotypes by middle childhood, but their gender categories are not as rigid as they were in early childhood, and individual children hold some aspects of stereotypes, but not others (Serbin et al., 1993).

There is evidence that gender schemas can be used increasingly flexibly as children mature, but in certain arenas, gender stereotypes remain powerful predictors of children's behaviour and interests. In the arena of academic achievement, stereotypes around boys' and girls' academic abilities are pervasive – for instance, the association of maths, athletics and technical subjects with masculinity, and reading, spelling, art and music with femininity is ubiquitous. But does this common stereotype have any influence on how children behave and how they achieve?

Cvencek et al. (2011, 2014) found that stereotyping had a powerful implication for children's sense of self and sense of their capacity. Looking at primary schoolchildren in the United States of America and in Singapore, researchers found that children who held a strong maths-gender stereotype (that maths was masculine) and a strong gender identity (that I am masculine/feminine) tended to see themselves in gender stereotypical ways. In other words, they looked at the patterns of associations between:

- me with male or me with female (gender identity)

- male with maths or female with maths (maths–gender stereotype)

- me with maths (maths self-concept).

In this study, the researchers found that for both sexes, gender stereotypes intensified with age, as did gender identification. That is, boys identified more strongly as masculine, and also drew on the stereotype that boys are better at maths. Girls identified more strongly with femininity over time, and used the stereotype that girls are not as good at maths. The effect was that, even when girls excelled at maths, they did not identify themselves as competent mathematicians. This indicates that gender identity has strong implications for both the construction of stereotypes and for the implications of these constructions for other elements of self-identity (see Figure 4.8).

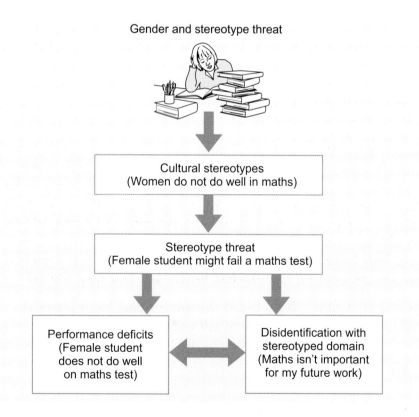

Figure 4.8   Stereotype threat: children who held a strong maths-gender stereotype tended to see themselves in gender stereotypical ways, regardless of maths ability

It is also interesting to note how adults draw on stereotypes in their interactions with children. Research suggests that many adults actively engage in stereotyping children's behaviour. How often have you heard parents describe their child's behaviour as 'typical boy' or 'typical girl' behaviour? In the classic 'Baby X' experiments, Condry and Condry (1976) showed adults a video of a baby. The baby in the video was either dressed in feminine or masculine clothes, and was labelled as either David or Dana. The same baby featured in both videos, and the baby behaved in exactly the same way. The baby was shown reacting to toys, and 200 adults were asked to rate the baby's responses. Overwhelmingly, the adults labelled the infant dressed in a masculine way as 'angry' and the infant dressed in a feminine way as 'frightened'. Powlishta (2000) found that adults were far more likely to rate children's personality traits as masculine or feminine than they were to rate the behaviour of adults. Why might this be? Is it possible that producing stereotypes is an important part of the way that we socialise gender for boys and girls? If our gender was genuinely determined in the uterine environment as the brain organisation theories reviewed earlier suggest, would there be such a strong social imperative to ensure that children were labelled and inducted into gender stereotyping? Other researchers found that parents' (and particularly mothers') implicit gender stereotypes predicted their children's stereotypes (Endendijk et al., 2013). In other words, when parents themselves used implicit gender stereotypes their children were more likely to hold them too. For instance, girls were more likely to draw on the 'maths is male, I am female therefore maths is not me' stereotype if their mother often complained about being 'rubbish at maths' herself. This indicates that parental attitudes to gender do have an influence on the emergence of gender stereotypes in their children, but that this influence was not as overt as models of socialisation might have predicted. It is not simply a case of observing and copying gendered behaviour – the cognitive processes that underpin the adoption of gender stereotypes are more subtle and more complex than basic socialisation models would suggest.

Pause for thought

Why do you think adults are more likely to rate children's behaviour as masculine or feminine than they are adult behaviour (Powlishta, 2000)?

Do you think this has anything to do with socialisation of children?

What does this tell us about the importance of connecting cognitive theories about gender categorisation to, for example, the ideas about gender identity development that we find in social learning theory?

It seems sensible to suggest, as Maccoby (2000) does, that gender development depends on the intersection of three factors:

- biological factors: including the influence of hormones, brain structure, and brain functioning

- social factors: for instance the strength of socialisation pressures

- cognitive factors: like the kinds of gender schemas held – knowledge of sex characteristics and social expectations of gender.

It is clear that gender socialisation does play a role in producing gender typing and gender identity. It also seems likely that our biology plays some role in the production of gendered labelling and gender identity.

But is the kind of social cognitive approach advanced by Maccoby, drawing together biological differences, socialisation and schemas, enough to explain the lived experience of gender? Is it enough to help us understand complex and varied experiences of gender that don't fit the presumed categories of male and female, of masculine and feminine?

4.3 Summary

A social cognitive approach sees gender identity and the development of gender typical behaviour and attitudes as a function of the intersection of biological factors, socialisation pressures and gender schemas. Socialisation refers to the processes through which we learn about gender and gender roles. This can occur through interactions in the family, relationships outside the family (peers, teachers, etc.) and other social influences, like gendered toys, media images, etc. These interact with cognitive factors, like schemas and stereotypes. Schemas are cognitive organising structures that provide a quick rule of thumb that individuals use to make sense of complex social information. Gender schemas summarise complex social information about gender and help us to make sense of our social world. They are stable but relatively flexible cognitive structures that are open to revision and recategorisation on the basis of new information and experience. Stereotypes are relatively rigid cognitive schemas that act in more limiting ways to reproduce dominant ideas about gender and can restrict individual's perception of their range of possible action. Social cognitive approaches suggest that our gendered responses to the world become relatively automated as a consequence of the operation of biology, social pressure and gender schemas.

5 Troubling gender – interactionist and social constructionist rereadings of gender identity

So far this chapter has considered the acquisition of gender identity and an understanding of gender difference in a way that assumes gender is a 'real' phenomenon – that the division of the world into male and female, and man and woman is a reasonable and sustainable one. But is it? Do humans really come in two kinds? Or is gender more complex than these dimorphic representations might suggest? And is it a 'real' biologically determined phenomenon?

5.1 Raising gender neutral children

Activity 4.3:   Raising gender neutral children

The following article from the *Daily Mail* reports on the parents' decision to raise their child in a gender neutral manner. Read the article and then answer the questions.

The baby who is neither boy nor girl: as gender experiment provokes outrage, what about the poor child's future?

Figure 4.9   Is it possible and/or desirable to raise babies as gender neutral?

Chubby-cheeked and fair-haired, Storm Stocker has the expression of permanent puzzlement familiar to parents of four-month-old babies.

But then this child has a lot to think about: such as whether he or she is a boy or a girl.

It won't be much help turning for guidance to Storm's brothers: Jazz, five, with long pigtails, a pink ear stud and sparkly pink dresses, and two-year-old Kio, with collar-length hair and a penchant for leggings.

Everyone who meets them thinks they are girls.

Still, even if they do sound as if they were named after family hatchbacks, Jazz and Kio got off lightly. Their parents David Stocker and Kathy Witterick have something more extreme for their third child.

In a move that has earned the Toronto couple the dubious title of the world's most politically correct family, they are raising Storm as 'genderless'.

The midwives who delivered the child had no uncertainty about Storm's sex – the baby isn't a hermaphrodite. It's just that the parents will be keeping it a secret until the child is old enough to 'choose' which gender he or she is most comfortable living with. Apart from the two siblings, a family friend and the two midwives, no one knows if Storm is biologically a girl or a boy.

The rest of the couple's friends and family – even the grandparents – were sent an email that announced: 'We've decided not to share Storm's sex for now – a tribute to freedom and choice in place of limitation.'

The couple admitted their wonderfully po-faced missive was initially met with silence. One can only imagine the emails and phone calls that passed between their loved ones as they digested this bizarre plan.

The couple say no one they told had a kind word to say about their decision. The grandparents were annoyed that they had to explain to friends that their grandchild was more of an 'it' than a 'he' or a 'she'.

Some friends accused the couple of imposing their ideology on the child; others chided that they had condemned Storm to a life of bullying.

But, naturally, the parents weren't dismayed. Repulsed by a world of what they see as pushy parents, they believe very young children can – and should – choose who they want to be, free from social norms about being male or female.

'I am saying to the world: "Please can you just let Storm discover for him/herself what s(he) wants to be?"' says Witterick.

Or, as her husband puts it: 'What we noticed is that parents make so many choices for their children. It's obnoxious.'

Those who know them insist Stocker, 39, and Witterick, 38, are well-meaning and devoted to their children. But in the interview they gave before the thunderclap of outrage sent them scurrying to close the curtains on their bizarre household, they emerge as beyond parody.

Stocker, a progressive teacher, wrote a textbook, *Math That Matters*, which urges teachers to stop using everyday objects in maths questions and instead work with issues such as homophobia, poverty, child abuse and racial profiling to 'spark discussion' and increase students' interest in 'social justice advocacy'.

(Sample question: A Chinese worker who makes my shoes earns what percentage of the price I paid for them?)

Their last family holiday was two weeks in Cuba staying with local families to learn about the wonders of Marxist revolution.

In their cluttered family home, Witterick says she was put out when, after the birth, the first question from 'even the people you love the most' was to ask if she'd had a girl or a boy. Well, yes, people do tend to ask that, but as Stocker adds, charmingly: 'That the whole world must know what is between the baby's legs is unhealthy, unsafe and voyeuristic. We know – and we're keeping it clean, safe, healthy and private (not secret!)'

Indeed, you don't usually have to pry about gender, but that's because you can work it out from other evidence.

But Storm's parents are offering no clues. The child is dressed in gender-neutral red and the couple are so determined to fight the 'tyranny of pronouns' that, after considering 'Z' (pronounced 'zee'), mum refers to Storm as 'she' — but 'imagining the "s" in brackets'.

It's hard to believe Storm's brothers will not blurt out the secret. Having said that, they don't seem to have a packed social life. Jazz is home-schooled (his mother uses a system called 'unschooling' in which the child is taught something only when he asks about it).

Given that he loves his pink dress because 'it really poofs out at the bottom', you can understand why he finds the idea of going to school 'upsetting'.

There are already signs of trouble ahead. At the local playground, two little girls refused to play with the 'girl boy', and a shopping trip ended in humiliating retreat when an assistant balked at the idea of selling a feather boa to a little boy.

Revealing not a jot of self-doubt, Jazz's parents insist their decision to go the whole gender-neutral hog with Storm came after Stocker found a book in his school library called *X: A Fabulous Child's Story*.

It's about a child with 'no gender' who plays football and weaves baskets.

The child ignores bullying and ends up stunning experts with how well-adjusted he/she is.

The story will strike many as naive, but Storm's parents found it 'compelling'.

The great irony, of course, about this family's scorn for gender is that they're obsessed with it. Even before he was weighed down with Storm's secret, Jazz was showing signs of confusion.

One of his favourite books is *10,000 Dresses*, the tale of a boy who likes to dress up. And in a birthday card to his father, he wrote: 'I love to do laundry with Dad.'

Granted, not all little boys want to play with toy cars, but are fashion and washing clothes normal enthusiasms for a five-year-old?

The parents insist they are giving their children freedom to express themselves. Critics tend to see a pair of crackpot liberals indulging in crude social engineering. When they went public with their decision, Stocker and Witterick may have assumed readers of the liberal Canadian newspaper the *Toronto Star*, would applaud, but instead hundreds emailed to express their horror.

'This is a perfect example of why you should have a licence to have children,' erupted one reader.

And the shockwaves have moved across Canada and beyond.

Perhaps this outlandish world of gender-free parenting would be comical if it weren't for the fact that experts fear it could be damaging.

'To raise a child not as a boy or a girl is creating, in some sense, a freak. It sets them up for not knowing who they are,' says Dr Eugene Beresin, a child psychiatrist at Massachusetts General Hospital.

Dr Harold Koplewicz, a leading U.S. child psychiatrist, said he was 'disturbed' that well-meaning parents could be so misguided.

'When children are born, they're not a blank slate. We do have male brains and female brains,' he says. 'There's a reason why boys do more rough and tumble play; there's a reason why girls have better language development skills.'

For him, 'the worst part of the story' is that the two older boys have to keep Storm's gender a secret — an act that other experts say will make them ashamed.

Intriguingly, this experiment may not be unique. In 2009, a Swedish couple announced, to a blaze of publicity, that they were raising their two-year-old child, Pop, as gender-neutral. Even now, we don't know if Pop is a boy or a girl.

A more tragic case suggests the biological facts are difficult to suppress. In 1966, David Reimer, a six-month-old boy from Winnipeg, Canada, lost his penis in a botched circumcision.

A psychologist persuaded David's mother he could be raised as a girl, so his genitals were partially converted to female ones. David became Brenda, but complained he never felt female. In 2004, he committed suicide, aged 38.

As for the Toronto experiment, experts doubt the parents can keep up the charade, particularly as studies show we cannot help but treat boys and girls differently.

Storm's mother says that if people want to take a peek when she changes a nappy, 'that's their journey'. The question of whether her youngest child will use the gents or the ladies is still some way off.

(Leonard, 2011)

- What is your reaction to the article?
- What assumptions is the journalist making about gender?
- What assumptions does the journalist make about the importance of gender in our culture?
- What assumptions does the journalist make about gender non-conformity?
- Can you see traces of the psychological theories we have reviewed so far in the article – in decisions made by the parents, in the reactions of the journalist, and in your own reactions?

5.2   Social constructionist and interactionist perspectives

Social constructionism
A theoretical approach that explores how human knowledge and meaning making is built through jointly constructed understandings of our world.

Social constructionist accounts argue that gender itself is socially constructed. In other words, it is more than our gendered behaviour and beliefs that have their origins in social processes and interactions. This approach emerged in sociology, with theorists like Cooley (1902) suggesting that social phenomena like gender identity are not 'made' through biological processes, but that gender is constituted in social processes. This is different from a socialisation perspective that sees society providing content for a pre-divided and sexed society. Socialisation does not question the reality of the basic categorisation of human beings as male or female, masculine or feminine. Rather the socialisation approach looks at how these pre-existing categories of being human (male and female) become populated with gendered content.

In contrast, social constructionist accounts argue that the notion of gender itself – the idea that humans come in two kinds – masculine and feminine – is something that is constituted socially. They argue that categories of gender are constructed socially, and do not have any inherent reality or meaning other than the one we give to them. Because our culture positions gender as so important, as so core, to human identity, it is perhaps difficult to imagine a space in which being 'a boy' or 'a girl' might not be the most important thing to know about a new baby. Gender differences in attitudes, behaviours and roles are found so consistently in so many different cultures that we tend to assume that this means that gender difference is natural and inevitable. However, it is important to remember that from culture to culture, there are significant variations in the 'content' of those gender differences. Men and women are not 'different' in the same ways from one culture to another, an observation that makes us question the degree to which all observed gender differences can sensibly be ascribed to biological factors.

Box 4.2   Crossing boundaries: building a social and developmental psychological account of masculinities and femininities

In their article 'The contextual specificity of masculinity and femininity in early adolescence', Jennifer Pickard Leszczynski and JoNell Strough (2008) draw together a social psychological account of gender identity, with a more developmental and experimental psychological approach to make sense of how young people negotiate gendered behaviour. They wanted to explore whether masculinity and femininity is best understood as a fixed trait, or as a flexible identity resource that was drawn on differently in varying situations and contexts.

To test this, they asked 80 young teens (40 boys and 40 girls) to take part in a block building game with a partner. The gender of the partner was varied, and the young people were asked to either play the game cooperatively or competitively. They explored how two situational factors – the instruction to cooperate or compete, and the sex of the partner they played with – affected young people's self-report of their masculinity and femininity. They found that both boys and girls had higher femininity scores when working with a girl peer than they did when working with a boy peer. They also found that stereotypically masculine traits emerged more strongly when the instructions were focused on cooperation. Leszczynski and

---

Strough (2008) argue that this challenges the more typical developmental view of gender identity development, which uses social cognitive and gender schema theory to argue that masculinity and femininity are *individual differences* that are stable and fixed. Rather, they suggest that while there may be relatively stable individual differences in masculinity and femininity, there are also contextual cues that raise the salience of masculine and feminine aspects of self in different contexts. By drawing together a traditional developmental account of gender identity with a social constructionist account that emphasises the importance of context in the performance of gender identity, they suggest that gender functions both as a trait (so that some people might fairly stably seem 'more masculine' or 'more feminine' in varying situations) and as a state (in which gender identity is more strongly expressed in situations that provoke a stronger performance of gender identity).

While Leszczynski and Strough do not challenge the notion of gender itself as a binary category, nonetheless their work represents an interesting inroad into mainstream developmental psychology, by drawing through social constructionist ideas about gender as context specific and performative in its nature. This allows some challenge to the notion that people simply 'are' masculine or feminine, and some space to begin to challenge the idea of gender as something that is determined by either biology or society, and that is a rigid feature of an individual's character.

Interactionism

In sociology, interactionism is the theoretical perspective that society is produced from people's social interactions.

The **interactionist** perspective (Cooley, 1902) suggests that our human interactions produce gender itself – not just our norms about what men and women should do. It further suggests that gender stratification is a result of human activity (the things we do) and meaning making (the way we make sense of our social world). Gender is constituted in the social meanings we share and produce. Gender is not a pre-given thing that maps straightforwardly on to pre-existing biological difference. We produce biological difference as meaningful through our social interactions (think again about the baby question: 'What is it?'). In this sense gender is about our interpretations about our social world, and the concepts we construct and use to make sense of that world. Cooley developed the concept of the 'looking glass self'. This theory indicates that we see ourselves through the mirror of our culture – that our identity is constructed based on how society sees us. Gender, therefore, is not something inherent to us, it is not something we bear as individuals. Rather gender is constructed as something meaningful and important in our social interactions. In this way gender *becomes* a core-identifier. This is an important idea for psychologists because of the way it denaturalises gender and gender assumptions. It challenges us to move beyond the psychological formulation of gender that takes gender as a given, and to think about other ways of doing gender or being gendered. This approach positions gender as fluid and malleable, rather than as fixed, stable and permanent.

West and Zimmerman (1987) suggested that gender is something *we do* rather than something *we are*. They used the term 'doing gender' to describe this more performative understanding of how gender is constituted socially. Think for example about the way girls learn to use their bodies, and the implications of this for the construction of feminine identities. In her essay 'Throwing like a girl', the philosopher Iris Marion Young (Young, 2005) explores how contemporary Western girls use their bodies in sport. She suggests that the reason girls often throw poorly is not because of any inherent biological inability. Rather, she argues, the 'girly throw' is characterised by what she terms 'inhibited intentionality': she suggests that in throwing a ball, girls simultaneously reach out with a sense that they can throw the ball, and hold back with a sense that they cannot. She argues that this 'double hesitation', built into girls' embodied experiences characterises feminine identities themselves. Our sense of ourself as feminine is in this sense performative – it is constituted in a series of embodied actions and social practices that produce our sense of ourselves as feminine. The way of being that characterises 'throwing like a girl' is expressed in many other femininised ways of being. For instance, it is well documented that professional women are often hesitant in applying for promotion. In this sense women are reaching forward with a sense that 'I can' (in seeking out a professional career) and holding back with a sense that 'I cannot' (in not applying for promotion). In the example of maths ability that we have already considered in this chapter, girls sense of capacity to do maths, their engagement with maths programmes is a gesture of 'I can', but their sense that 'maths is for boys, not for me' is an 'I cannot'. In this sense, Young argues, femininity is characterised by inhibited intentionality.

Think about the complex ways this kind of 'feminine comportment' might have built up. There is no single act of socialisation that results in this 'feminine comportment'. Nor are we the passive victims of gender stereotyping or other social forces. Rather we are actively engaged in the construction, production and reproduction of gendered identities in a range of performances of femininity.

Judith Butler (1990) also suggests that gendered and sexual identities are performative in their nature, and that masculinities and femininities are constructed in our social meaning making – our language and our social practices (our 'discourse'). In other words, there is no permanent, biologically 'real' gender identity, rather the categories of male and female, masculine and feminine are built up in language, and (re)produced in social practices. When we name a baby as 'a boy' we are calling them into being as a boy with all the attendant cultural meanings we attach to that. In this way, we have some capacity to either take on or resist our construction as masculine or feminine. We are not completely free to choose this because the social processes involved are complex and regulative in their nature – for instance there is considerable social censure around gender non-conformity that makes resistance to these dominant categories difficult. Also the naturalisation of gender in our culture means that gender normative behaviour is so taken for granted that alternative ways of being gendered or being 'agender' (i.e. not seeing yourself as having gender) are rendered almost unthinkable. Therefore, through our language and social practices, social norms can function to regulate us by opening up certain ways of being as possible, and closing down others.

It is still possible for us to resist dominant understandings of gender. Butler points to gender non-conformist acts, such as the performance art of 'drag' (where theatre performers dress and act as members of the other sex). She suggests that such performances subvert our taken-for-granted assumptions about gender, 'troubling' or challenging our assumptions that gender is permanent and stable. In her analysis of gender and sexuality, Butler suggests that it is not so much that we 'are' masculine or feminine, straight or gay, but rather that for example, we 'do' femininity or heterosexuality. Our understanding of ourselves as man or woman, boy or girl, is produced in the social divisions we construct in our culture, and individual boys and girls, men and women are expected to 'do gender' in a way that fits these categories. Our status as masculine or feminine is dependent on our performance of masculinity or femininity – how well we 'pass' as man or woman in a given set of gendered social arrangements.

We have already begun to think about the way that our assumption that humans come in two kinds, male and female, masculine and feminine, might have implications for people who do not neatly fit on to these binaries. When we discussed Kohlberg's theory of gender identity development, we considered how this approach to gender frames anyone who doesn't neatly fit binary gender patterns as making a 'gender mistake', a cognitive error. We also briefly discussed the way that this has been taken up by psychologists and psychiatrists concerned about what they term 'gender identity dysphoria'. But can a notion that gender comes in two types, and that anyone who does not neatly fit those two types is *ill*, really be sustained?

Liao et al. (2012, p. 598) argue that 'self-identification as male or female is not a fixed attribute waiting to unveil itself, rather an expression of complex, multiple and interactive developmental processes'. Our categorical understanding of gender as masculine and feminine (which relies on an understanding of gender as binary), and as stable and permanent means we tend to assume children must have a 'true gender' that maps simply and straightforwardly on to their 'true sex'. This creates significant difficulties for the growing number of adults and children who do not see their gender identity in this way. This is particularly visible for trans children – children whose gender identity is not the same as their assigned biological sex. Our cultural insistence that gender should be binary, and should be identified with our biological sex (termed 'cisgenderism' by transactivists) produces a climate in which gender norms are presumed and people who transgress normative constructions of gender are positioned as deviant or perverse. Natacha Kennedy (2012) argues that this climate of cisgenderism creates real developmental challenges for trans children, who must navigate not only their own gender identity, but cultural assumptions that problematise their gender identity. She suggests that these challenges explain higher rates of mental health difficulty among young trans people.

> ## Pause for thought
>
> Think about Kennedy's idea that cisgenderism presents developmental challenges for trans children. Might this explanation help us make sense of the distress experienced by David Reimer, in being shoe-horned into pre-existing gender categories?

Further, a growing number of people do not identify at all with the gender binary categories that have been normalised through our particular cultural assumptions about gender as fixed. Think about the child 'Storm' who we read about in Activity 4.3 at the beginning of this section. Much of the moral panic in the news article about this child is about the way a child who is not 'gendered' will necessarily be confused about their gender identity. This is seen as necessarily bad because of the cultural taken for grantedness of binary gender identities. But some theorists argue that it is useful to consider the possibility of 'other genders' beyond the binary constructs of masculinity and femininity that we are used to (Barker and Richards, 2015). Gender has perhaps always been more fluid than we think. For instance, how many girls do you know who went through a time of being 'a bit of a tomboy'? Gender is performed in a manner that is contextually responsive. For instance, can you think of times when it is appropriate for you to be 'more girly' or 'more manly' in particular spaces and times? Is your 'student' femininity or masculinity always the same as your 'down the pub' masculinity or femininity? Reynolds et al. (2001) argue that when being 'a bit of a tomboy' girls are appropriating identities in a fluid, contextual and nuanced way, subverting and playing with dominant notions of heterosexualised femininities. Many adults draw on different ways of being gendered in different contexts, suggesting that perhaps our gender identity is not quite as fixed as more traditional psychological explanations of gender identity development would indicate.

Pause for thought

As we have explored throughout this chapter, gender is a more complex phenomenon than we might initially assume. While intuitively we take it for granted as something we're 'born with', as we start to explore the various influences on the development of gender identity it becomes clear that seeing gender as *determined* by a single factor is not sufficient. This section on 'Troubling gender' used theoretical resources from within psychology and beyond to make sense of this complex phenomenon. These include theoretical resources from sociology (interactionism), philosophy (Iris Marion Young) and literary theory (Butler) that explore the complexity of gender identity and its construction. These interdisciplinary resources help us to consider the assumptions that are built into the discipline of psychology about the nature of gender identity *itself*.

The psychological theories we have reviewed up to this point assume that gender is a 'real thing' – that it is a bounded category, fixed and relatively stable over time. In other words, (mainstream) psychological theory tends to reproduce the dominant social assumption that gender comes in two kinds (masculine and feminine), and only really questions the way that these categories are *produced*. Is gender caused by biology, by cognition, or by socialisation? However, a more interdisciplinary perspective invites us to reflect on the taken-for-granted assumption that gender *is*. It invites us to explore how psychology as a discipline might be reproducing and naturalising these categories. The idea of gender as *performative* and as *socially constituted* moves us beyond just understanding how boys and girls develop gender identity. It helps us to explore how and why gender has come to be so important in our social world, and what the implications of this are for children growing up gendered. This framework takes us outside our usual psychological preoccupations with questions about nature versus nurture (are we born masculine and feminine, or do we learn?), to think about how gender works in our culture, how it is lived, and how we might start to challenge it's apparent 'naturalness'. An interdisciplinary perspective helps us to question whether the idea of gender as masculine *or* feminine is sustainable.

5.3 Summary

Social constructionist explanations of gender indicate that gender should not be understood as 'real' or taken for granted. In this approach, gender is understood as performative and socially constituted – we produce our understanding of what gender is through our social interactions and our social meaning making. Our sense of self as gendered is likewise socially constituted. Social constructionist ideas of gender suggest that gender identity is not a consequence of either innate tendencies or learned gendered roles. Rather gender is understood as a relatively flexible performance. We *do gender*, rather than *being gendered*.

Activity 4.4: Picturing genders

Look at the collage of images of gender available in contemporary culture (Figure 4.10).

Figure 4.10   Contemporary images of gender

How can you use psychological knowledge acquired through this chapter to make sense of these images?

6   Concluding thoughts

This chapter has considered a range of psychological answers to the question of whether boys and girls are born or made. Is gender natural and biologically pre-determined or does it emerge through social interactions? Evolutionary theory frames gender as an evolutionary adaptation that ensures reproductive fitness through a gendered division of labour around child rearing. You have considered how this might mean that gender is 'hard-wired' in human beings, and that brain structure and function is set in gendered ways in utero, producing pre-programmed sex differences. While there seems to be some evidence to support this notion of gender as hard-wired, the available evidence does not seem to explain the full range of gender differences or gender performance seen in contemporary society. You have considered the possibility that gender is simply learned through socialisation processes – that we learn to be masculine or feminine through our interactions with others. And you have reviewed social cognitive approaches that suggest our gendered behaviour and attitudes result in the production of gender 'schemas' that organise social information in gender typed ways. Finally, you have explored the possibility that gender might not naturally function in the binary way that psychology tends to presume, challenging the taken-for-granted notion that gender comes in two fixed types.

In understanding how children grow to be gendered, it is helpful to consider the range of possible explanations of gender identity: as biologically constituted, as socially determined, as cognitively constructed, or as socially constituted. While evolutionary theory might provide some useful historical explanations of the emergence of gender, and biological accounts might explain how this is embodied, these accounts are not sufficient to explain the complex and contextually bounded nature of gendered identities. Concepts like socialisation, cognitive schemas and stereotypes provide a useful understanding of how social knowledges about gender become incorporated in developing gender identities. But these explanations nonetheless reproduce notions that gender identities are fixed, stable and permanent. In the final section of this chapter, you were invited to consider what it might mean for psychology to build an understanding of gender that is less dependent on binary categories that position us as *either* masculine *or* feminine.

Further reading

- This chapter provides a clear, highly readable exploration of non-binary and other genders:

Barker, M.J. and Richards, C. (2015) 'Further genders', in Richards, C. and Barker, M.J. (eds) *The Palgrave Handbook of the Psychology of Sexuality and Gender*, London, Palgrave MacMillan.

- This book offers a thorough and rigorous critique of the science that underpins the notion of gender and sexuality as biologically determined:

Jordan-Young, R.M. (2010) *Brain Storm: The Flaws in the Science of Sex Differences*, Cambridge, MA, Harvard University Press.

- This is a classic text exploring the nature vs nurture debate in relation to the development of gender identity:

Money, J. and Erhardt, A.A. (1972) *Man & Woman, Boy & Girl*, Baltimore, MD, John Hopkins University Press.

- This classic article provides an early insight into the arguments that underpin much social constructionist thinking on gender identities, outlining the notion of gender as something that is 'performed' or 'done', rather than gender as something one *is*:

West, C. and Zimmerman, D.H. (1987) 'Doing gender', *Gender and Society*, vol. 1, no. 2, pp. 125–51.

References

American Psychological Association (APA) (2010) *Report of the APA Task Force on the Sexualization of Girls*, Washington, USA, APA. Available [online] at www.apa.org/pi/women/programs/girls/report-full.pdf (Accessed 3 April 2015).

American Psychological Association (APA) (2012) 'Guidelines for psychological practice with lesbian, gay, and bisexual clients', *American Psychologist*, vol. 67, no. 1, pp. 10–42.

Atay, Z., Turan, S., Guran, T., Furman, A. and Bereket, A. (2011) 'Puberty and influencing factors in schoolgirls living in Istanbul: end of the secular trend?', *Pediatrics*, vol. 128, no. 1, pp. 40–5 [Online]. Available at ww.ncbi.nlm.nih.gov/pubmed/21669888 (Accessed 25 July 2014).

Barker, M.J. and Richards, C. (2015) 'Further genders', in Richards, C. and Barker, M.J. (eds) *The Palgrave Handbook of the Psychology of Sexuality and Gender*, London, Palgrave Macmillan.

Baron-Cohen, S., Knickmeyer, R.C. and Belmonte, M.K. (2005) 'Sex differences in the brain: implications for explaining autism', *Science*, vol. 310, no. 5749, pp. 819–23 [Online]. Available at www.ncbi.nlm.nih.gov/pubmed/16272115 (Accessed 25 July 2014).

Berenbaum, S.A., Blakemore, J.E.O. and Beltz, A.M. (2011) 'A role for biology in gender-related behavior,' *Sex Roles*, vol. 64, no. 11–12, pp. 804–25 [Online]. Available at http://link.springer.com/10.1007/s11199-011-9990-8 (Accessed 25 July 2014).

Berkout, O.V., Young, J.N. and Gross, A.M. (2011) 'Mean girls and bad boys: Recent research on gender differences in conduct disorder', *Aggression and Violent Behavior*, vol. 16, no. 6, pp. 503–11 [Online]. Available at http://linkinghub.elsevier.com/retrieve/pii/S1359178911000784 (Accessed 27 July 2014).

Blakemore, S.J. and Choudhury, S. (2006) 'Development of the adolescent brain: implications for executive function and social cognition', *Journal of Child Psychology and Psychiatry, and Allied Disciplines*, vol. 47, no. 3–4, pp. 296–312 [Online]. Available at www.ncbi.nlm.nih.gov/pubmed/16492261 (Accessed 10 July 2014).

Blanton, R.E., Levitt, J.G., Peterson, J.R., Fadale, D., Sporty, M.L., Lee, M., To, D., Mormino, E.C., Thompson, P.M., McCracken, J.T. and Toga, A.W. (2004) 'Gender differences in the left inferior frontal gyrus in normal children', *NeuroImage*, vol. 22, no. 2, pp. 626–36 [Online]. Available at www.ncbi.nlm.nih.gov/pubmed/15193591 (Accessed 27 July 2014).

Brooks, K. (2008) *Consuming Innocence: Popular Culture and our Children*, Brisbane: University of Queensland Press.

Burman, D.D., Bitan, T. and Booth, J.R. (2008) 'Sex differences in neural processing of language among children', *Neuropsychologia*, vol. 46, no. 5, pp. 1349–62 [Online]. Available at www.pubmedcentral.nih.gov/articlerender. fcgi?artid=2478638&tool=pmcentrez&rendertype=abstract (Accessed 25 July 2014).

Buss, D.M. (1989) 'Sex differences in human mate preferences: evolutionary hypotheses tested in 37 cultures', *Behavioural and Brain Sciences*, vol. 12, pp. 1–49.

Buss, D.M. (2011) *Evolutionary Psychology: The New Science of the Mind*, 4th edn, Needham Heights, Allyn and Bacon.

Buss, D.M. and Schmitt, D.P. (2011) 'Evolutionary psychology and feminism,' *Sex Roles*, vol. 64, no. 9–10, pp. 768–87 [Online]. Available at http://link. springer.com/10.1007/s11199-011-9987-3 (Accessed 12 July 2014).

Bussey, K. and Bandura, A. (2004) 'Social cognitive theory of gender development and functioning', in Eagley, A.H., Beall, A.E. and Sternberg, R.J. (eds) *The Psychology of Gender*, New York, Guilford, p. 92.

Butler, J. (1990) *Gender Trouble: Feminism and the Subversion of Identity*, London, Routledge.

Carter, R., Silverman, W.K. and Jaccard, J. (2012) 'Sex variations in youth anxiety symptoms: effects of pubertal development and gender role orientation', *Journal of Clinical Child and Adolescent Psychology*, vol. 40, no. 5, pp. 730–41.

Cherney, I.D. and London, K. (2006) 'Gender-linked differences in the toys, television shows, computer games, and outdoor activities of 5- to 13-year-old children', *Sex Roles*, vol. 54, no. 9–10, pp. 717–26 [Online] Available at http://link.springer.com/10.1007/s11199-006-9037-8 (Accessed 10 July 2014).

Christova, P.S., Lewis, S.M., Tagaris, G.A, Uğurbil, K. and Georgopoulos, A.P. (2008) 'A voxel-by-voxel parametric fMRI study of motor mental rotation: hemispheric specialization and gender differences in neural processing efficiency', *Experimental Brain Research*, vol. 189, no. 1, pp. 79–90 [Online]. Available at www.ncbi.nlm.nih.gov/pubmed/18478211 (Accessed 12 July 2014).

Chung, W.C.J. and Auger, A.P. (2013) 'Gender differences in neurodevelopment and epigenetics', *European Journal of Physiology*, vol. 465, no. 5, pp. 573–84 [Online]. Available at www.pubmedcentral.nih.gov/ articlerender.fcgi?artid=3654067&tool=pmcentrez&rendertype=abstract (Accessed 25 July 2014).

Condry, J. and Condry, S. (1976) 'Sex differences: a study of the eye of the beholder', *Child Development*, vol. 47, no. 3, p. 812 [Online]. Available at www. jstor.org/stable/1128199?origin=crossref (Accessed 11 June 2015).

Cooley, C.H. (1902) 'The looking glass self', in Lemert, C. (ed.), *Social Theory: The Multicultural Readings*, 5th edn, Philadelphia, Westview Press, pp. 142-53 (this edition 2013).

Cvencek, D., Meltzoff, A.N. and Greenwald, A.G. (2011) 'Math-gender stereotypes in elementary school children', *Child Development*, vol. 82, no. 3, pp. 766–79 [Online]. Available at www.ncbi.nlm.nih.gov/pubmed/21410915 (Accessed 18 July 2014).

Cvencek, D., Meltzoff, A.N. and Kapur, M. (2014) 'Cognitive consistency and math-gender stereotypes in Singaporean children', *Journal of Experimental Child Psychology*, vol. 117, January 2014, pp. 73–91 [Online]. Available at www.ncbi.nlm.nih.gov/pubmed/24141205 (Accessed 25 July 2014).

Diamond, M. (1997) 'Sex reassignment at birth. Long-term review and clinical implications', *Archive of Pediatric Adolescent Medicine*, vol. 151, no. 3, pp. 298–304.

Eagly, A.H. and Wood, W. (2011) 'Feminism and the evolution of sex differences and similarities', *Sex Roles*, vol. 64, no. 9–10, pp. 758–67 [Online]. Available at http://link.springer.com/10.1007/s11199-011-9949-9 (Accessed 25 July 2014).

Egan, R.D. and Hawkes, G.L. (2008) 'Endangered girls and incendiary objects: unpacking the discourse on sexualization', *Sexuality and Culture*, vol. 12, no. 4, pp. 291–311 [Online]. Available at http://link.springer.com/10.1007/s12119-008-9036-8 (Accessed 19 July 2014).

Endendijk, J.J., Groeneveld, M.G., Berkel, S.R., Hallers-Haalboom, E.T., Mesman, J. and Bakermans-Kranenburg, M.J. (2013) 'Gender stereotypes in the family context: mothers, fathers, and siblings', *Sex Roles*, vol. 68, no. 9–10, pp. 577–90 [Online]. Available at http://link.springer.com/10.1007/s11199-013-0265-4 (Accessed 30 July 2014).

Geary, D.C. (2005) *The Origin of Mind: Evolution of Brain, Cognition and General Intelligence*, Washington, American Psychological Association.

Geary, D.C. (2010) *Male, Female: The Evolution of Human Sex Differences*, 2nd edn, Washington, American Psychological Association.

Gilmore, J.H., Lin, W., Prastawa, M.W., Looney, C.B., Vetsa, Y.S.K., Knickmeyer, R.C., Evans, D.D., Smith, J.K., Hamer, R.M., Lieberman, J.A. and Gerig, G. (2007) 'Regional gray matter growth, sexual dimorphism, and cerebral asymmetry in the neonatal brain', *The Journal of Neuroscience: The Official Journal of the Society for Neuroscience*, vol. 27, no. 6, pp. 1255–60 [Online]. Available at www.pubmedcentral.nih.gov/articlerender.fcgi?artid=2886661&tool=pmcentrez&rendertype=abstract (Accessed 26 July 2014).

Gmitrova, V., Podhajecká, M. and Gmitrov, J. (2009) 'Children's play preferences: implications for the preschool education', *Early Child Development and Care*, vol. 179, no. 3, pp. 339–51 [Online]. Available at www.tandfonline.com/doi/abs/10.1080/03004430601101883 (Accessed 25 July 2014).

Grumbach, M. and Conte, F. (1998) 'Disorders of sex differentiation', in Wilson, J., Foster, D.W., Kronenberg, H and Larsen, P.R. (eds.), *Williams Textbook of Endocrinology*, 9th edn, Philadelphia, W.B. Saunders, pp. 1303–427.

Heltsley, M. and Calhoun, T.C. (2003) 'The good mother: neutralization techniques used by pageant mothers', *Deviant Behavior*, vol. 24, no. 2, pp. 81–100.

Hines, M. (2011) 'Gender development and the human brain', *Annual Review of Neuroscience*, vol. 34, pp. 69–88 [Online]. Available at www.ncbi.nlm.nih.gov/pubmed/21438685 (Accessed 25 July 2014).

Jaruratanasirikul, S., Chanpong, A., Tassanakijpanich, N. and Sriplung, H. (2014) 'Declining age of puberty of school girls in southern Thailand', *World Journal of Pediatrics*, March, pp. 1–6 [Online]. Available at www.ncbi.nlm.nih.gov/pubmed/24668235 (Accessed 25 July 2014).

Jordan-Young, R.M. (2010) *Brain Storm: The Flaws in the Science of Sex Differences*, Cambridge, MA, Harvard University Press.

Jordan-Young, R.M. (2012) 'Hormones, context, and 'brain gender': a review of evidence from congenital adrenal hyperplasia', *Social Science & Medicine*, vol. 74, no. 11, pp. 1738–44 [Online]. Available at www.ncbi.nlm.nih.gov/pubmed/21962724 (Accessed 25 July 2014).

Kennedy, N. (2012) 'Cultural cisgenderism: consequences of the imperceptible', *Psychology of Women Section Review*, vol. 15, no. 2, pp. 3–10.

Kohlberg, L. (1966) 'A cognitive-developmental analysis of children's sex-role concepts and attitudes', in Maccoby, E.E. (ed.), The Development of Sex Differences, Stanford, CA, Stanford University Press, pp. 82–173.

Leinbach, M.D., Hort, B.E. and Fagot, B.I. (1997) 'Bears are for boys: metaphorical associations in young children's gender stereotypes', *Cognitive Development*, vol. 12, no. 1, pp. 107–30 [Online] Available at http://linkinghub.elsevier.com/retrieve/pii/S0885201497900320 (Accessed 12 June 2015).

Lenroot, R.K. and Giedd, J.N. (2010) 'Sex differences in the adolescent brain', *Brain and Cognition*, vol. 72, no. 1, pp. 46–55 [Online] Available at www.pubmedcentral.nih.gov/articlerender.fcgi?artid=2818549&tool=pmcentrez&rendertype=abstract (Accessed 10 July 2014).

Leonard, T. (2011) 'The baby who is neither boy nor girl: as gender experiment provokes outrage, what about the poor child's future?', *The Daily Mail*, 28 May [Online]. Available at www.dailymail.co.uk/news/article-1391772/Storm-Stocker-As-gender-experiment-provokes-outrage-poor-childs-future.html (Accessed 15 November 2014).

Leszczynski, J.P. and Strough, J. (2008) 'The contextual specificity of masculinity and femininity in early adolescence', *Social Development*, vol. 17, no. 3, pp. 719–36.

Liao, L.-M., Audi, L., Magritte, E., Meyer-Bahlburg, H.F.L. and Quigley, C.A. (2012) 'Determinant factors of gender identity: a commentary', *Journal of Pediatric Urology*, vol. 8, no. 6, pp. 597–601 [Online]. Available at www.ncbi.nlm.nih.gov/pubmed/23158728 (Accessed 25 July 2014).

Maccoby, E.E. (2000) 'Perspectives on gender development', *International Journal of Behavioral Development*, vol. 24, no. 4, pp. 398–406.

Martin, C.L. (1989) 'Children's use of gender-related information in making social judgments', *Developmental Psychology*, vol. 25, pp. 80–8.

Martin, C.L. (1993) 'New directions for investigating children's gender knowledge', *Developmental Review*, vol. 13, pp. 184–204.

Martin, C.L. and Halverson, C. (1981) 'A schematic processing model of sex typing and stereotyping in children', *Child Development*, vol. 52, no. 4, pp. 1119–34.

Martin, C.L. and Ruble, D. (2004) 'Children's search for gender cues. Cognitive perspectives on gender development', *Current Directions in Psychological Science*, vol. 13, no. 2, pp. 67–70 [Online]. Available at http://cdp.sagepub.com/lookup/doi/10.1111/j.0963-7214.2004.00276.x (Accessed 30 July 2014).

Miller, D.I. and Halpern, D.F. (2014) 'The new science of cognitive sex differences', *Trends in Cognitive Sciences*, vol. 18, no. 1, pp. 37–45 [Online]. Available at www.ncbi.nlm.nih.gov/pubmed/24246136 (Accessed 14 July 2014).

Money, J. and Erhardt, A.A. (1972) *Man & Woman, Boy & Girl*, Baltimore, MD, John Hopkins University Press.

Nagy, Z., Westerberg, H. and Klingberg, T. (2004) 'Maturation of white matter is associated with the development of cognitive functions during childhood', *Journal of Cognitive Neuroscience*, vol. 16, no. 7, pp. 1227–33 [Online]. Available at www.ncbi.nlm.nih.gov/pubmed/15453975 (Accessed 12 June 2015).

Nolen-Hoeksema, S. (2001) 'Gender differences in depression', *Current Directions in Psychological Science*, vol. 10, no. 5, pp. 173–76.

Opplinger, P. (2009) *Girls Gone Skank: The Sexualization of Girls in American Culture*, Jefferson, NC, McFarland.

Pardun, C.J., L'Engle, K.L. and Brown, J.D. (2005) 'Linking exposure to outcomes: early adolescents' consumption of sexual content in six media', *Mass Communication & Society*, vol. 8, no. 2, pp. 75–91.

Pinker, S. (2003) *The Blank Slate*, New York, Penguin.

Poulin-Dubois, D., Serbin, L.A., Eichstedt, J.A., Sen, M.G. and Beissel, C.F. (2002) 'Men don't put on make-up: toddlers' knowledge of the gender stereotyping of household activities', *Social Development*, vol. 11, no. 2, pp. 166–81.

Powlishta, K.K. (2000) 'The effect of target age on the activation of gender stereotypes', *Sex Roles*, vol. 42, no. 3-4, pp. 271–82.

Reynolds, M.W., Wallace, J., Hill, T.F., Weist, M.D. and Nabors, L.A. (2001) 'The relationship between gender, depression, and self-esteem in children who have witnessed domestic violence', *Child Abuse & Neglect*, vol. 25, no. 9, pp. 1201–6 [Online]. Available at www.ncbi.nlm.nih.gov/pubmed/11700692 (Accessed 12 June 2015).

Rutter, M. (2007) 'Psychopathological development across adolescence', *Journal of Youth and Adolescence*, vol. 36, no. 1, pp. 101–10.

Serbin, L.A., Poulin-Dubois, D. and Eichstedt, J.A. (2002) 'Infants' responses to gender-inconsistent events', *Infancy*, vol. 3, no. 4, pp. 531–42.

Serbin, L.A., Powlishta, K.K. and Gulko, J. (1993) 'The development of sex typing in middle childhood', *Monographs of the Society for Research in Child Development*, vol. 2, no. 1, pp. 1–93.

Slaby, R.G. and Frey, K.S. (1975) 'Development of gender constancy and selective attention to same-sex models', *Child Development*, vol. 46, no. 4, pp. 849–56.

Stoet, G., O'Connor, D.B., Conner, M. and Laws, K.R. (2013) 'Are women better than men at multi-tasking?', *BMC Psychology*, vol. 1, no. 1, p. 18. [Online]. Available at www.biomedcentral.com/2050-7283/1/18 (Accessed 19 July 2014).

West, C. and Zimmerman, D.H. (1987) 'Doing gender', *Gender and Society*, vol. 1, no. 2, pp. 125–51.

Wood, W. and Eagly, A.H. (2002) 'A cross-cultural analysis of the behaviour of women and men: implications for the origins of sex differences', *Psychological Bulletin*, vol. 128, pp. 699–727.

Yakolev, P.I. and Lecours, A.R. (1967) 'The myelogenetic cycles of regional maturation of the brain', in Minkowski, A. (ed.), *Regional Development of the Brain in Early Life*, Oxford, Blackwell, pp. 3–65.

Young, I.M. (2005) *On Female Body Experience: 'Throwing Like a Girl' and Other Essays (Studies in Feminist Philosophy)*, Cary, NC, Oxford University Press.

Zahn-Waxler, C., Shirtcliff, E.A. and Marceau, K. (2008) 'Disorders of childhood and adolescence: gender and psychopathology', *Annual Review of Clinical Psychology*, vol. 4, pp. 275–303 [Online] Available at www.ncbi.nlm.nih.gov/pubmed/18370618 (Accessed 15 July 2014).

Zosuls, K.M., Ruble, D.N., Tamis-LeMonda, C.S., Shrout, P.E., Bornstein, M.H. and Greulich, F.K. (2009) 'The acquisition of gender labels in infancy: implications for gender-typed play', *Developmental Psychology*, vol. 45, no. 3, pp. 688–95.

Zucker, K.J., Bradley, S.J., Kuksis, M., Pecore, K., Birkenfeld-Adams, A., Doering, R.W., Mitchell, J.N. and Wild, J. (1999) 'Gender constancy judgments in children with gender identity disorder: evidence for a developmental lag', *Archives of Sexual Behavior*, vol. 28, no. 6, pp. 475–502 [Online]. Available at www.ncbi.nlm.nih.gov/pubmed/10650437 (Accessed 12 June 2015).

Chapter 5

Can people really change? Changing self-identity and 'other' relationships across the lifespan

Sarah Crafter

Contents

—

1   Introduction

My eldest daughter first stood up in a school assembly when she was five years old. The pupils at her school had been invited to make a hat for an 'Easter Bonnet' competition. She probably wouldn't have been so keen to know, while she was cutting, sticking and gluing, that as one of the winners of the competition she would be required to collect her prize in front of the whole school. The reason for this is that my daughter would have been described as an 'extremely shy' child. She looked so scared doing this; it was very difficult to watch as a parent. She stood at the front of the school hall, with tense shoulders up near her ears, and visibly shook. However, she did it!

While shyness in children may be perceived as cute, it is not generally valued in adulthood. So, over the years there was a lot of gentle nudging from her family (and sometimes the schools she went to) to be brave and do things she was not comfortable doing. At the time of writing this, she is undertaking a university course that requires her to give a presentation on her work, in front of her peers and tutors, every week. More than this, she tells me she is actually starting to enjoy them.

What does this tell us about the changes to my daughter's sense of 'self'? What roles have family, teachers and peers had in helping to shape that exceedingly shy five-year-old into a more confident young woman? Is shyness an underlying characteristic that she has learned to cover up, or has the culmination of all those experiences and interactions with others allowed her to construct an altered sense of who she is? How has her self-identity changed as she engages in different life transitions?

Pause for thought

How have you changed since your childhood? (If you prefer, imagine you are one of your friends and answer the question from their point of view.) Write down three words or phrases that come to mind.

Now imagine you have bumped into someone you haven't seen since leaving school. What kinds of changes would they see in you?

> Now think about how some of those changes came about. What role did other people play, such as family, friends, work colleagues? Perhaps there were particular activities or major events in your life that led to changes?

These kinds of questions have been a central thread within the study of lifespan developmental psychology. A number of theorists within developmental psychology, some of whom are discussed within this chapter, have devoted their time to the study of 'stability' and 'change' as we develop. There has been a strong assumption within developmental psychology that who you are, and what happens in early childhood, *determines* a pattern or pathway through to adulthood. But as you go through this chapter, you will be asked to question this assumption.

In this module you have covered many different aspects of psychology, such as cognition, biology, and the social aspects of studying human beings. This chapter will focus on the self and our relationships with others. Studies of the self can be broadly placed under the title of '**identity**'. Identity is a way of making sense of who we are, in a way that reflects our interactions and responses to others (Wetherell and Talpade Mohanty, 2010). For example, is my daughter's shyness a stable part of her self-identity or have her interactions with others meant she has reconstructed how she sees herself over time? For Erikson, a leading figure in the early work on lifespan development, identity is a critical feature of the study of human development. He wrote in 1950:

> The study of identity, then, becomes as strategic in our time as the study of sexuality was in Freud's time.
>
> (Erikson, 1950, p. 242)

Section 2 of this chapter will look at the study of stability and change across the lifespan by introducing you to longitudinal research. It will then use Erikson's work to examine how developmental psychology has understood change as a series of steps or stages (see Chapters 3 and 4). Section 2.3 asks what role culture, context and history might play in influencing our identity. Finally, the concept of transition will form the basis for the penultimate section and the chapter will finish by looking at our self identity and how we are influenced by our relationships with others.

Identity
Identity is a way of making sense of who we are, in a way that reflects our interactions and responses to others.

Learning outcomes

On completing this chapter, you should:

- be able to identify how normative assumptions about childhood and development have influenced research in developmental psychology

- understand the concept of stability and change within developmental psychology

- be able to link issues of self with identity and examine the role of key relationships in people's lives.

2   Stability, change and life transitions

At the core of modern developmental psychology has been the attempt to understand the physical and psychological changes that human beings undergo as they grow older. A substantial part of this work has been based on the study of what people can do (particularly children and adolescents) at different ages. It is obvious that people change, physically and psychologically, as they grow, but developmental psychologists are interested in *how* that process occurs. For example, should we think about our lifespan in blocks of time or stages like childhood, adolescence, middle age or old age? This is certainly a very popular and old idea. Shakespeare wrote about the seven ages of man in his 'All the world's a stage' monologue to include the infant, the school-boy, the lover, the soldier, the justice, the pantaloon and finally, old age (Figure 5.1). (Look up the poem on the internet if you would like a description of each stage.)

Figure 5.1   The seven ages of man
(Source: Mulready, 1838)

The idea is very familiar, and it therefore appeals to our common sense. But perhaps, rather than being characterised by discrete stages, development is a more gradual process, with a smooth trajectory that reaches an endpoint in old age. Equally, you may know people who don't fit either of these patterns – the young carer who undertakes adult responsibilities, the 30-something who never seems to grow up (popularly characterised as the Peter Pan figure), or the adult with learning difficulties who looks physically mature but is not mentally 'mature'. This chapter will introduce you to theorists who have studied development as discrete stages or steps and those who later critiqued this approach. First though, let's have a quick look at the role that longitudinal studies have played in developmental psychology in helping us understand how people change (or don't change) across their lifespans.

2.1   What can longitudinal studies tell us?

It is undoubtedly difficult to capture change over time through research. However, one way to look at change and stability over time is to take a group of people and study them over a long period of time, known as a longitudinal study. We could, of course, observe the changes our own children go through over time in the form of an observational diary. This was famously done by Darwin (1877) in his paper 'A biographical sketch of an infant'. However, these descriptions, while interesting, wouldn't tell us much about the changes of other children from different backgrounds. We might also be subject to criticism because the observations of our own relatives are more likely to be biased.

Although longitudinal studies are hard to do because maintaining contact with the same group of people across time is challenging, and such studies are expensive, they are considered a very useful resource. A prominent example of a large-scale longitudinal project in the UK is the Millennium Cohort Study. In this research, 19,000 children were recruited at the beginning of the twenty-first century with the aim of understanding the range of physical, cognitive, social and emotional changes they undergo over time. This work is particularly interesting because it allows researchers to map the links and patterns between measurements of poverty, ethnicity and mobility (see Hansen et al., 2010). Two other prominent nationally representative cohort studies are:

* the Medical Research Council's National Study of Health, a project that followed individuals from their birth in 1946 into older age

- the National Child Development Study (NCDS), which followed individuals born in 1958 and showed links between childhood disadvantage and adult challenges at ages 23 and 33 (see Elliot and Vaitilingam, 2008, for a rich overview of the study).

There are also media programmes, such as the UK's Child of Our Time, which capture visual examples of the kind of changes that people can undergo as they develop.

Nevertheless, it is worth viewing some of the 'maps' or 'trajectories' between childhood and adulthood with some scepticism. A considerable amount of work within developmental psychology is based on the assumption that what happens in childhood *'determines'* outcomes in adulthood (Warin, 2010). The area of extreme childhood deprivation provides fertile ground for further exploration. For example, a large number of studies link early institutional deprivation with later physical, cognitive and social problems (see Lawler and Gunnar, 2012). Children who have experienced profound institutional deprivation, for instance, tend to be physically much smaller and tend to remain smaller than their peers once they reach adulthood (Sonuga-Barke et al., 2010). However, research has also shown that children in good quality childcare, or those adopted early, can show signs of reversing the consequences of early deprivation in all domains, including cognitive and social-emotional (Lawler and Gunnar, 2012). Others have highlighted that children respond to stressful experiences with a great deal of variety, and many display a high degree of resilience (Rutter, 1972).

The specific study of the self in longitudinal research is rarer. One excellent exception is the work of Jo Warin (2010), who documented the changes to self of a group of ten young people between the ages of three and seventeen years (some of the young people dropped out of the study). Warin collected observational and interview data from the children, their parents and other carers, such as early years and school teachers. Warin describes the contradictory accounts of identity held between teachers, parents and the children themselves, often to the point where it seemed like they are all talking about a different child. One participant, Shelley, for instance, had a very shaky start in school with a teacher describing her as aggressive (though this mystified Warin who never observed such behaviour). Yet, after a positive time at secondary school, Shelley had ambitious hopes for her future.

Let us now look at how significant figures in developmental psychology have tried to make sense of *how* that process of change might occur.

2.2   Stability and change as steps or stages

In other modules or chapters, you may have encountered a variety of significant figures within developmental psychology who have looked at different aspects of development as a series of stages: for example, Jean Piaget was interested in how children's thinking changes over time in discrete stages. In Chapter 3, you were introduced to Kohlberg's stages of moral development, which drew on the work of Piaget to show how moral judgements changed in distinct ways as children pass through each stage. Other researchers have similarly based their work on steps or stages. Since this chapter is mainly concerned with identity, it will mostly focus on the work of Erikson, who was interested in the changes to how we feel about ourselves across our lifespan; that is, in changes to our identity.

It is curious that Erikson named his developmental stages as the 'Eight Stages of Man' (1950) because this resonates with Shakespeare's seven stages described at a much earlier time in history. In his treatise on the stages of 'man' Erikson argues that development depends on sameness and continuity between the self and the outer world of the individual. For example, in his first stage 'Trust v. Mistrust', Erikson suggests that the infant comes to trust in the continuity and sameness of care provided by the 'mother'. A break in the continuity of care from this outer world can lead to negative emotions that the child turns in on itself: their inner world. You can see how, from this perspective, identity is perceived as a constant struggle to find some consistency between the 'self s/he would like to be and the self s/he believes is attributed to her or him by others' (van Meijl, 2010, p. 65). In other words, there is 'mutuality' between the individual and the social world they inhabit. For Erikson, sameness and continuity throughout the lifespan are the basis for a well-adjusted or 'normal' personality. Erikson's stages can be broadly summarised as shown in Table 5.1.

Table 5.1   Erikson's psychosocial stages

Approximate age	Stage categories
First year	*Trust v. mistrust* Infants learn that they can trust others to care for their basic needs, or they come to mistrust them
Second year	*Autonomy v. shame and doubt* Children learn to exercise their will and to control themselves, or uncertainty leads them to doubt themselves
3–6 years	*Initiative v. guilt* Children start to enjoy initiating their activities and becoming accomplished. If they are not allowed to take their own initiative they feel guilty about trying to be independent
6–11 years	*Industry v. inferiority* Children learn to be valued and competent by adults and peers, or they develop feelings of inferiority
Adolescence	*Identity v. role confusion* Adolescents establish a sense of personal identity in their social group, or they become confused about who they are and what they want to do with their life. They develop a vocational identity
Early adulthood	*Intimacy v. isolation* This stage is geared towards finding life companions, or risk feeling lonely and isolated
Middle age	*Generativity v. stagnation* Adults are geared towards work and guiding the next generation, or life becomes stagnated
Old age	*Integrity v. despair* People look back on their life and try to make sense of it as a meaningful experience, or they despair about unachieved goals and hopes

It is important to note though, that like Piaget's work, each of Erikson's stages shows a discrete break or difference from the previous stage. In Piaget's work, a seven-year-old child learns how to organise information logically in a way that they would have been incapable of at an earlier stage of development. In a similar vein, Erikson understood that each stage of development led to new ways of interacting between the self and others. He believed problems could occur if each stage did not provide the continuity to psychologically master the next stage. So, poor adjustment to school might reflect the 'failed promises of earlier stages' (Erikson, 1950, p. 227). Another example would be Erikson's suggestion that adolescence was one of the key stages for cementing a stable sense of identity. One of the key 'resolutions' for this stage involved making 'commitments' and establishing a personal 'ideology'. According to this, an individual would leave adolescence having established a secure identity that might also include a stable occupation (Kroger and Marcia, 2011).

Erikson's work, though over 60 years old, remains popular today, and stage-related ideas about development have been very pervasive in psychology. But much of this work takes for granted Erikson's assumptions about the 'correct', 'normal' or most 'well-adjusted' way to develop. In contemporary Western society, how often can we say that young people leave adolescence with a stable occupational identity? What happens if your life does not fit this 'normal' pathway? For example, Merriam et al. (2001, p. 176) describe how being HIV-positive 'suspends development' because the disease is a threat to our ideas of a 'normal' life cycle. The lack of attention to lives that do not follow a 'normal' pathway has led some developmental psychologists to be critical of stage perspectives on development (Burman, 2008). They argue that work like Erikson's is a problem in two ways:

1 It does not acknowledge sufficiently how the context of our lives might influence our ability to go through the stages in a way that is considered 'well-adjusted'.

2 It presupposes that the stages set out by theorists such as Erikson are the only correct or right pathway.

To develop these points, let us explore in more depth Erikson's 'Generativity v. Stagnation' stage. Erikson does not provide ages but it is safe to assume this stage refers to middle and late-middle adulthood. Despite this stage forming a significant portion of our adult lives, Erikson devotes only half a page to it in his book *Childhood and Society*. He suggested that this stage is primarily concerned with 'establishing and guiding the next generation' (Erikson, 1950, p. 231). Failure to do so would lead to 'mutual repulsion', 'individual stagnation' and 'interpersonal impoverishment'. Clearly, this stage only fits with a certain 'script' for life that assumes adulthood will be geared to raising children. This view of a 'normal' adult life neglects to take into account other life trajectories such as couples who choose not to or cannot have children, women orienting their lives towards career goals or the consequences of unexpected events like divorce (Slater, 2003). There is a danger here that a description of the changes that some individuals undergo is inflated into a prescription about normal development for everyone.

While we should acknowledge that Erikson was writing in a particular time (his seminal work was developed in the 1950s), his approach did not sufficiently account for the role of social and cultural contexts. For example, a study by Descartes (2006) examined parents' views on giving financial aid to their adult children in the USA at a time of economic uncertainty. She found that some of her participants were happy to give money or accommodation to their adult children and grandchildren. Others, though, felt this violated their 'script' about adult independence (Figure 5.2).

Figure 5.2   An adult child living at home with disgruntled parents

One white American mother explained how she had clashed with her husband and developed conflicting feelings about helping out their daughter:

> It's probably a weakness that I have. I've been accused, correctly, justly so, of helping my younger daughter too much ... Financially I just help too much. And I do it not because of them, not because of my daughter or son-in-law ... they got themselves into bankruptcy ... My concerns are always the grandkids. They're the innocent victims. When my daughter and son-in-law are screwing

up their life really big time … if it impacts the kids, it … gets to me. And I step in.

(Descartes, 2006, p. 143)

Erikson's stages would suggest that individuals have already settled into a steady work plan during the previous stage of 'Intimacy v. Isolation', so here you see how contextual economic uncertainty shapes the processes and practices of individuals. In this instance, two stages collide, instead of development playing out in a neat sequence of stages. More than that, it is easy to see how violating our expectation about 'normal' adult development has a bearing on the relationships with other people in our lives.

Breaking up development into stages inevitably encourages researchers to focus on change by chronological age. It is worth questioning whether 'age' is the best way to look at patterns of development. It was not until the late 1800s that people, in the industrial world at least, recorded or took note of their age (Rogoff, 2003). This is still likely to be the case in many parts of the world. For example, Bril et al. (1989) compared mothers' representations of child rearing and development in one Western culture (France) and two non-Western cultures (the Bambara of Mali and the Bakongo of Kongo-Brazzaville). While there were subtle differences between the two non-Western cultures, there were more striking differences between the Western and non-Western cultures. Essentially, the French mothers computed their child's age in terms of months or weeks and tended to use numerical indices as an indication of their child's development. The Bambara and Bakongo mothers, by contrast, compared one skill to another. For example, all the women in the non-Western sample agreed that toilet training could only be achieved once the child had learned to walk. Therefore, age was not the key issue for these parents; rather, other developmental milestones were the frame of reference for their children's achievements.

measuring development — western vs non western cultures.

There are also consequences to children's lives when they violate expected 'norms' of childhood. In a research project I was involved in, our team looked at children's work. We asked young people in the UK what jobs they thought it was appropriate for a 14-year-old to do. All of our participants thought it was alright for a 14-year-old to have a Saturday job or do babysitting. However, most said that caring for a disabled parent imposed too much responsibility on someone that age. Moreover, missing school or giving money to parents at 14 years old was a violation of 'age-appropriate' activities. That said, a number of the young people told us they would put family obligations first if it was necessary. This could include missing school to care for family members in some capacity or finding work to take financial burdens away from parents (see Crafter et al., 2009; O'Dell et al., 2010). Children's work presents an interesting challenge to certain notions of the 'appropriate' childhood because in many cultures and contexts it is common, and often necessary, to give financial support to parents (see O'Dell et al., 2013).

2.3   Change as a cultural-historical phenomenon

Pause for thought

Have a look at the image in Figure 5.3 and consider ways in which life is different now.

Figure 5.3   Image from the Second World War

When we look at old photos or read diaries or books from a previous time, it is not hard to see how our cultural and social contexts have changed too. It is worth asking ourselves how our own developing identities and relationships with others are shaped by changing histories and the communities to which we belong. There are two key figures whose work is prominent within developmental psychology who can help to do this: Lev Vygotsky and Urie Bronfenbrenner. First, though, read this story of Taiwanese-born academic, Dora Dien.

Dien was born in 1936 in Taiwan, when it was still under Japanese rule. Taiwan had had a complex history moving between Chinese and Japanese occupation/rule. Dora Dien, then eight years old, was oblivious to this changing and often antagonistic history. Instead, she describes her efforts to be a 'perfect Japanese girl' (Dien, 2000, p. 11) who held a Japanese name and spoke the Japanese language. When Japan was defeated in the Second World War, she was shocked to find her parents rejoicing over the return of a Chinese heritage that Dora had not even known existed. Almost overnight, Chinese names were re-established, a Chinese school education commenced, and the Chinese language was now spoken. Her father was able to take a job as a school principal, a post that previously only a Japanese person could hold.

The experience described by Dien is instructive because it shows how wider political contexts can have a profound impact on the life histories and personal histories of the individuals within a society. It also indicates how such contexts may impact on identity development. Dien changed her identity from a 'perfect Japanese girl' to someone who could describe herself as 'well rooted in my Chinese identity' (Dien, 2000, p. 13). The changes described by Dien reflect the view of her 'self' as produced through dialogues and interactions with others, so that her sense of self developed from the social judgements of others in her community (Holland and Lachicotte, 2007). In later life she studied in the USA, married an American man and described wanting to be the 'best American mother I could possibly be' while striving 'not to be a possessive and controlling traditional Chinese mother' (Dien, 2000, p. 14). Dien's story also shows that our development across the lifespan is influenced as much by our past, as it is by our present, and even our future.

The study of social, cultural and historical processes in psychology is often accredited to the work of Lev Vygotsky and his sociocultural theory. Vykotsky (1978) – and many academics who subsequently built on his work – believed that psychological phenomena are mediated by our interactions with tools or artefacts. Tools can be something concrete like a computer, or something symbolic, like the language we speak. Many of the tools or artefacts and the activities that are mediated by them (such as our ability to speak to one another) are passed down through historical experience. Chapter 2 provided an example of an adult pointing at a teddy bear to garner the shared attention of a young child. From a sociocultural theory perspective, the pointing gesture can be viewed as a tool to mediate social interaction between the infant and caregiver. The act of gesturing and its associated meaning (i.e. 'hey, look at that') is something that the parent, and the parent's parent before them, and so on, passed on through generations.

Supporters of Vygotsky's work, then, would argue that children are not born into a vacuum, but enter into a world of established practices and pre-organised identities. The well-known work of paediatrician Aidan MacFarlane (1977) provides a good example. Macfarlane recorded conversations between mothers, fathers and medical specialists straight after birth. Recorded in Britain in the 1970s, they show how gendered identities of the newborns were already being shaped through, or mediated by, the parents' language. Comments about a newborn girl were typically 'I wanted a boy .... it can't play rugby' and 'she's a beaut, Jo' or as one medical practitioner said 'often tactically best to have a girl first – she can help with the washing up'. What this example beautifully illustrates is the way these parents used their own cultural past experience to construct an identity, and future pathway, for their new baby (see also Cole, 2006 or Valsiner, 2005). In Chapter 4 on gender development you read about the negative consequences that can result from trying to fit within the 'normative' expectations set up by cultural gender expectations.

As well as looking at change and stability between our past, present and future, we can also look at identity and our relationships to others across a variety of different contexts. Urie Bronfenbrenner (1979) suggested that the changing and developing person is always in interaction with a changing and evolving environment. He saw the ecological environment as a nest of structures or settings placed within each other, namely the microsystem, mesosystem, exosystem and macrosystem. The microsystem is a place of face-to-face interactions, activities and roles such as the home or school. This setting has been the focus of a lot of laboratory work within developmental psychology. There has been less work that addresses the mesosystem, which is the interrelation between two or more settings in which the individual is actively present. For an adult this might mean negotiating between a secular workplace and attending a church group. The exosystem is one or more settings that the person is not actively a part of, but may have an effect on them. The classic example is how a child might be affected by the stress a parent is experiencing at work. The macrosystem consists of customs, laws, cultural values and beliefs and resources. For example, the various school curriculums in different countries influence the activities that occur within those schools.

In most developmental psychology textbooks you will find a pictorial representation of Bronfenbrenner's model as shown in Figure 5.4.

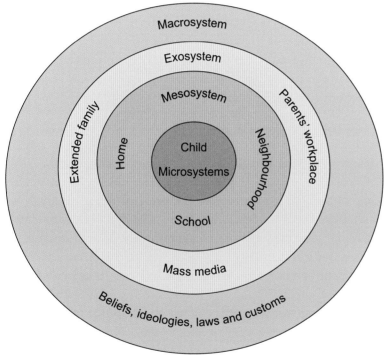

Figure 5.4 Bronfenbrenner's model

So what can our cultural histories and ecological system settings tell us about our identity and the complex set of relationships we have with others? Let us turn to a fascinating study by a team of geneticists, archaeologists, linguists and social psychologists, which is looking at the diasporas involved in 'making Britain'. Population genetics, or testing peoples' **DNA**, makes it possible to link back to our ancient past. With the growing interest in genealogy, there has been a surge of interest in people wanting to find out more about their ancestry. Social psychologist, Marc Scully, and colleagues looked at the links between

Deoxyribonucleic Acid (DNA)
DNA is the hereditary material in humans and most other organisms that is largely located in the cell nucleus. DNA contains the instructions needed for an organism to develop, survive and reproduce. A portion of DNA is passed to offspring from their parents.

genetic ancestry, DNA testing and people's imagined identity with a remote past (see Scully et al., 2013, p. 922). When people in the North of England were invited by the project team to have their DNA tested to see if they had Viking ancestry in their remote past, Scully and colleagues were interested to understand how their imagined identity linked with the present. When respondents were asked whether they would be disappointed if the DNA results did not support their assumptions of being of Viking descent, answers included, 'I have always assumed that I was of Viking descent', 'Just sure feeling I am Viking', 'I am very proud of York and its people and its Norse roots and feel it is my clan'. Scully et al.'s (2013) findings suggest that as we develop into adulthood, some of us are not just concerned with our immediate cultural past, such as where we are born or what we can remember of our childhood (these kinds of memories were talked about in Chapter 2). We are also concerned with a more distant past. More than that, these imagined pasts are strongly tied to our sense of identity or 'feelings'.

Roseneil (2009) writes about how the traces of the lives of others who are dead (such as fathers, mothers or partners) permeate our everyday lives. She describes this as a 'haunting', but from a sociocultural perspective it could be viewed as past experiences and interactions with others linking with our self-identities of the present. Roseneil details an interview with Ben, a man in his early fifties, who describes himself as 'Black English'. He describes, across two interviews, the influence his now-dead father had on his life, saying 'Cos he told us to be self-sufficient and stand up for ourselves … I come from [the] school of, you don't turn your cheek. You know, it's an eye for an eye … That's how I were brought up … We've all got his photo in our homes, just as a permanent reminder' (Roseneil, 2009, p. 419). Ben describes using the words of his deceased father to make life decisions long after his father had passed away.

Intergenerational studies are also an insightful way to understand change and stability of identity between our cultural past and our imagined future. The study of fatherhood provides a very interesting example of how we can bring together the ideas of Vygotsky, about practices as cultural and historical, alongside Bronfenbrenner's focus on the ecology of multiple contexts. Brannen and Nilsen (2006) (also Nilsen and Brannen, 2014) interviewed the father, grandfather and great-grandfather of three-generation families where the youngest fathers had a child under ten years of age. They were interested in the continuities and discontinuities in fatherhood across the three generations. Their results highlighted the role that wider structures, or the macrosystem, played in the changes to fatherhood over time. The middle generation, born during the Second World War, went through rapid life transitions from school, to work, to marriage and family life very early on. The transitions of the great-grandfathers, and current father generation, were generally more prolonged with an extended youth. The younger generation, unlike the previous two, lived with partners before marriage. However, being a more 'work-focused' father rather than a 'child-focused' father was not necessarily a value or practice shared across generations within the same family. For some of the current generation, those in higher status jobs were working longer hours which reshaped what it meant to be a father. Those with less demanding work roles, including some of the grandfathers, could identify themselves as 'family men' because they were heavily invested in their families as well as, or instead of, work.

Box 5.1   Crossing boundaries: the sociology of material objects (Bell and Bell, 2012)

Our past, traditions and cultures are not only captured through our identities or the way we see ourselves, but also through material objects that are sometimes passed down through generations. The most obvious kinds of objects that people pass down are photo albums, scrapbooks and works of art, such as paintings or sculptures.

Mary and Susan Bell, two sisters from Maine USA, described the process of examining and sorting the material objects collated by their family. When they moved their 83-year-old mother into an assisted-living home they found themselves with an overflow of furniture, household items, letters and other objects. In the course of sorting these items they began to write a dialogue that reflected their individual responses and experiences surrounding specific objects. They also argue that the objects represent the structural changes that were occurring in the USA during the twenty-first century and the shared experiences of American sons and daughters whose parents came of age during the Depression, the Second World War and the Cold War.

Take the picture of King, the family dog, as an example (see Figure 5.5). This was the only 'treasured' object that resonated with both sisters (who had a seven-year age gap) as a shared childhood

---

experience. For both sisters the photo represented a happy family, loyalty but also the trauma of family moves and upheaval. Their father's work often took them abroad for two years at a time and the dog was always left behind. Susan wrote in her diary every day, at the time, how much she missed him. There is also a family story accompanying the dog. He tried to follow the family home one time, walking 40 miles, until his feet bled. Susan found him. He later died on one of their trips abroad.

Figure 5.5   King, the family dog

(Source: Bell and Bell, 2012)

Pause for thought

Think of two objects that are important to you, either passed down through family or collected by yourself.

What story or feelings surround the material object? Does the material object link to any of your family or friends?

2.4   Transition – new ways of looking at stability and change

---

Activity 5.1:   The story of Simon

In her book *Stories of Self*, Jo Warin (2010) describes the qualitative longitudinal study mentioned earlier where she follows the lives of a small group of young people from nursery age to late teenage-hood. One of her participants is Simon. Simon describes a moment when he is 15 years old and is physically attacked by a group of boys from his school. He subsequently missed 18 months of school and the incident had a negative effect on his school exams. Here Simon describes his anger towards his attackers and people who 'batter' others.

> When you're walking around [school] people are getting battered. It's not on. Like them that did me, said 'Oh we were just doing it for a laugh' but I nearly came out of it blind in one eye. I've still got a gap there in me chest [indicates]. They kicked me and punched me. Bit of a black eye as well. All sorts ... I'm so wary now of what's happening. After it happened I was just sleeping all the time. Just staying in bed. Watching telly. I had to build it up gradually. Like, first time I went into town after I got attacked I was really panicking. Breathing rate went up. Heart rate had gone up. Everything really. Sweating was constant.

> (Warin, 2010, p. 125)

From reading this extract, in what ways has Simon changed following his attack?

Discussion

Simon later went on to tell Jo that he now went to the gym every day, took self-defence classes and played football. Jo saw these activities as a way of Simon strengthening his self-identity. Contemporary scholars might call the process of change that Simon underwent as 'transition'. A transition may refer to a move from one physical location to another (e.g. moving schools) or a forward trajectory in age (e.g. change through growing up), or a change to who we are (Crafter and Maunder, 2012).

Section 2.2 wrestled with the idea of development as stages and the challenges this raises for everyday lives. Section 2.3 looked at development against a backdrop of the wider social, cultural and historical communities to which we belong. When change is viewed as a transition, rather than a stage, however, it opens up possibilities for looking at change as something dynamic and ongoing. Change can simultaneously alter our emotions, the way we look at the world around us and our physical bodies (Zittoun, 2006). This perspective also allows us to study transitions as consequential, because they have an impact on the individual and the social context they are part of (Beach, 1999; Crafter and Maunder, 2012). Sometimes these are quite dramatic, like Simon's experience in the excerpt above. But others take place over a longer period of time, like my daughter steadily overcoming her 'shyness' through ongoing interactions and experiences.

Transitions have largely been studied in two different ways (Hviid and Zittoun, 2008). The first is by measuring what has happened to a person *after* they have made a transition, commonly known as measuring outcomes. For example, Zeedyk et al. (2003) surveyed pupils, parents and teachers in the last year of primary school and after the first year of secondary school, about the primary to secondary school transition. One significant *outcome* was that all three groups at both primary and secondary level were concerned about bullying above everything else. This is very useful but doesn't tell us much about what was happening during the *process* of that transition. The second way to study transition is to look at how individuals change when faced with new challenges, and most importantly for this chapter, how this alters who we are. Therefore the concept of transition incorporates a key psychological element about the altering of 'one's sense of self'.

Academic studies have looked at the dramatic changes that pre-empt a transition as 'fateful' moments (Giddens, 1991) or ruptures (Zittoun, 2006). For Giddens, 'fateful moments' are:

> when individuals are called on to take decisions that are particularly consequential for their ambitions, or more generally for their future lives. Fateful moments are highly consequential for a person's destiny ... Fateful moments are times when events come together in such a way that an individual stands, as it were, at a crossroads in his [sic] existence.
>
> (Giddens, 1991, pp. 112–13)

While the concept of 'fateful moments' draws our attention to big life changing events that are both planned and unforeseen, the idea of 'fate' is perhaps too slippery for our purposes and does not attend too deeply to the psychological elements that are part of the process. For example, in the story above, Simon experienced a 'fateful moment' when he was physically attacked. However, from a psychological point of view, this is not our only concern. It is the subsequent change to his identity that is really interesting. The concept of 'rupture' allows us to look at the different psychological processes involved in significant change. Zittoun (2006) describes four forms of rupture that an individual can experience:

1   Change in the cultural context (perhaps as a result of war, natural disasters or new technology).

2   Change of, or within, a person's sphere of experience (such as the move to a new country, the arrival of a sibling or a new boss at work).

3   Change in the relationships and interactions with objects and others (a child leaving home or reading a life-altering book).

4   Change from within a person (bodily changes like illness or getting older).

Clearly these four forms are highly interconnected. For instance, a war can precipitate the move to a new country, and therefore the experience of engaging with a new sphere of experience. They are also deeply personal and subjectively defined, so an event might be experienced as a rupture by one person but not by another. Let me give you another example. Hale and Abreu (2010) studied the life transition of young people (aged 11–18 years) moving from Portugal to Britain and the ruptures they experienced negotiating school as a new sphere of experience. These authors report that for many, the migration experiences were highly emotional and full of pain, loss and hope. This quote by Livia, who was 17 years old when she was interviewed, speaks to the uncertainty that is a part of experiencing a rupture:

> I was feeling I was losing my strength. I don't know why. Basically I was changing everything, from house to family and friends, school and everything. I felt I was losing … well, one of the things we built – family, friends, our environment and the familiar atmosphere around us. Um, I cried a lot as well when I

came over. It was difficult but once you get over it you don't think any more, but it was still there at the back of my mind. [...] It sounded as though it would be a bit difficult for me – obviously in a new school, new friends and everything is sort of different. So I got really worried and I got there really scared. All those people looking at me and I thought 'Oh my God, what am doing? I don't know if I'm sure about this.'

(Hale and Abreu, 2010, p. 403)

What is particularly interesting about this study is the way the authors capture change over a longer transitional period and across different spheres of experience. For example, a number of their participants described the negative emotions they experienced on arrival in Britain as temporary, though some took longer to get used to it than others. Many of the students felt torn between their English and Portuguese identities across different spheres of experience (i.e. home and school). In other words, at home the students were speaking the Portuguese language, maintaining Portuguese values and cultural practices. At school they were learning the English language, socialising with English friends and discovering new values and practices. Other examples from the literature on migration show how hope for a better life weighed against tremendous stress, often long-term separations among family members and grief over the loss of the familiar (Suárez-Orozco et al., 2008). One young girl said 'The day I left my mother I felt like my heart was staying behind ... I felt as if a light had extinguished' (Suárez-Orozco et al., 2008, p. 63). These authors found that those young people experiencing the longest separations and the most complicated reunifications also had the greatest decline in academic performance.

Becoming a new parent is also a good example of a rupture in the trajectory of one's life, and is often followed by a period of transition as the new parent(s) adjust to the new identity of parenthood. One interesting aspect of new parenthood is choosing the baby's first name. Names are symbolic and connected to identity, either our own or a group's (Zittoun, 2004). I remember when my husband and I were choosing baby names we discounted some because they represented a bully at school or the naughty child in class. So names link to our cultural past, but also feature as part of our ideas for the future. We sometimes imagine our child as an adult and think how the name would suit the adult version. We may also use cultural resources, like books from our past, for baby name inspiration. Thus, there is a link between the identity of that book character and the identity being shaped by the parents for their new baby.

The above example illustrates nicely how the development of an identity not only begins early in life (or even before someone is born) but that the self is inextricably linked through our relationships with others and our imagined future. Figure 5.6 is an illustration by artist Ed Fornieles that is said to depict the family he may have had with his now ex-girlfriend. The next section explores this self–other relationship in more depth and questions what role it might play in identity development.

Figure 5.6 An illustration of an imagined future family by artist, Ed Fornieles

2.5   Summary

This section has looked at development as a step or stage process and some of the issues this raises when considering looking at people whose life trajectory does not fit with a set pathway. It has explored how cultural, social and historical context has the power to challenge assumptions about stability and change as we develop.

Through the theoretical ideas laid down by Vygotsky and Bronfenbrenner, it has explored how our cultures, social contexts and even our histories play a role in shaping our identities. Although there is some continuity embedded in these ideas, structural changes at the macro level, like a change in government, have the power to alter our lives. While some practices, like gestures taught to our babies, remain stable, other activities are susceptible to change.

3   Self–other relationships

It has been established that for stage-related theorists, like Erikson, there is an underlying adherence to a continuity of self across time and place. The study of the self within developmental psychology is both prolific and deeply complex, with multiple ways of looking at how we use and 'hold' information about ourselves. Schaffer (2006) tries to capture this complexity by calling the self a 'self-system', defining it as:

> The multifaceted theory that all individuals construct in the course of development as to who they are and how they fit into society, based on a sense of continuing identity at the core of one's awareness.
>
> (Schaffer, 2006, p. 74)

While many philosophers have written about the self, it is William James (1890) who has had the most significant impact on our understanding of the relationship between the self and other in psychology. For James, there were two aspects of the self: the *I* and the *Me*. The *I* is often referred to as the 'self-as-knower', which is the part of our personal identity that sees our self today as the same as it was yesterday. In other words, that part of the self that has continuity and stability. James also wrote that the *I* is the part of the self that 'remembers those which went before, and knows the things they knew' (James, 1890, p. 400). The *Me*, referred to as 'self-as-known', recognises the extension of those things that you might call 'mine'. This could be anything from material possessions such as your house, to other people, such as your husband/wife and children. For James, the *Me* was that part of the self that was linked to our social interactions. You have seen in Chapter 2 how this idea was later taken up by scholars like Bowlby, investigating the role of the mother in shaping the child through interactions (Bowlby, 1969).

3.1   Self-awareness, self-concept and self-esteem

Since the work of James, the study of self in mainstream psychology has formed into three distinct aspects of study: **self-awareness, self-concept** and **self-esteem**. All three approaches have their basis in the notion of a continuous self.

Self-awareness
Self-awareness is the very first step in the formation of the self and refers to the realisation by children that they are distinct human beings existing separately from those around them.

Self-concept
Self-concept refers to the description or image that a child uses to describe themselves.

Self-esteem
Self-esteem refers to the evaluation or value that a child attaches to their personal qualities.

The study of self-awareness came about because psychologists wanted to understand at what point young children saw themselves as a distinct and separate entity from the people around them. The work of Lewis and Brooks-Gunn (1979) is the most well-known and oft-cited work. They conducted the Mirror Test (sometimes known as the rouge test) (Figure 5.7) which was designed to identify when infants recognised themselves in the mirror. They did this by asking mothers to paint their child's nose with red lipstick. The children ranged from 9–24 months. The mothers were instructed to tell the infant they were rubbing away dirt. The mothers were then asked to encourage their child to look in the mirror. The researchers recorded different types of behaviour shown by the child such as facial expressions, vocal expressions, and gesture. Although many children interacted with the mirror (tapping it or kissing it), only children aged from 15 months onwards actually touched the spot where the lipstick mark was. Therefore, they understood that they were looking at their own reflection. The authors suggested this was a sign they were beginning to develop a sense of self.

Figure 5.7   Rouge test

Self-concept has also been a key feature of the study of self within developmental psychology and aims to understand how children represent or categorise themselves either by physical characteristics ('I have brown eyes') or by psychological characteristics ('I am outgoing'). While this enables us to understand how people *describe* themselves, the study of how people *evaluate* themselves is called self-esteem (Schaffer, 2006). Therefore self-esteem is about people asking 'how good am I?' or attaching some kind of value to others' judgements. For James, there was a distinction between the *real* self and the *ideal* self. If an individual's feelings about their *real* self are very low, or the *ideal* self seems unreachable, then this evaluation may lead to poor self-esteem. Self-esteem is interesting because it is a concept that has been adopted into everyday language with little critical questioning.

Developmental psychologists have sometimes assumed that self-esteem can be measured using techniques similar to those used to measure intelligence. The problem is that whenever you have a measurement scale, there is always a value judgement attached to it; you are either at the low end or the high end. Scholars critical of self-esteem scales regard such judgements as a problem in themselves. If you imagine being in a mental health situation, being labelled with low self-esteem will inevitably be perceived as a negative assessment. McEachron-Hirsch (1993) writes about a number of myths perpetuated by studies of self-esteem. One is that women, minorities and the poor have lower self-esteem than men, non-minorities and the more affluent. The problem is that many of the studies have been flawed because minority groups from one socio-economic level were compared with non-minority groups from another. Moreover, the social situation may lead to unanticipated reporting of self-esteem. For example, one common myth is that children who are high achieving will have high self-esteem. This is not always the case. In a study by Boaler (1997), when asked, children in both the top and bottom 'sets' in mathematics classrooms identified themselves as being unhappy with the set they were in. Children in the top set were just as likely to give themselves a poor value judgement about their mathematics learning.

The studies mentioned above suggest that concepts of self-awareness, self-concept and self-esteem are problematic in a number of other ways. They could be considered to be overly static, with an underlying assumption that there is a continuity across both the lifespan and different contexts. There is a common myth associated with self-awareness, self-concept and self-esteem: that it is formed primarily in the first five years of life, regardless of subsequent life events or experiences (McEachron-Hirsch, 1993). The perpetuation of this myth means there is little room for recognising change in people as they grow, or change across different contexts. Let's return to the story of my 'shy' daughter that was introduced at the beginning of this chapter.

Although she was very 'shy' at school, in other micro contexts, like the home, she was pretty gregarious. I also mentioned that she had grown in confidence over the years, perhaps in part because of the people and activities she engaged with.

If we accept that the self is subject to change as well as stability across the lifespan and different contexts, perhaps what is needed is a different way of conceptualising the self. This is where the concept of self-identity becomes useful because identity can help us understand the 'self' as value-laden, linked to emotion, other people and context (Warin, 2010). The next section will approach self-identity as a dialogue and interaction with others.

3.2   Self-identity and interactions with others

One of the limitations of the approach on identity by scholars like Erikson, and those working within the arena of self-concept and self-esteem, is that the group or community to which one belongs is either ignored or placed in the background. Henri Tajfel's (1972) work on intergroup processes (discussed in Book 1 of this module) is often described as the basis for more contemporary ideas about the way social context influences individual tendencies (Reicher et al., 2010). Tajfel's work provided a conceptual bridge to link the individual with the social. As you can see from our discussions above, Vygotksy's (1978) work has also served a similar purpose.

Work within the area of critical and cultural psychology has likewise looked towards the role played by communities in examining our self-identities. In his conceptual framework *Communities of Practice*, Etienne Wenger (1998) describes how the things that we do (our practices) and the way our identities are shaped, have a lot to do with the communities we belong to. For example, belonging to a community who share an interest in rock climbing will shape what members do with their time and how they feel about themselves. As well as being able to identify with our communities, we should also be able to negotiate our role and place with that community.

Wenger (1998, p. 189) goes on to describe three other elements to what he describes as the 'social ecology of identity':

- Engagement – through our direct experience of the world, the ways we engage with others, and the ways these relations reflect who we are

- Imagination – through our images of the world, both personal and collective, that locate us in various contexts

- Alignment – through our power to direct energy, our own and that of others.

When we engage with others we get to see what effects we have on the world around us. Of course, through our engagement we may also be excluded if, for example, our ideas are ignored or rejected. We might present our work colleagues with a new idea, only to have other members of the group tell us it won't work. We sometimes identify with the communities of our imagination, without actually engaging in face-to-face contact. Newspapers or the internet are good examples because they enable us to envisage others sharing our opinion about a particular story. Zittoun (2006), for instance, writes about the power of books and music to change oneself.

Activity 5.2:   Imagination and the arts

Take a piece of paper and draw yourself in the middle of it. Around the drawing of yourself write down a book, a piece of music, a piece of art and a film or TV programme that have made big impressions on your life. You don't have to include all of these things and can add anything else you like (e.g. a poem or perhaps a smell). For each item write down why it was so important to you. Was it attached to a big moment of change or something more subtle? Does the item connect to a person, persons or community? Perhaps it is linked to a particular time and place? How does this item of 'imagination' link to how you feel about yourself and your identity?

Zittoun (2006, p. 130) describes the case of Julia, a young woman who used the band the Manic Street Preachers to help her overcome two ruptures: the death of her grandmother and the move to university.

Julia describes the music acting as a companion during her grief as well as an influence in her move from conservative to left-wing politics.

Alignment is about more than just belonging to a community, it also involves sharing a practice and joining your energies with theirs for some kind of joint enterprise. You can be with someone without engaging in what they do. For example, at work, you might align with other members of a union in joint activity, or indeed work alongside union members without being part of the union practices.

In my own work I take a sociocultural approach (the basis of which is formed by Vygotksian ideas) to look at identity as three processes that occur in a constant negotiation between the self and other people:

- Identifying the other – This is the process through which the individual comes to gain an understanding of social identities of others that are given by society.

- Being identified – This is an amalgam of community and personal identity because it begins with the individual coming to understand identities extended to themselves by others.

- Self-identification – This refers to the internalised and individual level of identity that ensues after the previous levels have been negotiated in the course of participation in communities of practice (see Abreu and Cline, 2003 and Crafter and Abreu, 2010).

To give you an example of how these processes of identity can play out in relation to an aspect of real life, read the following three sections of an interview transcript with a ten-year-old girl called Monifa. Monifa was interviewed in a multicultural British school about her achievement in mathematics, which was rated by the teachers as high. Her parents were both from Nigeria but she had spent all her school years in Britain.

In this first extract, you see an example of how she identifies with other people in the classroom. In an attempt to explain what makes someone 'good at maths', she provides a range of identifications related to her classmates, who, like her, are in the top set at school.

Sarah   Some children do better at maths than other children. Can you tell me why you think those children are good at maths?

Monifa   Well, like Chiranjiv, who's the best person in maths, he gets it from his sister. And Ryan was just born naturally with it, so it just depends really. Some people are just born naturally, some people get it from their parents.

Equally, Monifa is aware of being 'identified by others' in particular ways in relation to her learning. This next excerpt particularly details the role her parents play in shaping her identity in the future (which also links well with our previous discussions about the role of the imagined future in shaping who we are).

Sarah   Do you know what you would like to do when you grow up? Can you tell me about it?

Monifa   I was gonna be either a singer or I would be doing computers and like a business where I would be doing computers and all that. Because my dad has really taught me so I understand a lot, so that's what I would be.

Sarah   Do you know what your mum and dad would like to see you do? Can you tell me about it?

Monifa   My dad wants me to do computing and my mum wants me to be a singer. And like my mum is saying that she wants me to be in a choir and all that, but my dad wants me to stay at home so he can teach me a lot of things. And he takes me to his office and all that so.

Sarah   So you're piggy in the middle?

Monifa   [Monifa and Sarah laugh] yeah.

Monifa uses the identity extended by others to shape her self-identity, a process that Vygotksy described as internalisation. Similarly, you can see here how Monifa identifies herself as 'good at maths' but in a way that links with her identification of another person, namely her father.

Sarah   You said that [mathematics] was one of your best ones, how do you know, what gives you the idea that you're good at maths?

> Monifa   Because like, when I do it I understand it more, I don't know why. Maybe it's because my dad was a maths teacher and that it just runs through the family because all his family is good at maths. So I'm just good at maths as well.

In many ways Monifa is shaped by others, her parents in particular, by what they give her: namely, a positive identity around mathematics (supplemented by her success at school) which she then internalises as part of her self-identity. While Monifa talks about what her parents 'give her', identity can also be shaped by loss or rejection. In a different study by Bagnoli (2003), the author details how the experience of loss can influence the process of identity construction in young people. One of the interviewees was a boy called Barnie, who woke one morning, aged 16, to find his mother and sister had left, leaving only a note for him and his father. This event, which could easily be described as a rupture, changed how he saw his own identity and his relationship with his father. Their relationship towards each other became more like 'friends' than 'father and son' and he wrote in his diary that he worried he was becoming more like his father:

> After that happened it changed, before it was a father–son relationship, now it's more … We're friends, erm … I live with him at the moment, I'm staying … but it's almost as if we're like two people that live in the same house, two mates who live in the same house, we get on, and that's about it, it's not really a father–son relationship anymore.
>
> (Bagnoli, 2003, p. 210)

Barnie was 25 years old when he was interviewed but had written in his diary at the time:

> Spent much of the day in my room, away from dad, who seemed to spend a lot, if not all, of the day, sat on the sofa watching the television. He didn't get dressed all day. I couldn't face being in the room with him. Having spent the last two days on my own, I fear that I will end up like him. (25 May 1998)
>
> (Bagnoli, 2003, p. 211)

Barnie's self-identity is positioned as a reflection of the other, his father. However, Barnie also demonstrates his resistance to internalising this identity. Barnie describes how he observed the behaviour of his father and sought to resist engaging in a similar practice.

3.3 Summary

This section began by introducing Schaffer's concept of a self-system as a means of capturing different aspects of the self, known as self-awareness, self-concept and self-esteem. These concepts are rooted in the idea of a continuous self. The section then grappled with the complexity of a changeable self, whereby identity is understood as different positions that we take in interaction with others. The section concluded with some illustrations of how this might work in practice.

4   Concluding thoughts

So what have we learned by examining stability and change in relation to our own identities, and our relationships with others over the lifespan? The first point is that we are fascinated with understanding the pathways or trajectories of our own lives and those of others. Sometimes we have a 'sliding doors' moment in our life (a moment when one makes a decision that changes the trajectory of a life path) and we ask 'if I had made a different decision, what would my life be like now?'. Researchers and psychologists working in the area of longitudinal studies (such as Warin, 2010) have attempted to capture those patterns of development over long periods of time. What many of those longitudinal studies have shown is that broad patterns are useful in policy terms because they can address inequalities in people's life experiences. For example, we know that there are links between poverty and educational outcomes. Nonetheless, we must be careful not to *assume* that someone born into poverty cannot excel educationally, or construct a positive sense of identity. In other words, what happens in childhood does not necessarily *determine* outcomes in adulthood.

This chapter has also questioned the over-emphasis placed upon stability of the self across the lifespan that underlies much of the work by developmental psychologists who look at development as stages or steps. Stages presuppose that developmental trajectories are experienced in a universally similar way regardless of cultural context, history, and personal, social or political change. More than this, people whose lives do not fit a 'normal' life progression are often seen as a problem or in need of 'fixing'. This chapter has considered a range of examples that link change to identity development over the lifespan. Some of these changes are small or gradual, whereas others are more dramatic, with a 'rupture' leading to an alteration to an individual's sense of self.

Finally there was a closer focus on how a detailed understanding of the self has developed in the academic literature. The studies on 'self systems' (self-awareness, self-concept and self-esteem) have been largely built on the premise of the contained self, who categorises and evaluates themselves in a way that remains fairly stable over time. But we also looked at the self as something that can only be constructed in relation to others; that is, through our engagement and alignment with communities and our practices. In sum, studying self–other identities over a lifespan is complex, partly because we are drawn to the comfortable idea of stability in our lives but also because we recognise life can be rife with instability and change.

Further reading

- This book provides a powerful insight into the way change occurs to our sense of self when we engage in different cultural contexts:

Kondo, D.K. (1990) *Crafting Selves: Power, Gender, and Discourses of Identity in a Japanese Workplace*, Chicago, University of Chicago Press.

- This is a classic book that outlines the key ideas of Lev Vygotksy and how these ideas influenced our notions of development:

Van der Veer, R. and Valsiner, J. (1991) *Understanding Vygotksy: A Quest for Synthesis*, Oxford, Wiley-Blackwell.

- This in-depth paper provides an account of how the self changes in a global world when times seem uncertain. The paper discusses how we manage our identities and emotions to make sense of change:

Hermans, H.J.M. and Dimaggio, G. (2007) 'Self, identity, and globalisation in time of uncertainty: a dialogical analysis', *A Review of General Psychology*, vol. 11, pp. 31–61.

References

Abreu, G.de and Cline, T. (2003) 'Schooled mathematics and cultural knowledge', *Pedagogy, Culture & Society*, vol. 11, no. 1, pp. 11–30.

Bagnoli, A. (2003) 'Imagining the lost other: the experience of loss and the process of identity construction in young people', *Journal of Youth Studies*, vol. 6, no. 2, pp. 203–17.

Beach, K.D. (1999) 'Consequential transitions: A sociocultural expedition beyond transfer in education', *Review of Research in Education*, vol. 24, pp. 101–39.

Bell, M.E. and Bell, S.E. (2012) 'What to do with all this "stuff"? Memory, family and material objects', *Interdisciplinary Journal of Storytelling Studies*, vol. 8, no. 2, pp. 63–84.

Boaler, J. (1997) 'When even the winners are losers: evaluating the experiences of the 'top-set' students', *Journal of Curriculum Studies*, vol. 29, no. 2, pp. 165–82.

Bowlby, J. (1969) *Attachment and Loss: Vol. 1. Attachment*, New York, Basic Books.

Brannen, J. and Nilsen, A. (2006) 'From fatherhood to fathering: transmission and change among British fathers in four-generation families', *Sociology*, vol. 40, no. 2, pp. 335–52.

Bril, B., Zack, M. and Nkounkou-Hombessa, E. (1989) 'Ethnotheories of development and education: a view from different cultures', *European Journal of Psychology of Education*, vol. 4, no. 2, pp. 307–18.

Bronfenbrenner, U. (1979) *The Ecology of Human Development: Experiments by Nature and Design*, Cambridge, MA, Harvard University Press.

Burman, E. (2008) *Deconstructing Developmental Psychology*, Hove, Routledge.

Cole, M. (2006) *Cultural Psychology: A Once and Future Discipline*, Cambridge, MA, The Belknap Press of Harvard University Press.

Crafter, S. and Abreu, G. de (2010) 'Constructing identities in multicultural learning contexts', *Mind, Culture and Activity*, vol 17, no. 2, pp. 1–17.

Crafter, S. and Maunder, M. (2012) 'Understanding transitions using a sociocultural framework', *Educational & Child Psychology*, vol. 29, no. 1, pp. 10–18.

Crafter, S., O'Dell, L., Abreu, G. de and Cline, T. (2009) 'Young peoples' representations of "atypical' work in English society", *Children and Society*, vol. 23, no. 3, pp. 176–88.

Darwin, C. (1877) 'A biographical sketch of an infant', *Mind*, vol. 2, pp. 285–94.

Descartes, L. (2006) 'Put your money where your love is: parental aid to adult children', *Journal of Adult Development*, vol. 13, no. 3–4, pp. 137–47.

Dien, D.S. (2000) 'The evolving nature of self-identity across four levels of history', *Human Development*, vol. 43, no. 1, pp. 1–18.

Elliot, J. and Vailtilingam, R. (2008) 'Now we are 50: key findings from the National Child Development Study' [Online]. Available at tinyurl.com/kxo5tbh (Accessed 21 February 2015).

Erikson, E. (1950) *Childhood and Society*, London, Imago Publishing Company Ltd.

Giddens, A. (1991) *Modernity and Self-identity: Self and Society in the Late Modern Age*, Cambridge, Polity Press.

Hale, H. and Abreu, G. de (2010) 'Drawing on the notion of symbolic resources in exploring the development of cultural identities in immigrant transitions', *Culture & Psychology*, vol. 16, no. 3, pp. 395–415.

Hansen, K., Joshi, H. and Dex, S. (2010) *Children of the 21st Century: The First Five Years*, Bristol, Policy Press.

Holland, D. and Lachicotte, J.R. (2007) 'Vygotsky, Mead, and the new sociocultural studies of identity', in Daniels, H., Cole, M. and Wertsch, J.V. (eds) *The Cambridge Companion to Vygotsky*, New York, Cambridge University Press, pp. 101–35.

Hviid, P. and Zittoun, T. (2008) 'Editorial introduction: transitions in the process of education', *European Journal of Psychology of Education*, vol. 23, no. 2, pp. 121–30.

James, W. (1890) *The Principles of Psychology*, Cambridge, MA, Harvard University Press (this edition 1981).

Kroger, J. and Marcia, J.E. (2011) 'The identity statuses: Origins, meanings, and interpretations,' in Shwartz, S.J., Luyckx, K. and Vignoles, V.L. (eds) *Handbook of Identity Theory and Research*, New York, Springer, pp. 31–53.

Lawler, J.M. and Gunnar, M.R. (2012) 'Implications of research on post-institutionalized children for practice and policy in early education', in Pianta, R.C. (ed.) *Handbook of Early Childhood Education*, New York, The Guildford Press, pp. 457–79.

Lewis, M. and Brooks-Gunn, J. (1979) *Social Cognition and the Acquisition of Self*, New York, Plenum Press.

Macfarlane, A. (1977) *The Psychology of Childbirth*, Cambridge, MA, Harvard University Press.

McEachron-Hirsch, G. (1993) 'Self and identity formation', in Mceachron-Hirsch, G. (ed.) *Student Self-esteem: Integrating the Self*, Lancaster, Pennsylvania, Technomic Publishing Company Inc., pp. 1–18.

Merriam, S.B., Courtenay, B.C. and Reeves, P.M. (2001) 'Time and its relationship to development in the life course: some reflections from a study of HIV-positive adults', *Journal of Adult Development*, vol. 8, no. 3, pp. 173–82.

Mulready, W. (1838) *The Seven Ages of Man*, London, Victoria and Albert Museum.

Nilsen, A. and Brannen, J. (2014) 'An intergenerational approach to transitions to adulthood: The importance of history and biography', *Sociological Research Online*, vol. 19, no. 2.

O'Dell, L., Crafter, S., Abreu, G. de and Cline, T. (2010) 'Constructing "normal childhoods": young people talk about young carers', *Disability and Society*, vol. 25, no. 6, pp. 643–55.

O'Dell, L., Crafter, S. and Montgomery, H. (2013) 'Children and work', in Clark, A. (ed.) *Childhoods in Context*, Milton Keynes, The Open University, pp. 213–62.

Reicher, S., Spears, R. and Alexander Haslam, S. (2010) 'The social identity approach in social psychology', in Wetherell, M. and Talpade Mohanty, C. (eds) *The SAGE Handbook of Identities*, London, Sage Publications Ltd., pp. 45–62.

Rogoff, B. (2003) *The Cultural Nature of Human Development*, Oxford, Oxford University Press.

Roseneil, S. (2009) 'Haunting in an age of individualization: subjectivity, relationality and the traces of the lives of others', *European Societies*, vol. 11, no. 3, pp. 411–30.

Rutter, M. (1972) *Maternal Deprivation Reassessed*, Middlesex, Penguin Books Ltd.

Schaffer, R.H. (2006) *Key Concepts in Developmental Psychology*, London, Sage Publications Ltd.

Scully, M., King, T. and Brown, S.D. (2013) 'Remediating Viking origins: genetic code as archival memory of the remote past', *Sociology*, vol. 47, no. 5, pp. 921–38.

Slater, C.L. (2003) 'Generativity versus stagnation: an elaboration of Erikson's adult stage of human development', *Journal of Adult Development*, vol. 10, no. 1, pp. 53–65.

Sonuga-Barke, E.J., Scholtz, W. and Rutter, M. (2010) 'Physical growth and maturation following early severe institutional deprivation: do they mediate specific psychopathological effects?', *Monographs of the Society for Research in Child Development*, vol. 75, no. 1, pp. 143–66.

Suárez-Orozco, C., Suárez-Orozco, M.M. and Todorova, I. (2008) *Learning a New Land: Immigrant Students in American Society*, Boston, MA, Harvard University Press.

Tajfel, H. (1972) 'Experiments in a vacuum', in Israel, J. and Tajfel, H. (eds) *The Context of Social Psychology*, London, Academic Press, pp. 69–119.

Valsiner, J. (2005) *Culture and Human Development*, London, SAGE Publications Ltd.

Van Meijl, T. (2010) 'Anthropological perspectives on identity: From sameness to difference' in Wetherell, M. and Talpade Mohanty, C. (eds) *The SAGE Handbook of Identities*, London, Sage Publications Ltd., pp. 63–81.

Vygotsky, L. (1978) *Mind in Society: The Development of Higher Psychological Processes*, Cambridge, MA, Harvard University Press.

Warin, J. (2010) *Stories of Self: Tracking Children's Identity and Wellbeing Through the School Years*, Stoke-on-Trent, Trentham Books Ltd.

Wenger, E. (1998) *Communities of Practice: Learning Meaning, and Identity*, New York, Cambridge University Press.

Wetherell, M. and Talpade Mohanty, C. (2010) *The SAGE Handbook of Identities*, London, Sage Publications Ltd.

Zeedyk, M.S., Gallacher, J., Herderson, M., Hope, G. and Husband, B. (2003) 'Negotiating the transition from primary to secondary school: perceptions of pupils, parents and teachers', *School Psychology International*, vol. 24, no. 1, pp. 67–79.

Zittoun, T. (2004) 'Symbolic competencies for developmental transitions: the case of the choice of first names', *Culture & Psychology*, vol. 10, no. 2, pp. 131–61.

Zittoun, T. (2006) *Transitions: Development through Symbolic Resources*, Greenwich, Information Age Publishing.

Chapter 6

Conclusion: the challenges and opportunities of an integrative approach

Rose Capdevila, Gemma Briggs, John Dixon

Contents

1   Introduction

Your module textbooks have journeyed through four traditions of psychological research: from social to cognitive, from cognitive to biological, and from biological to developmental psychology. In the course of this journey, you have considered some of the everyday questions that fascinate psychologists: Why do we help one another? Is seeing believing? How does the brain work? What is the point of childhood? You have also considered some of the methods that psychologists use to address such questions, reviewed the evidence they have gathered, and weighed up the varying – and sometimes competing – explanations they have produced. The main aim of your three textbooks, then, has been to convey the breadth of psychological research. That is, they have showcased the discipline's richness and variety: from studies of the fine-grained neurology of the human brain to studies of large-scale intergroup conflict; from studies of basic processes of auditory cognition to studies of how we respond to complex stimuli such as jazz; from studies of early emotional development in children to studies of adult relationships of friendship and love.

Yet this variety also creates tensions, complexities and debates. Indeed, in this concluding chapter, we argue that it raises important questions about the very nature of psychological inquiry and about how the field could, or should, develop in the future. Specifically, the chapter revisits an overarching theme of the module, which concerns the need to produce psychological knowledge that crosses the traditional boundaries between social, cognitive, biological and developmental perspectives in an attempt to create *integrative* knowledge. We begin by reminding you of some of the topics that you have covered in DE200 and by celebrating the diversity of psychology.

2   The diversity of psychology

Pause for thought

You first saw Table 6.1 in Book 1, Chapter 1. Looking at it again, can you see how your understanding of social, cognitive, biological and developmental psychology has developed?

When you first encountered this table, it was intended to give you some sense – however preliminary – of the core features of the four psychological sub-disciplines covered in DE200. Although it offered a useful starting point, this table did not really capture the nature of each sub-discipline in any depth. It stood in lieu of the many hours of reading, thinking and learning that you have now (almost) completed! As you approach the end of the module, you should be better able to appreciate how psychologists working in each of these sub-disciplines have contributed to knowledge.

Table 6.1   Four psychological sub-disciplines and their core characteristics

	Sub-discipline			
	Social	Cognitive	Biological	Developmental
Core focus	The relationship between individual psychological processes and the social and cultural contexts in which they unfold	The mental processes through which we perceive, think and reason about the world	The role of biology and neurology in human psychological functioning and behaviour	The psychological changes that occur across the lifespan, from early infancy to later life
Illustrative topics	Social cognition Attribution Attitudes Group processes and intergroup relations Close relationships Social constructionism	Attention Study of perception Learning Memory Thinking Language Consciousness Cognitive neuropsychology	Biological bases of behaviour Hormones and behaviour Behavioural genetics Neuroimaging Neuropsychology Evolutionary psychology	Childhood, adolescence and lifespan development Development of attachment Social relations Cognitive and language development Social and cultural contexts of development
Most commonly used methods of data collection	Experiments Questionnaires Observation Interviews Diary method Visual methods	Experiments Interviews Observation Questionnaires Tests and scales	Experiments Interviews Observation Questionnaires Tests and scales	Experiments Interviews Observation Tests and scales Diary method Visual methods
Most commonly used methods of data analysis	Statistical Thematic Discursive	Statistical	Statistical	Statistical Thematic Discursive
Examples of practical applications	Health promotion, prejudice and conflict reduction, advertising and marketing, team building	Improving decision making, advising on safe practice (e.g. driving behaviour), accessing memory (e.g. cognitive interviewing)	Improving outcomes for patients who have suffered brain damage, developing treatments for neuropsychological disorders (e.g. Parkinson's disease)	Advising parents and carers, designing educational programmes and strategies, providing support for those facing developmental challenges (e.g. autism)

2.1 Social psychology

As you discovered in the opening chapters of the first textbook, social psychologists are interested in the interaction between individual psychological processes and the broader contexts in which they unfold. Henri Tajfel, one of the sub-discipline's central figures, expressed this idea as follows: 'Social psychology must include in its theoretical and research preoccupations a direct concern with the relationship between human psychological function and the large scale social processes which shape this function and are shaped by it' (Tajfel, 1981, p. 7).

By 'large scale social processes', Tajfel meant phenomena such as collective norms and values, relations between groups, political ideologies, and social institutions. He felt that the project of understanding how these broader social factors shape individual behaviours gives social psychology its distinctive character. Tajfel's own work, for example, explored several of the topics that you covered in Book 1. He investigated how individuals' membership of social groups – embedded in wider relations of intergroup status, conflict and cooperation – shapes their sense of identity (Book 1, Chapter 3), readiness to conform to particular social norms (Book 1, Chapter 2), willingness to mistreat (Book 1, Chapter 4) or help others (Book 1, Chapter 5), and tendency to form particular kinds of social attitudes (Book 1, Chapter 7). At the same time, Tajfel and many later social psychologists also recognised that basic psychological processes may, in turn, shape wider social processes. The interaction between the social and the psychological is not a one-way street. Thus, as Book 1, Chapter 8 illustrated, social cognitive structures such as schemas, stereotypes and attributions not only allow us to make sense of the world, but also lead us to act in ways that reproduce the social order.

At the centre of social psychological research, then, is the attempt to grapple with a paradox. On the one hand, it is possible to view much of what is called human 'psychology' as a mere reflection of wider social factors: family dynamics, situational pressures, group dynamics, the language that our culture makes available to us and that shapes how we understand the social world. On the other hand, it is also possible to view much of what we call 'society' as the accumulation (or sedimentation) of basic features of human psychology and associated behaviours: the cognitive processes through which we perceive and organise information about the social world, the emotions and motivations that shape our reactions to others, the genetic factors that lead us to participate in relationships of cooperation, altruism, aggression and exclusion.

This paradox has inspired passionate debates within social psychology and raised important questions. How, for example, do we weigh up the relative influence of psychological and social factors in producing any given instance of social behaviour? It is a platitude to suggest that we should always look for an interaction between both kinds of factors. Most social psychologists – indeed most psychologists – would agree with that. The more interesting questions concern how the relationship between the social and the psychological is best conceptualised and studied. Which factors should be prioritised and why? How might they work together to shape our actions? Similarly, if social psychologists are to achieve their goal of studying the relationship between the individual and the social world, then do they require methods that go beyond the traditional experimental focus that dominates many other areas of psychology? Do they need alternative methods in order to explore, for example, the role of conversational dynamics in social influence (Book 1, Chapter 2), group identification in crowd behaviour (Book 1, Chapter 3) or dehumanisation in events of genocide (Book 1, Chapter 4)?

Social psychologists have addressed such questions in many different ways and have provided many kinds of different answers. However, they agree on at least one thing: we are, at our most fundamental level, creatures whose behaviours cannot be understood outside of the relational, situational, cultural and political contexts in which we are embedded. By putting this irreducibly *social* conception of the human being at its heart, the field of social psychology arguably offers a distinctive vision not only on how to understand human psychology, but also on how to change it. Many social psychological interventions are based on the idea that if we can change contexts then we can change people. For example, interventions to reduce discrimination have historically sought to abolish institutional structures of ethnic and racial segregation (see Book 1, Chapter 4), while interventions to change health behaviours have targeted the collective norms and beliefs that shape our attitudes towards food, sexuality and substance misuse (Book 1, Chapter 7).

2.2   Cognitive psychology

As you have discovered in your textbooks, particularly in Book 2, cognitive psychologists consider how sensory information is taken in and processed. They are interested in the specific processing mechanisms that exist to enable us to carry out normal everyday tasks such as remembering the items on our shopping list or learning to play an instrument. Cognitive psychology is a relatively young sub-discipline of psychology. It was only in Ulric Neisser's (1967) book that the term 'cognitive psychology' was first introduced, as an alternative to the behaviourist theories that had taken centre stage for several years. By proposing a break from the behaviourist tradition, Neisser suggested that psychologists had far more to investigate than simply visible behaviours – instead, mental processes could, and should, be investigated. Neisser claimed that cognitive psychology encapsulates:

> ... all processes by which the sensory input is transformed, reduced, elaborated, stored, recovered, and used. It is concerned with these processes even when they operate in the absence of relevant stimulation, as in images and hallucinations ... Given such a sweeping definition, it is apparent that cognition is involved in everything a human being might possibly do; that every psychological phenomenon is a cognitive phenomenon.
>
> (Neisser, 1967, p. 1)

This contention gave rise to a new type of psychological inquiry, where psychologists devised tasks aimed at identifying the mental processes required for their completion. Based on these findings, cognitive psychologists could then attempt to identify the processing stages and mechanisms required for everyday tasks, such as learning to read or paying attention to a particular stimulus.

Given this grounding, cognitive psychologists often propose models for behaviours that take the form of interconnected 'boxes in the brain'. These theoretical models aren't designed to identify *where* in the brain a particular behaviour or action derives from; rather they attempt to identify *how* incoming information is (or is not) processed. As demonstrated in Chapter 6 of Book 2, these models can help psychologists to identify where in a process a difficulty lies. For a patient with anomia, for example, the problem may be at the retrieval stage, rather than the recognition stage, or it may lie somewhere between the two. For this reason, the connections (or arrows) between these boxes are just as important as the boxes themselves. The type of error made by different patients helps to inform how the model should be constructed.

As a further example of the theoretical approach taken by cognitive psychologists, think back to Chapter 2 of Book 2, which asked whether or not we can do two things at once. Several models of attention were outlined, all of which follow a similar pattern, based on the assumption that tasks have three stages: input, cognition and response. These could be represented by three boxes with linking arrows, as shown in Figure 6.1. However, this kind of basic model needs elaboration in order to identify specifically which aspects of 'cognition' are required for acceptable task performance.

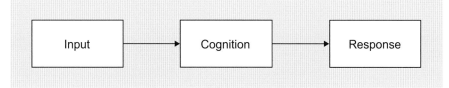

Figure 6.1   A basic cognitive model for task performance

Cognitive psychologists have therefore built on this model, in various different ways, to account for differences in task performance between individuals and type of task. The working memory model, for example, divides up the 'cognition' box into three areas: a central executive and two slave systems specialised for tasks requiring different resources (see Figure 6.2).

When presented with two simultaneous tasks, such as writing a letter and listening to music, the different slave systems process the relevant information. Nevertheless, a failure at this 'cognition' stage, or an overload to cognitive resources may result in either no response being offered (e.g. you stop writing in the middle of your letter) or an inappropriate response being offered (e.g. you write down the song lyrics instead of your intended message). These types of failures are interesting to cognitive psychologists because they help them to identify different processing mechanisms, or component parts, of the models they propose. These models can then help them to design investigations to answer specific research questions, such as those explored throughout Book 2.

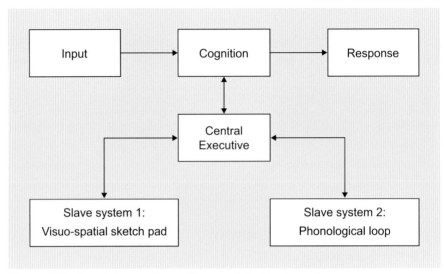

Figure 6.2   An elaborated cognitive model of task performance

Cognitive psychologists often use computer-based analogies to describe their models and discuss the different 'information processing' mechanisms that humans employ. They also consider how we have a limited processing capacity; much like a computer hard drive we have finite 'space' and resources available to us. This approach is useful because it isolates the specific area of interest – an investigation can be tailored to focus on one box in the model, or the connection between two boxes. It is also useful in terms of identifying how different cognitive resources are organised. Identifying this organisation can help us to understand how we go about completing tasks, as well as why we make errors.

While a great benefit of cognitive psychology is its scientific approach which allows for the isolation of individual processing strategies, it is also apparent that the interplay between the different areas is crucial. Thus the areas of perception, attention, learning and language all interact at some level. As you have seen, attention is required for accurate perception – without full attention we can be blind to changes in a visual scene, and when we divide our attention between two tasks, our visual search behaviour may alter, affecting our perception (Chapter 3 of Book 2). Similarly, our experience of the world affects how we learn new skills and information. This perceptual learning has an impact on how we process new information, meaning that experience affects perception as well as speed of learning (Book 2, Chapter 4). As an example of this, think back to Chapter 1 of Book 2 where you were introduced to different models of perception and the notion of bottom-up (data driven) and top-down (conceptually driven) processing. The hollow mask illusion nicely demonstrated the interplay between these two types of processing, where a person's previous experience of faces affects their perception of a novel face-like object.

As our experience of the world can differ from what is actually presented to us, cognitive psychologists have devised different ways of investigating perception, attention, learning and language that do not rely on an individual's memory or subjective experience of a task. The use of eye tracking, for example, has enabled researchers to identify when participants look at but fail to process visual information. For example, drivers who talk on the phone consistently notice fewer hazards than undistracted drivers. Dual-tasking drivers have also been shown to fixate on items in the driving scene that they later claim not to have seen (Chapters 2 and 3 of Book 2). In this context, the use of reaction time data is also useful – a dual-tasking participant may take much longer to react to an event than an undistracted participant, but when cross-referenced with eye tracking data it is possible to identify that a hazard was viewed but not seen (as no reaction was made). This allows the researchers to test their theoretical box models: the sensory information was taken in, but due to a lack of attentional resources, it wasn't processed at a high enough level in order for perception to occur, explaining why the participant didn't react to the hazard and claimed not to have seen it – thus the problem lies in the 'cognition' box of the model.

The cognitive tradition offers varied but consistent support to Neisser's contention that every psychological phenomenon is a cognitive phenomenon. As exemplified throughout Book 2, the applications of cognitive psychological research are vast and far-reaching and their use of experimental design demonstrates a methodical, scientific approach to psychological inquiry.

2.3   Biological psychology

As you have discovered throughout the module, the nature versus nurture debate is interwoven through almost any psychological question we investigate. The biological perspective focuses primarily on the nature side of the debate and investigates the biological and neurological bases of behaviour. Biological psychologists therefore look at the physiology of the human body and brain in order to answer questions about the behaviours we exhibit. They investigate how the central nervous system and hormones function to affect behaviour, and how different behaviours, such as drinking alcohol, taking drugs or exercising, can affect us both internally and externally in the behaviours we exhibit. They also focus on neurological data and investigate the contribution of different brain areas, or communication between areas, to particular behaviours. In comparison to cognitive psychology, the biological approach to research has been around for many years. The notable case of Phineas Gage, an unfortunate railway worker who suffered a serious brain injury after an iron rod penetrated his skull, has been the focus of research and discussion on cognitive function and plasticity since 1848.

Biological psychology is also comparative, and early roots of this branch of the biological approach stem back to Darwin's (1859) *On the Origin of Species by Means of Natural Selection*. As such, the approach explores the biological differences, at a genetic level, between species in order to help explain human capabilities and the evolution of our skills and behaviours. Hand-in-hand with this comes an additional focus on inheritance of genes, allowing researchers to assess to what extent abilities are genetic (i.e. driven by nature, and passed on through our genes) or environmental (i.e. driven by nurture). Finally, biological psychologists are interested in how sensory information enters the body. By assessing the physiology of our sensory organs, they can understand how sensory information is taken in and communicated throughout the body (as highlighted in Chapter 1 of Book 2).

The stance taken by biological psychologists leads them to use highly specialised, experimental approaches to collecting their data. Through the use of drug studies, advanced scanning techniques (e.g. fMRI) and case studies, they are able to identify how drugs affect specific neurotransmitters (Book 2, Chapter 5), how hormones can alter our moods (Book 2, Chapter 5) and how damage to particular brain areas can alter cognitive function (Book 2, Chapter 6). As an example of research in this area, think back to Chapter 5 of Book 2 where the effects of illegal drugs on mood were considered. By identifying exactly how a drug acts on an individual, biological psychology can assist greatly in our understanding of drug taking. For instance, this approach can explain which drugs, over a long period of use, can alter brain structure (plasticity), leading to changes in sensitisation, which in turn causes the individual to want more of the drug. While other sub-disciplines also help greatly in our understanding of addiction (e.g. cognitive psychology can explain conditioned responses and social psychology can tell us about the role of social influence in both addiction and treatment), the biological approach provides the backbone to understanding the effects of drugs on the brain. The applications of such research are far-reaching: drug studies on patients suffering from specific conditions, such as Parkinson's or Alzheimer's disease, can help us to identify some of the biological bases to these conditions.

The other branch of biological psychology you have encountered is neuropsychology. Think back to Chapter 6 of Book 2 where you learned about language function following stroke. The unique contribution of neuropsychologists here is through scanning studies (e.g. Figure 6.3). By comparing patterns of activation in brain areas known to be associated with language of stroke patients and controls, they are able to identify the degree of plasticity possible. Scanning studies can also identify lesion sites and different pathways of neural communication following a stroke, allowing for a measurement of the degree of neural plasticity a patient shows.

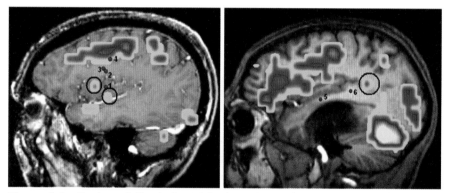

Figure 6.3   Brain activity during object naming in two different patients

As you have seen, when this approach is teamed with tests of cognitive function, neuropsychologists are able to paint a far clearer picture of the brain areas associated with 'normal' language ability as well as identifying double dissociations in stroke patients.

2.4   Developmental psychology

In many areas of psychology, research focuses on the reactions of adult individuals at a single point in time. Although its limits are widely recognised, the 'one shot' experiment conducted with undergraduate students remains at the heart of much psychological research and our main source of knowledge about many psychological topics. Such work has virtues, of course, and it has taught us a lot; but it arguably presents a rather static and narrow picture of the nature of human psychology. By contrast, developmental researchers are concerned fundamentally with how individuals *change* over time. This requires them to move beyond synchronic 'snapshots' of human psychology in order to explore the lived experience and psychological functioning of individuals across their entire lifespans.

The most influential work in this field has focused on the psychological development of infants and young children, which often displays extraordinarily rapid bursts of growth. As Erik Erikson (1950, p. 255) once remarked, there is 'in every child at every stage a new miracle of vigorous unfolding'. Consider, for example, the research that you encountered in this book, which explored how children acquire the ability to 'read' others' minds (Book 3, Chapter 2), reason about morality (Book 3, Chapter 3), and recognise gender (Book 3, Chapter 4). As this research indicates, in a relatively short space of time, young children evolve from creatures with little awareness of others' feelings and thoughts, a limited sense of right and wrong, and scant recognition of their own and other's gender into moral beings with a sophisticated 'theory of mind' and a nuanced appreciation of the gendered nature of social reality and relationships.

In recent years, developmental psychology has moved increasingly beyond its traditional focus on child psychology in order to explore psychological change (and stability) across the entire human lifespan, from cradle to grave. As Chapter 5 of Book 3 elaborates, for instance, such researchers have tracked how our self-concept evolves from childhood through adolescence into adulthood and finally old age. In so doing, they have been able to address some fascinating questions. What aspects of ourselves remain stable over time and what aspects are malleable and subject to transformation? If a girl is shy and introverted as a child does her personality stay this way as she grows older? How might her early development of self-identity affect the relationships she forms with others over the course of her life?

The challenge of addressing such questions has shaped the conceptual and methodological evolution of developmental psychology. Conceptually, for example, the field has devised a number of stage theories to account for the nature of human development. To cite one famous instance: the theory of moral reasoning proposed by Lawrence Kohlberg (1976) proposed a developmental sequence in which individuals move from a punishment–reward orientation (*pre-conventional morality*) to a focus on conventional norms and values (*conventional morality*) to, at least in some cases, a complex system of personal judgement in which the individual weighs up potentially competing moral principles in order to decide what is right or wrong for themselves (*post-conventional morality*). Each stage, Kohlberg argued, is marked by a core set of defining characteristics and, crucially, each stage must be navigated successfully before an individual can progress to a 'higher' level of moral reasoning (see Chapter 3, Book 3).

Critics of stage theories such as Kohlberg's, as you have seen, argue that development is a continuous, rather than stepped, process. They also argue that the idea of universal 'stages' is too inflexible to capture the cross-cultural, situational, and contextual variability of human development. They worry, too, about the social and political consequences of conceiving some developmental trajectories as 'normal', and others as 'abnormal' or 'disordered'. Nevertheless, stage theories such as Kohlberg's illustrate a common resolution to a challenge faced by all developmental psychologists: the need to devise concepts and theories that are able to make sense of the complex *developmental changes* that unfold over the course of individual lives.

This challenge also registers at a methodological level. Because they have to track changes over time, developmental researchers often require specialist methods of data collection and analysis. For example, they rely on longitudinal research designs to a greater extent than psychologists working in other sub-disciplines (e.g. see Book 3, Chapter 5). They must also adapt conventional research methods in order to explore human responses at the extremes of the human life cycle. How, for example, does one measure infants' emotional and cognitive capacities when they are not yet capable of speech and, frankly, all too readily distracted from the serious business of psychological research? The chapters presented in this third book of your module are dotted with illustrations of the ingenious techniques that developmental researchers have fashioned in order to meet this challenge, ranging from tasks designed to access young children's 'theory of mind' to tasks designed to tap their emerging understandings of self, gender and morality.

Perhaps the most significant contribution of developmental psychology, however, lies in the field's (re)conceptualisation of the nature of the human subject. In other sub-disciplines, a standard image of this subject is presupposed. He or she is typically a young to middle-aged

Western adult, whose psychological capacities and responses can be investigated and explained as though they are fully formed (and relatively fixed). The person at the heart of developmental psychology, by contrast, is someone whose capacities and responses are constantly 'on the move' and never quite finalised. Moreover, developmental approaches have been more ready than other approaches to explore the impact of culture on the individual, including the impact of growing up in non-Western societies. By thus prioritising the inherent dynamism and cultural context of psychological processes over time, the field of developmental psychology has made its most vital contribution to knowledge. To echo Erikson, the field has found its definition in the study of the 'vigorous unfolding' of our cognitions, emotions, behaviours and relationships.

3 Crossing boundaries and the future of psychology

Section 2 celebrated the diversity of psychological research, as exemplified by work produced within the sub-disciplines of social, cognitive, biological and developmental psychology. Yet how are we to make sense of this diversity? Is it a good thing that we have all of these sub-disciplines, serviced by specialists plugging away on their own, often rather arcane, research questions and talking only occasionally to colleagues working in other areas? Might such diversity suggest that the various traditions of psychological research are not only *different* from one another, but also potentially *incompatible*? Perhaps they ultimately offer contradictory accounts of the nature of human psychology?

The most obvious response here, of course, would be to argue that diversity is inherently good, that it should be embraced, and that psychologists should seek to build integrative perspectives that can take advantage of a full range of work in the field. Certainly, this has been an overarching message of this module. Every chapter of your three textbooks has cited examples of research that crosses sub-disciplinary boundaries. It is now time for us to concede, however, that building a truly 'integrative perspective' on any psychological topic is easier said than done (Figure 6.4).

"I THINK YOU SHOULD BE MORE EXPLICIT HERE IN STEP TWO."

Figure 6.4   'Then a miracle happens'

3.1   Challenges to an integrative approach

3.1.1   Ontological challenges

Ontology
The philosophical study of the nature of being, existence or reality.

The first challenge is arguably the most fundamental. It raises debates about the very nature of the person lying at the heart of psychological research, what philosophers might refer to as debates about **ontology**. As you have seen, different sub-disciplines offer different core images of this 'basic nature', and even within sub-disciplines, debates rage about the kinds of psychological beings we are. The subject of biological psychology, for example, is a material being, comprised of brain tissues, genes, neurons, hormones, synapses and so on. This biological makeup is viewed as laying the foundations not only for basic perceptual responses (e.g. recognition of sounds and visual patterns in the environment) but also for complex social behaviours such as altruism, aggression, empathy and love. The subject of social psychology, by contrast, is a being defined primarily in terms of its relationships with others. Many social psychologists would argue that our social behaviour is ultimately irreducible to our biological makeup or indeed other factors 'internal' to the individual. As Ian Burkitt eloquently puts it in his book *Social Selves*: 'Suppose we tried to understand human beings from a different perspective, as social selves rather than self-contained individuals. From such an angle, we would try to see human beings inside their essential connections to other people' (Burkitt, 1991, p. 1).

While these two core images of the nature of the human subject of psychology are not necessarily directly opposed – as work on social neuroscience demonstrates – they do open up quite different ways of thinking about the nature of human psychology and different perspectives on the likely or most important causes of how we feel, think and act. To explain the origins of collective conflict as the result of genetically inherited predispositions to fear or hate others, for example, is very different from explaining it as the result of competition among individuals who identify with opposing social groups and who have been socialised to believe in the legitimacy of their own group's cause.

3.1.2   Conceptual, methodological and epistemological challenges

Partly because they presuppose such different core concepts of the human subject of psychology, sub-disciplines also tend to develop very different kinds of core concepts and theories and to prioritise different kinds of methodological techniques. At a deeper level, their practitioners may even hold competing ideas about the kinds of knowledge that the discipline should be producing, and how the validity of that knowledge should be evaluated. That is to say, they may hold contrasting approaches to questions of **epistemology**.

To return to our previous example, social psychological theories of prejudice tend to favour concepts (and theories) that link together individual behaviours and social structures. Thus, Sherif's model (Book 1, Chapter 4) explained the origins of individual prejudice as a function of realistic intergroup conflict for scarce resources within particular social environments, drawing on concepts such as group identity, group norms, negative goal interdependence, superordinate goals and intergroup competition. By contrast, biological work on prejudice has tended to focus on underlying neurological processes, developing theories of how the activation of particular brain regions (e.g. the Amygdala, located deep within the brain's medial temporal lobe) may be associated with particular emotional and behavioural

Epistemology
The philosophical study of the nature and validity of knowledge, addressing the question how can we (best) know what we know?

responses (e.g. fear and avoidance), often in response to immediate social stimuli (e.g. skin colour). As a general observation, one might note that work in these two areas of psychology simply does not overlap to any meaningful extent: it focuses on different processes, operating at different levels of analysis, using different core concepts and perhaps even very different constructions of the nature of prejudice itself. Our point is that the question of how such radically different perspectives might be integrated in order to devise a unified theory is not one that yields a straightforward or immediately obvious answer.

Adding to the difficulties of this project are the different methodological priorities of researchers working within each sub-discipline. Although the use of experimental methods is common in both fields, social psychologists tend to emphasise the study of everyday behaviour and experience in real social contexts to a greater extent than biological psychologists and, as such, they use methods designed to access such behaviour and experience, including self-report measures, naturalistic observation, field studies, and interviews. For many biological psychologists, such methods yield limited insight at best into the deeper workings of the human brain. They prefer instead to take advantage of a suite of techniques designed to access the biological foundations of our thoughts, feelings and actions, including EEG, PET scans and fMRI. Yet, just as biological psychologists might be sceptical of the value of self-report or interview methods in providing a suitably 'objective' index of our basic psychology, so social psychologists are sceptical about whether brain-imaging methods can provide meaningful information about how we operate psychologically in real world settings. They wonder, for example, if a methodology based on getting people to lie down, motionless, alone and often rather uncomfortable in a brain-imaging chamber is the most useful way to explore the interaction between the individual and the social world. What can such a method really tell us about family relationships, love, national identity, stereotyping, conformity, crowd violence and all the other complex forms of social behaviour you considered in Book 1?

Underlying these methodological and conceptual tensions, as you may have picked up, something deeper lurks, though it often remains in the shadows. This is a more fundamental clash of perspectives about the very nature of psychological knowledge and about what kind of science the discipline of psychology represents. We can express this clash in terms of a rather simplistic opposition, which nevertheless has heuristic value. Should psychology be modelled on the advances of other 'hard' sciences such as physics, biology or chemistry? Accordingly, should we be seeking to derive universal laws of human behaviour, based upon gathering objective, observable, replicable facts and formulating theories that can be subjected to the acid test of experimentation? Or is psychology more akin to the social and human sciences and thus based more appropriately on the analysis of the contextually specific meanings that underpin human experience and behaviour? And when might we need to choose between the two approaches?

It is beyond the scope of this chapter to unpack the complexities of this opposition. As you progress in your psychology career, you will have the opportunity to encounter more sophisticated treatments of such epistemological debates. At this stage, we simply want to encourage you to think about its implications for the overall message of DE200, which emphasises the importance of building accounts of human psychology that benefit from social, cognitive, biological and developmental psychology and move us towards a unified perspective. We have outlined in this section some reasons why this may be easier said than done. In the next section, we sign off by imagining the opportunities an integrative approach may afford us.

3.2 Opportunities of an integrative approach

Your three textbooks have exposed you to many studies that have attempted to transcend the traditional boundaries between the sub-disciplines of psychology. This section begins with a final example that explores a challenge faced by many people across the world each year – the process of recovering from a stroke. We want to use this example to make a simple point: if we want to address the most basic psychological questions effectively (e.g. how do individuals recover from a stroke?), then we are often required to cross sub-discipline 'boundaries'. The nature of the question itself often demands that we cultivate an integrative imagination.

To demonstrate this point, think back to Chapter 6 of Book 2 where you read about patients recovering from a stroke. As you have seen, recovering from a stroke can be a lengthy process as well as traumatic for both the sufferer and their family and friends. In some cases, recovery is sudden and dramatic, with few obvious long-term deficits in function, yet in others the effects can last far longer or indeed be permanent. Research has tended to focus on the loss of specific abilities following a stroke, most notably language and movement, but the impact on the individual is often wider reaching. Among other problems, they may experience: loss of independence; inability to work; changes to their relationships with loved ones; reduced mobility; and poor memory as well as loss of language or decreased abilities.

So how can the different branches of psychology contribute to our understanding of stroke recovery, and how can they work together to help formulate real world applications for their findings, which will, in turn, benefit patients? As you learned in Chapter 6 of Book 2, many stroke victims develop aphasia (a specific language impairment) in one form or another. As demonstrated by individual case studies, this is characterised by problems with language comprehension or speech production. When investigating the language ability of an aphasic patient, cognitive psychologists can use a battery of tests to assess abilities in object naming, word comprehension and speech production. As you have seen, these can require patients to name images shown on flashcards, describe an object to an experimenter, or categorise words into groups. Based on responses to these tests, cognitive psychologists can then formulate theoretical models (box and arrow models) to help identify the distinct processing of component parts of language. Such models can help greatly in identifying where (in the model) specific language impairments may be located (e.g. at the semantic level, or at the retrieval stage). If a patient can describe the object in question but cannot immediately name it, then there may be a problem in the connection between the boxes, which slows down retrieval. The existence of double dissociations (where aphasic patient A can complete task 1 but not task 2, whereas aphasic patient B can complete task 2 but not task 1) enable these models to encompass data from different patients to create a more reliable and predictive model. As such, they are incredibly helpful in generating hypotheses about the nature of the impairment from which a particular stroke victim is suffering and, thus, informing the development of rehabilitation and coping strategies.

Neuropsychologists, by contrast, can assess an aphasic patient using a different but complementary approach. They can take fMRI scans to assess brain activity as well as identifying lesion sites and other areas that have been damaged by the stroke. They can compare the scans of different patients to identify both common and distinct areas of damage in order to attempt to identify brain regions that may be critical to language production and comprehension. Furthermore, neuropsychologists can assess plasticity at a neurological level (i.e. they can assess physical changes to the brain as well as changes to brain activity during a task), allowing additional understanding of how recovery occurs, at what rate, and of how different brain areas can compensate for damage to others.

However, as is hopefully becoming clear, it is the combination of both the cognitive and the neuropsychological approaches – cognitive neuroscience – that is the most informative and complementary approach to understand specific language impairment. The interplay between these sub-disciplines allows for discussion of specifically *what* the language problems are as well as *where* they are represented in the brain and *how* recovery occurs. The combination of different methods, sources of data, and theoretical models allows psychologists to produce a richer, more holistic perspective on stroke recovery and to benefit from methodological cross-fertilisation (e.g. of cognitive assessments and brain-imaging techniques).

In a similar way, thinking about how a developmental or social psychologist might approach the question 'How do individuals recover from a stroke?' has the potential to enrich our understanding. Developmental research suggests, for example, that strokes may have quite different consequences for children than for adults. The so-called **Kennard principle** may apply here, suggesting that the earlier damage from a stroke occurs, the better an individual's chance of recovery. At the same time, differences in recovery rates between children and adults depend, too, on whether or not a child has achieved a particular set of developmental landmarks (e.g. language acquisition) at the time of the stroke. Developmental neuropsychologists, for example, have found that children who suffer a stroke before or during literacy acquisition (between the ages of 2–6 years) tend to demonstrate poorer reading ability and verbal processing capabilities than those who suffer a stroke after literacy acquisition (Pitchford, 2000). These findings tie together research from developmental psychologists on so-called 'critical periods' for language acquisition with research from neuropsychologists on lesion sites and executive function following a stroke.

Kennard principle
A principle suggesting that the earlier in the lifespan of an individual an event of brain damage occurs the more likely it is that he or she will have some form of recovery.

Support and rehabilitation for stroke victims has more recently received considerable attention in social psychology, which provides a different set of insights from those we've already discussed. Social psychology has focused not so much on what goes on in the stroke victim's head, but, as you may have surmised, on the relationship between these internal factors and the social environment in which the patient must manage their life. After all, the consequences of a stroke exist not only inside the head of individuals, or in purely physical problems of communication, movement or coordination: they also impact on the individual's relationships with others as well as their associated sense of autonomy, independence and identity. While a cognitive or developmental neuroscientist might explain specific deficits in language processing following a stroke or recovery rates in terms of neural plasticity, a social psychologist might investigate how this experience has impacted on the individual's ability to engage with the world, to be a parent, to go to work, to socialise, to pursue hobbies and interests – all of those things that make up our day-to-day life – as well as how these elements are implicated in recovery and rehabilitation.

Most psychological research on health outcomes, such as recovery from serious illness, has traditionally focused on individual level factors (e.g. personality, personal lifestyle, genetic factors). However, social psychologists (e.g. Haslam et al., 2008; Jetten et al., 2012) have found evidence that emphasises the importance of social relationships and identities in shaping not only our social but also our physical well-being. This approach works towards providing opportunities for the patient to pursue a meaningful and realistic role within the community. Rather intriguingly, they argue that having a strong social identity and social network can combat the negative effects of unhealthy individual behaviours about which we are constantly being warned.

Another important consideration is that stroke affects not only the individual who manifests the physical symptoms but also their families, friends and carers. Research has found that providing support for carers, as well as stroke victims, contributes to positive outcomes for all those affected (Corr et al., 2003). Hence, by taking the social contexts and processes through which recovery occurs as central, and thus moving the level of analysis beyond the self-contained individual, such a perspective opens up new forms of intervention.

Our main point is that research produced within different traditions of psychological inquiry can often be combined to produce a more holistic or novel perspective, especially when such research converges on a common, everyday question. The question of how individuals are able to recover from a stroke, for example, illustrates rather beautifully the possibilities of work that seeks to cross conventional boundaries and draw on the full range of psychological evidence, theories and methods.

4   Concluding thoughts

One of the most powerful professional associations of psychologists is the American Psychological Association (APA). It boasts well over 130,000 members belonging to 54 different specialist divisions of psychology. It publishes many of the most influential books and journals in our field. On its official website, the APA defines the discipline of psychology as follows:

> Psychology is the study of the mind and behaviour. The discipline embraces all aspects of the human experience – from the functions of the brain to the actions of nations, from child development to care for the aged. In every conceivable setting from scientific research centers to mental healthcare services, 'the understanding of behaviour' is the enterprise of psychologists.
>
> (APA, 2015)

Having approached the end of your journey through four of the major sub-disciplines of psychology, what do you make of this definition? What research topics, studies or psychological theories does it call to mind? What does it capture about the overall project of our discipline and what does it leave out? What kinds of opportunities, challenges and debates does it open and what does it hide or push to the margins? Perhaps most important, what psychological questions, methods and approaches have gripped you?

In a discipline that is so varied, so rich, so filled with contradictions as ours, the main objective of our three module texts has simply been to get you to think about such questions in more rigorous and imaginative ways.

Further reading

Instead of suggesting new material for you in this concluding chapter, we invite you to reread the introduction to Book 1 and to reflect on how much you have learned during the module.

References

American Psychological Association (APA) (2015) 'How does the APA define "psychology"?', Washington, APA Support Center.

Burkitt, I. (1991) *Social Selves: Theories of the Social Formation of Personality*, London, Sage.

Corr, S., Capdevila, R. and Phillips, C. (2003) 'Using Q methodology to evaluate a day service for younger adult stroke survivors', *Operant Subjectivity: The International Journal of Q Methodology*, vol. 27, no. 1, pp. 1–23.

Darwin, C.R. (1859) *On the Origin of Species by Means of Natural Selection, or the Preservation of Favoured Races in the Struggle for Life*, London, John Murray.

Erikson, E. (1950) *Childhood and Society*, New York, W.W. Norton.

Haslam, C., Holme, A., Haslam, S.A., Iyer, A., Jetten, J. and Williams, W.H. (2008) 'Maintaining group memberships: social identity continuity predicts well-being after stroke', *Neuropsychological Rehabilitation*, vol. 18, no. 5–6, pp. 671–91.

Jetten, J., Haslam, C. and Haslam, S.A. (eds.) (2012) *The Social Cure: Identity, Health and Well-being*, Hove, Psychology Press.

Kohlberg, L. (1976) 'Moral stage and moralization: The cognitive-developmental approach', in Lickona, T. (ed) *Moral Development and Behavior: Theory, Research, and Social Issues*, New York, Holt, Rinehart & Winston, pp. 84–107.

Neisser, U. (1967) *Cognitive Psychology*, Englewood Cliffs, NJ, Prentice-Hall.

Pitchford, N.J. (2000) 'Spoken language correlates of reading impairments acquired in childhood', *Brain and Language*, vol. 72, no. 2, pp. 129–49.

Tajfel, H. (1981) *Human Groups and Social Categories*, Cambridge, Cambridge University Press.

Glossary

Adult Attachment Interview (AAI)

An interview that taps into adult representation of attachment by assessing general and specific recollections of the relationship they had with their primary caregiver when they were children.

Agency

The capacity of an individual to act or take action.

Androgens

Male sex hormones.

Attachment

A positive social and emotional two-way bond between an infant and another person who is usually the primary caregiver.

Deoxyribonucleic Acid (DNA)

DNA is the hereditary material in humans and most other organisms that is largely located in the cell nucleus. DNA contains the instructions needed for an organism to develop, survive and reproduce. A portion of DNA is passed to offspring from their parents.

Determinist

The philosophical idea that external causes, rather than human agency, causes behaviour, identity and social interactions.

Developmental science

The scientific study of age-related changes including, but not limited to, changes in thinking, emotions, behaviour and social relationships.

Egocentrism

A lack of awareness that other people have views, thoughts, feelings, beliefs about the world that may differ from your own.

Emotional contagion

The spreading of emotion from person to person.

Empiricism

Empiricist positions focus on knowledge that is gained from observation or experience. Empiricism argues whatever morals we have as adults must have been learned during childhood. Under this view moral development can be thought of as a process of acquiring behaviours and internalising the standards and values of a society.

Enactive experience

In social learning theory, enactive experience refers to circumstances where individuals learn through direct personal action and experience.

Epigenetics

From the Greek 'around' the gene, epigenetics studies how the environment regulates how particular genes work within an individual's lifetime.

Epistemology

The philosophical study of the nature and validity of knowledge, addressing the question how can we (best) know what we know?

Essentialism

The idea that objects have an essence that makes them what they truly are. Gender essentialism is the notion that human identities are essentially gendered, i.e. that being masculine or feminine is a core part of being human and that our gendered essence is determined by biology.

Experience sampling

This method involves asking participants the same few questions at a time, multiple times a day.

Factor analysis

A technique that generates a set of factors that summarises the relationships between variables in acorrelation matrix.

Gender

The socially constructed roles, actions, thoughts, feelings and behaviours that a particular culture associates with being men or women or being masculine or feminine.

Gender dimorphism

The assumption that gender comes in two kinds, masculine and feminine, that maps only sexual dimorphism.

Gender identity

A person's sense of self as gendered. Typically this is understood as your feeling of being masculine or feminine.

Gender identity disorder

A diagnostic category describing people whose gender identity is different from their assigned biological sex.

Gender schema theory

A social cognitive theory that suggests that children learn about what it means to be masculine or feminine from their culture.

Identity

Identity is a way of making sense of who we are, in a way that reflects our interactions and responses to others.

Individualistic approach

A broad classification of culture that makes society answer to the needs of the individual. This framework emphasises individual choice, personal autonomy, and rights.

Innate

Characteristics or abilities present in an individual from birth.

Interactionism

In sociology, interactionism is the theoretical perspective that society is produced from people's social interactions.

Intersex

Having ambiguous sex characteristics. For example, having features of both male and female genitalia.

Kennard principle

A principle suggesting that the earlier in the lifespan of an individual an event of brain damage occurs the more likely it is that he or she will have some form of recovery.

Longitudinal study

Studies that monitor and chart the development of psychological variables over long periods of time.

Maternal sensitivity

The ability of a primary caregiver (not necessarily the mother) to respond appropriately and promptly to the signals of the infant.

Mind map

A type of diagram used to visually organise information where associated ideas are connected to (branch out from) central ideas.

Mobile conjugate reinforcement paradigm

A technique used to study infant memory whereby an overhead mobile is attached to an infant by a ribbon tied to their leg. The infant gradually learns that if they kick their leg they can make the mobile move.

Moral domain

A moral sense that is thought to relate to issues of harm, fairness and rights.

Moral dumbfounding

A gut reaction that an act or thought is morally wrong, but an inability to articulate why it is wrong.

Moral foundations theory (MFT)

A theory that proposes several innate and universally available psychological systems are the foundations of 'intuitive ethics'. These moral foundations, it is argued, developed in humans because it helped us solve adaptive challenges in our evolutionary past.

Musical consonance

Pleasant sounding intervals.

Musical dissonance

Unpleasant sounding intervals.

Nativism

Nativist positions focus on knowledge that is organised in advance of experience. It argues moral knowledge and emotions are an instinct; a product of our evolutionary history with a strong genetic basis.

Naturalistic observations

A study where researchers take advantage of naturally occurring events, rather than themselves manipulating variables.

Nature

The inherited biological predispositions of the individual.

Non-binary gender

Gender identities that are not neatly categorised as either masculine or feminine; sometimes referred to as genderqueer. Binary gender classifies gender into two: masculine and feminine.

Nurture

'Non-nature' influences on development such as personal experience and the social and cultural environment.

Observational learning

Learning that takes place by watching the action of others, and the consequences of those actions.

Ontology

The philosophical study of the nature of being, existence or reality.

Predisposition

An inclination or tendency beforehand to have particular characteristics or to act or behave in a particular way (often associated with 'nature').

Prospective cohort study

A study where a group of similar individuals (cohorts), who differ with respect to certain factors under study, are followed over time to determine how these factors affect particular outcomes.

Proto conversations

An early interaction between an adult and infant before the infant can speak involving a two-way and turntaking exchange of gestures, sounds and facial expressions viewed as a 'practice' conversation.

Randomised interventions

Where individuals are allocated 'at random' (by chance alone) to receive a particular intervention.

Rhythmic engagement

The extent to which infants physically move in response to musical patterns and whether their movements align with temporal aspects of the music.

Self-awareness

Self-awareness is the very first step in the formation of the self and refers to the realisation by children that they are distinct human beings existing separately from those around them.

Self-concept

Self-concept refers to the description or image that a child uses to describe themselves.

Self-esteem

Self-esteem refers to the evaluation or value that a child attaches to their personal qualities.

Sex

Biological characteristic of being male or female.

Sexual dimorphism

Categorisation of organisms into two sex types: male and female; the physical or behavioural differences associated with biological sex.

Sexual selection

In evolutionary theory, sexual selection is a mechanism of natural selection. Natural selection refers to the way that organisms that are better adapted to their environment are more likely to survive and reproduce. Sexual selection refers to the selection of characteristics that makes individuals in a species more attractive to the opposite sex, and therefore more likely to enjoy reproductive success.

Social cognitive models

The cognitive processing of social information, including perceiving, considering and explaining people, events, relationships and social issues.

Social constructionism

A theoretical approach that explores how human knowledge and meaning making is built through jointly constructed understandings of our world.

Social conventions

Behaviours that serve to coordinate social interactions in social systems such as rules about clothing and food. They are argued to be arbitrary and changeable.

Socialisation

The process whereby we learn and adapt to social norms.

Sociocentric approach

A broad classification of culture that places the needs of groups and institutions first and subordinates the needs of individuals. This framework emphasises duties, social harmony, obedience to authority, and hierarchy.

Testosterone

The hormone that stimulates the development of male secondary sex characteristics.

Theory of mind

The ability to recognise that you have mental states, i.e. thoughts, feelings and beliefs, and to understand and be able to infer the mental states of others.

Transactional models

A view of development where the environment 'transacts' with the individual over time to produce developmental outcomes; thus, both the individual and environment determine the course of development.

Tuition

In social learning theory, being taught expected behaviours and attitudes explicitly and directly.

Visual recognition memory techniques

Tests of infant memory involving the visual presentation of novel and familiar stimuli.

Acknowledgements

Grateful acknowledgement is made to the following sources:

Every effort has been made to contact copyright holders. If any have been inadvertently overlooked the publishers will be pleased to make the necessary arrangements at the first opportunity.

Cover
Copyright © iStockPhoto.com/Sololos

Text
Activity 4.3: Leonard, T. (2011) 'The baby who is neither a boy nor girl: As gender experiment provokes outrage, what about the poor child's future?', The Daily Mail, 28 May 2011, Copyright © Solo Syndication.

Figures
Figure 1.1 top left: Copyright © Photobank.ch/Shutterstock; Figure 1.1 centre left: Copyright © Amana Images Inc/Alamy; Figure 1.1 bottom left: Copyright © Robert Harding Picture Library/Alamy; Figure 1.1 top right: Copyright © Alex Segre/Alamy; Figure 1.1 centre right: Copyright © KZENON/Shutterstock; Figure 1.2 bottom right: Copyright © Aviv Small/ZUMA Press/Alamy; Figure 2.1: Copyright © Nigel Pavitt/Getty Images; Figure 2.3: Copyright © Science Photo Library/Alamy; Figure 2.4: Copyright © James Ross/Getty Images; Figure 2.5: Copyright © Shotshop GmbH/Alamy; Figure 2.6: Copyright © Katrina Wittkamp/Getty Images; Figure 2.7: Copyright © Amana Images Inc/Alamy; Figure 2.8: Copyright © Blend Images/ Alamy; Figure 2.10: Copyright © Christina Kennedy/Alamy; Figure 2.11: Copyright © Ian Shaw/Alamy; Figure 2.12: Copyright © Chris Whitehead/Getty Images; Figure 2.13: Copyright © Ezra Shaw/ Getty Images; Figure 2.14: Copyright © Cultura RM/Alamy; Figure 2.15: Copyright © Cultura RM/Alamy; Figure 3.1: Copyright © Bahri Altay/Shutterstock; Figure 3.2: Copyright © GameKeeper, This file is licensed under the Creative Commons Attribution-Share Alike Licence http://creativecommons.org/licenses/by-sa/3.0/; Figure 3.3: Copyright © Jason Hetherington/Getty Images; Figure 3.5: van der Duim, D. (2008) 'Self-scorable MFQ30', MoralsFoundations.org; Figure 3.6: McNemey, S. (2011) 'Jonathan Haidt and the moral matrix: Breaking out of our righteous minds', Scientific American.com 8 December 2011; Figure 3.7: Copyright © Steve McPhee; Figure 3.8:

Index

and stroke recovery 264, 265, 266
theoretical models of 250–1
Cohen, D.B. 99
collaboration
in young children 121, 124–5
communities
and self-identities 228–9, 230
and social and cultural identity 213
Condry, J. 170
Condry, S. 170
conversations
and non-verbal communication 67
proto conversations 68
Cooley, C.H. 178, 180
cooperation in young children 120–1
cultural influences
on attachment 55–7
on childhood experiences 43–4
musical preference in infants 9–10
cultural variations
in childrearing and development 211
in moral development 111–13, 118
and moral foundations theory 114
Cvencek, D. 168–9

Dahl, R. 82
Damasio, A.R. 126, 127
Damon, W. 105
Darwin, C.
'A biographical sketch of an infant' 205
On the Origin of Species by Means of Natural Selection 254
Davies, R. 31
depression
and bullying 75
and emotional reactions to music 16
and gender 152
Descartes, L. 210–11
descriptive approach to morality 95, 129–30
development
of memory in infants and young children 59–62
developmental psychology 245, 255–8
core characteristics of 247
and experimental research 255–6
nature of the human subject 257–8
neuropsychology and stroke recovery 265
research methods 257

see also childhood; infants; lifespan developmental psychology; young children
Dien, D. 213
dimorphism
sexual and gender 146
diversity of psychological research 245, 246–58, 259

ecological environment
Bronfenbrenner's model 213, 214–15
egocentrism, development of 62–4, 71, 81
emotional reactions to music 11–16
enactive experience
and gender identity development 160–2
environmental influences
in child development 48–51
in infant attachment 54–5
on moral development 98–100
epigenetics and moral development 99–100
epistemology 261
and the integrative approach to psychology 261–3
equality
and sharing behaviour 124–5, 126
Erikson, E. 202, 256, 258
Childhood and Society 209
stages of psychosocial development 207–11, 212, 225
evolutionary psychology
and gender 147–50, 187
and moral behaviour 125–7, 128, 129
and moral foundations theory 114–15
evolutionary theory
sexual selection in 147–50
exosystems in developmental psychology 214, 215
experimental psychology
'Baby X' experiments 170
and developmental psychology 255–6
and infant attachment 53–5
and the integrative approach 262–3
and music cognition
in infants 8–10
on prosocial behaviour in infants 123–4
studies of memory development in infants 61–2
eye tracking 104, 253

fairness
and moral development 101, 104, 111, 112
and moral foundations theory 113, 116
and sharing behaviour in children 125